Beading Projects Illustrated

Beading Projects Illustrated

Georgene Lockwood

A member of Penguin Group (USA) Inc.

Publisher:
Marie Butler-Knight

Editorial Director:
Mike Sanders

Managing Editor:
Billy Fields

Executive Editor:
Randy Ladenheim-Gil

Senior Development Editor:
Christy Wagner

Production Editor:
Megan Douglass

Copy Editor:
Krista Hansing

Book Designer:
William Thomas

Proofreader:
Mary Hunt

Photographer:
Georgene Lockwood

ALPHA BOOKS

Published by the Penguin Group

Penguin Group (USA) Inc., 375 Hudson Street, New York, New York 10014, USA

Penguin Group (Canada), 90 Eglinton Avenue East, Suite 700, Toronto, Ontario M4P 2Y3, Canada (a division of Pearson Penguin Canada Inc.)

Penguin Books Ltd., 80 Strand, London WC2R 0RL, England

Penguin Ireland, 25 St. Stephen's Green, Dublin 2, Ireland (a division of Penguin Books Ltd.)

Penguin Group (Australia), 250 Camberwell Road, Camberwell, Victoria 3124, Australia (a division of Pearson Australia Group Pty. Ltd.)

Penguin Books India Pvt. Ltd., 11 Community Centre, Panchsheel Park, New Delhi—110 017, India

Penguin Group (NZ), 67 Apollo Drive, Rosedale, North Shore, Auckland 1311, New Zealand (a division of Pearson New Zealand Ltd.)

Penguin Books (South Africa) (Pty.) Ltd., 24 Sturdee Avenue, Rosebank, Johannesburg 2196, South Africa

Penguin Books Ltd., Registered Offices: 80 Strand, London WC2R 0RL, England

International Standard Book Number: 978-1-59257-605-0
Library of Congress Catalog Card Number: 2007928976

09 08 07 8 7 6 5 4 3 2 1

Interpretation of the printing code: The rightmost number of the first series of numbers is the year of the book's printing; the rightmost number of the second series of numbers is the number of the book's printing. For example, a printing code of 07-1 shows that the first printing occurred in 2007.

Printed in the United States of America

Contents at a Glance

Contents

Part 3: Beading for Your Home 127

Appendixes

Introduction

Throughout the ages, beads have delighted and intrigued us. Since the dawn of civilization, beads were used as a means of exchange, served as a way to identify class and position, and were worn as things of beauty. These little orbs made from the most common to the most precious materials on Earth have found their way into the hearts and minds of peasants and kings, movie stars, and aging hippies. And today, as ever, people are beading their world.

When I wrote *The Complete Idiot's Guide to Beading Illustrated* (Alpha Books, 2004), my aim was to create as many "baby beaders" as I could, giving my readers the skills and the confidence to tackle any beading project or technique their hearts desired, creating beaded jewelry, accessories, and decorative items they could be proud to give or keep for themselves. I wanted them to be able to both follow a pattern or "recipe" and understand basic design principles well enough to try their own variations and combinations. Many of you were able to use that book to discover your very own "bead dreams," and I'm pleased to say I've been asked to create a companion book of projects to help take you to the next level. Welcome to *The Complete Idiot's Guide to Beading Projects Illustrated!*

With this book, you will be able to take any number of beadwork techniques, from weaving both on and off a loom, to twisting and wrapping wire, to doing embroidery, embellishment, and knotting with beads, and create more than 30 projects, each with variations you can make your very own. What I hope you will do with this book is pick a beading technique you've learned and would like to perfect or attempt a new technique you've never tried, and jump right in. I've included a review of all the techniques used in the projects, and if you have my first book, you can refer to it for even more detailed instructions. Each project is designed to perfect a particular skill you can easily adapt to other applications while creating something useful and beautiful for yourself or someone you love. I've included plenty of things to wear, of course, but there are also lots of projects to add pizzazz to everyday things, from the boudoir to the dining room table.

I've used beads I had in my stash or some I bought specifically for some of the projects I've designed for you. Wherever possible, I've given you sources for the materials I've used—if not exactly, then companies that offer choices that are very close. As you'll find when you get bitten by the beading bug (or maybe you have already?), there's always room for more beads! Adapt these projects to your own style or color preferences.

So grab your pliers and a fistful of beads, and let's get started!

How to Use This Book

When you're working on a bead project, I wish I could be there to give you some tips, explain a term, warn you about some of the things not to do, or tell you a story or two like I would in one of my classes or demonstrations. The next best thing to being there is to provide you with the most complete instructions possible, accompany them with lots of close-up and friendly illustrations so you can see exactly what's going on at each step, and interject all those extra things that will make your beading experience a smooth and happy one.

With that in mind, this book is organized into four parts:

Part 1, "Jewelry for You (and Other Loved Ones)," is all about *you* and yours. These projects are for you to wear or give as gifts to the special people in your life. In Part 1, you create plenty of jewelry to add some sparkle to ears, wrists, and necklines.

Part 2, "Accessories … to Fun!" shows you ways to add some glitz to your wardrobe, both your everyday duds and special-occasion finery.

Part 3, "Beading for Your Home," brings some sparkle to where you live. And these projects are great for gifts, too. This part shows you how to bring a little beading into any room in the house.

Part 4, "Celebrate With Beads!" gives a seasonal twist to your beadwork and shows you how to incorporate beautiful beaded items into your special celebrations and important events.

In the back I've included some appendixes. One lists suppliers used in projects, plus my favorite magazines, websites, online groups, guilds, and societies and events. The other is a comprehensive list of books used for reference and recommended for further reading, as well as some helpful visual media.

Extras

Throughout this book, you'll find four information boxes that provide you with help or extra information as you're reading:

Crimps!

Check these boxes for warnings to help you avoid common mistakes and pitfalls as you're working.

Pearls

Here is where you'll find tips to make your beading easier and more fun.

Beadwise

Get the skinny on terms you may be unfamiliar with in these boxes.

Embellishments

Look here for ways to "raise the bar" on your creativity.

Acknowledgments

First and foremost, I want to thank Bobbi Wicks for her endless hours of help and encouragement. Her designs for projects and variations help make this book everything that it is.

Special thanks also go to Rowena Tank for her whimsical mobile design, her artistic sense, and for her amazing ability to get the word out.

My heartfelt gratitude to: Donna Dickt, for helping solve the mysteries of engineering large beaded flower pieces; Don and Dianne at Arizona Gems and Minerals for steering me toward the right findings and equipment; Helby/the Bead Smith, SoftFlex, Via Murano and Beadalon for providing samples to work with and loads of information; the kind folks at The Bead Cellar and Bejeweled Software for their wonderful programs and their support. Thank you all.

And as always, thanks to my husband, Jim Lockwood, for his patience and perseverance while I scattered beads from one end of the house to the other. And to my three cats: I don't need anymore help, thank you very much!

Trademarks

In This Part

Jewelry for You (and Other Loved Ones)

As a beader, you can have all the jewelry you want, made especially for you to suit your tastes and your wardrobe! If you buy something new to wear, you can accessorize with the perfect piece of jewelry for a fraction of what you'd pay in department stores or pricey boutiques. Sound too good to be true? Well, it's not! With a few basic beading skills and a little creativity, you can look like a star or a runway model—on a budget (although no one but you will know you didn't pay top dollar for your bling).

Besides having the perfect jewelry to wear yourself, you can create beaded gifts that are totally unique and personalized for the special people in your life. Ready? Turn the page, because in Part 1, I show you how!

CHAPTER

1

Ears Up!

In This Chapter

- Creating showy chandelier earrings to dress up any occasion
- Weaving a beaded bead that creates lots of visual interest
- Working an all-in-one earring from a single piece of wire

The ears have it when it comes to showing off your beading skills. From understated to downright over the top, earrings always make a fashion statement.

The three projects in this chapter will put you on the right path to a bevy of beaded beauties.

Chandeliers for Your Ears

Skill level: Beginner

What you need:

- 14 (6mm) Swarovski Light Colorado AB crystal bicone beads
- 30 (5mm) Swarovski Indian Red crystal bicone beads
- 22 (4mm) Swarovski Light Colorado AB crystal bicone beads
- 1 pair of gold-filled French ear wires
- 10 inches of gold-plated fine cable chain
- 18 inches (22-gauge) gold-filled wire (half hard)
- 2 (5mm) gold-filled jump rings
- Plastic film canister
- Chain nose pliers
- Flush wire cutters
- Round nose pliers

Techniques and skills needed:

- Basic wirework loops

No matter where you look, movie stars, pop divas, and runway models are wearing eye-catching chandelier earrings. With their swing and shine, these earrings bring out the gypsy in us all!

Our version uses wire, chain, and crystals, and it's quick, quick, quick! If you're in a hurry, you can try one of the many premade metal chandelier *findings* and whip up a pair in no time, but even our "made from scratch" version is done in a New York minute!

Beadwise

A **finding** is any one of various manufactured or hand-fabricated pieces other than beads, usually made of metal, that are used to make jewelry or other beaded items. Clasps, crimps, and ear wires are examples.

Using only these few beads and findings, you can create a fabulous pair of showy chandelier earrings.

Here are the three tools you need for this project.

The basic design of this pair of earrings begs for variations, and I'll show you a few after we make our first pair. Using crystals gives them a very showy look, but you can easily dress them down with different beads.

Pearls

Flat nose or *chain nose* pliers? You'll often see these labels used interchangeably. What's the difference? Flat nose pliers have flat inner and outer edges. Chain nose pliers have flat inner edges but are rounded on the outside. The pliers you see in the photographs are technically chain nose pliers.

Making Wirework Dangles

If you haven't done wirework before, don't worry. It takes a little practice, but you'll get the hang of it soon enough. You can find a complete tutorial in my book, *The Complete Idiot's Guide to Beading Illustrated*, but here's a quick review.

You can make wire dangles in a couple of ways. Basically, you're creating a stack of beads with some sort of stopper at the bottom and a loop at the top. You can use a head pin, which looks like a common sewing pin with a head on one end and a blunt end on the other. These come in many gauges and lengths, and you'll want to match the length as closely as you can to the required length of your dangle, to avoid wasting material.

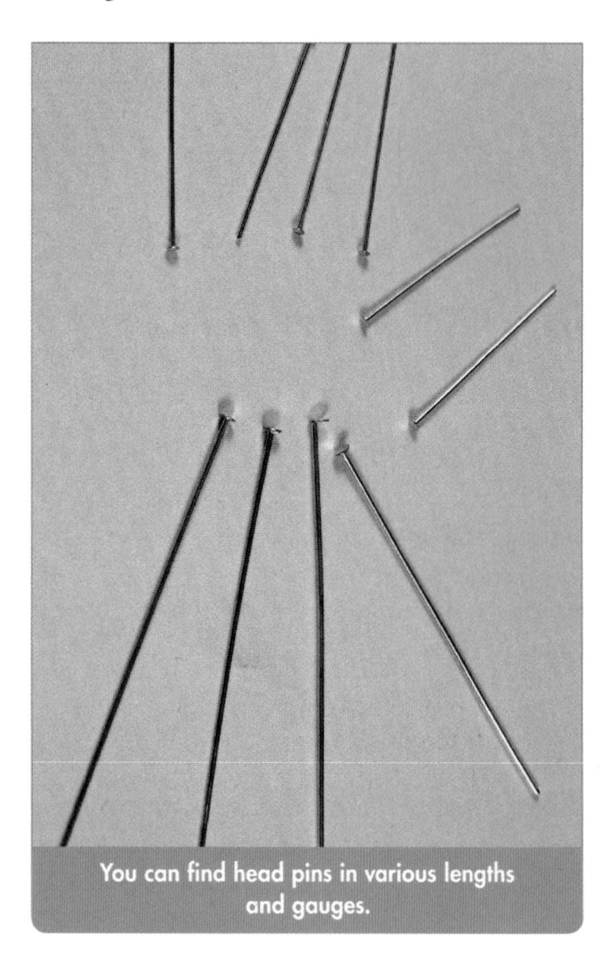

You can find head pins in various lengths and gauges.

You can also make your own head pins. Just take your chain nose pliers, turn up a tiny bit of one end of your wire, and squeeze.

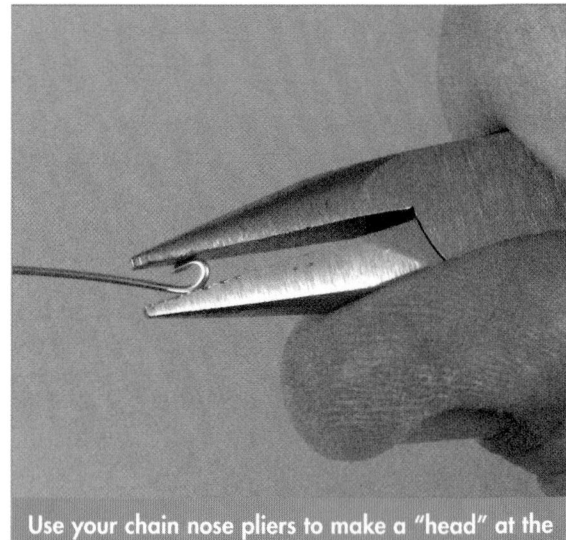

Use your chain nose pliers to make a "head" at the end of your wire.

Pearls

Here's a handy trick: keep a 10mm bead nearby if you're making a lot of dangles using simple loops. Just slip the 10mm bead on your wire, cut off the wire just above the bead, and slip off the bead. Voilà! You'll cut the right length—¼ inch—every time.

If you want, you can even flatten the end a bit with a ball-peen hammer. This little nub not only keeps your beads in place, it also creates a decorative tip on your dangle.

After you've put your beads on your head pin, the next step is to create a loop at the top end. You can make one of two kinds of loops: a simple or rosary loop, or a wrapped or closed-circuit loop. The simple loop is quicker and easier, but the wrapped loop is stronger and less likely to open. This is especially important when the loop is going to hold some weight or the loop could pull open. A wrapped loop also adds another decorative element to your dangle. For this project, because the dangles are light and don't cause any real pressure on the loops, we're going to use simple loops.

To make a simple loop, put your beads on the head pin in the desired order. At the top of your stack of beads, cut the wire to leave ¼ inch bare wire.

Using your fingers, bend the wire at a 45-degree angle. You can use your chain nose pliers to get it started, but you could chip the top bead if you don't remove the pliers before completing your bend. Don't bend the wire too far.

Bend the wire at a 45-degree angle at the top of your dangle.

Then, using your round nose pliers, bend the wire back toward the center into a loop.

Be sure the loop is completely closed, and take care to keep your loops uniform by starting at the same point on your round nose pliers each time. With some practice, you'll make near-perfect loops every time!

Pearls

One way to help make your loops uniform is to mark your round nose pliers so you bend the wire at the same point every time. You can mark your pliers at different intervals with a permanent marker, although this is apt to wear off in time. You could also score your pliers with a small triangular file.

Use your round nose pliers to make a simple loop.

Crimps!

Use good flush cutters to cut your wire because you want a nice clean cut. Using dull pliers or ones that are too heavy-duty for the job can leave you with burrs and a mashed end.

Earring Assembly

After a quick review of the basics of making simple wire loops, now you're ready to make your earrings! Here's how you do it:

1. Cut 2 pieces of gold wire 2½ inches in length.
2. Cut 4 pieces of gold chain 1¾ inches in length for each of the sides of the earrings (I used about 21 links) and 2 pieces ¼ inch in length for the center dangle (I used three links of chain for this part).

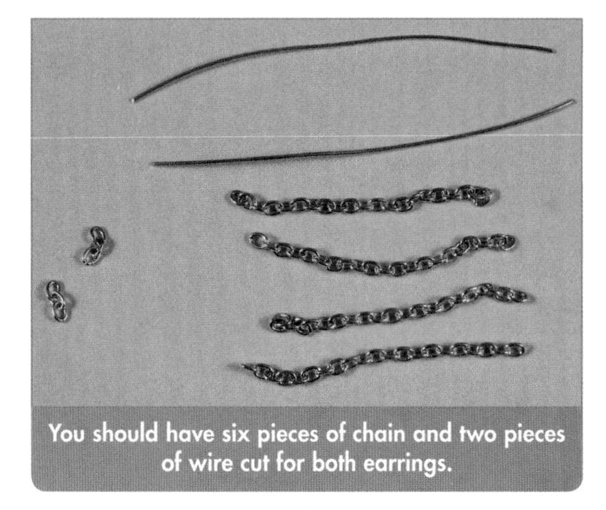

You should have six pieces of chain and two pieces of wire cut for both earrings.

3. Make 14 head pins (or use premade ones), and separate them into two groups of 7.

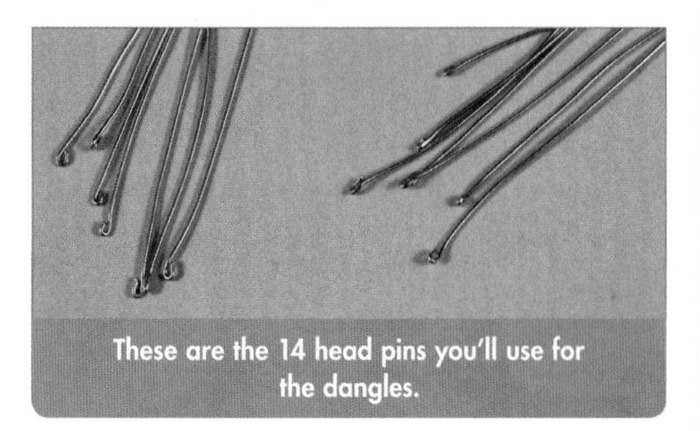

These are the 14 head pins you'll use for the dangles.

4. Bend one piece of cut wire (from step 1) over the film canister. It should be a gentle bend. Repeat with the second wire. Using the canister helps you make identical curves for both earrings.

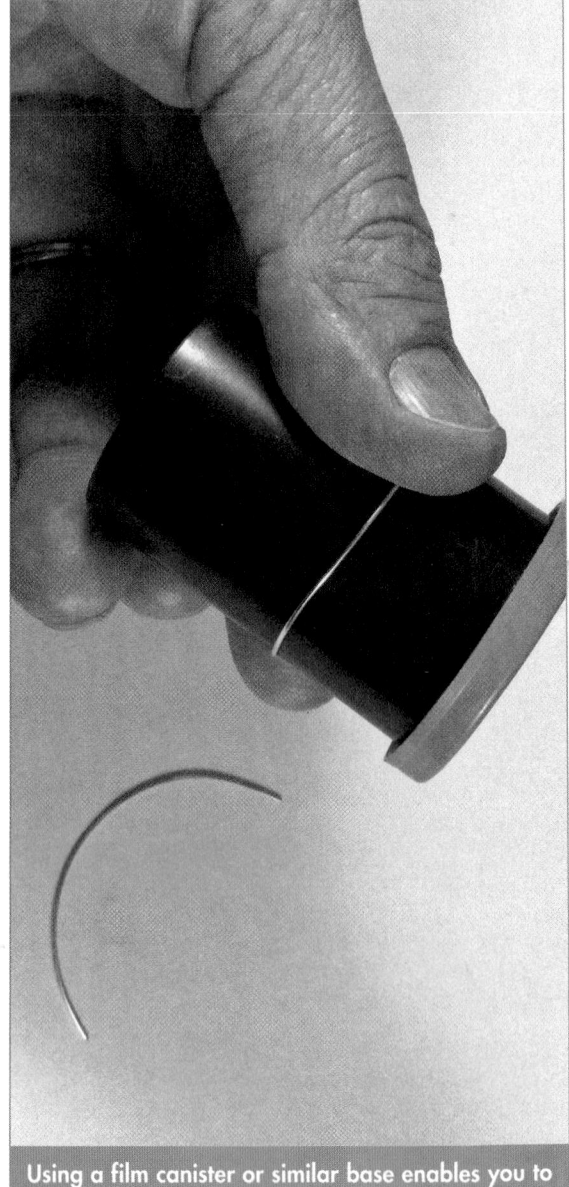

Using a film canister or similar base enables you to get a gentle, even bend for both earrings.

Pearls

A quick way to cut several pieces of chain all the same length is to cut one and then suspend it from the first link from a head pin or eye pin. Let the chains hang down, and cut at the bottom even with the first piece of chain. This keeps you from having to count each link to get all of the chain lengths even.

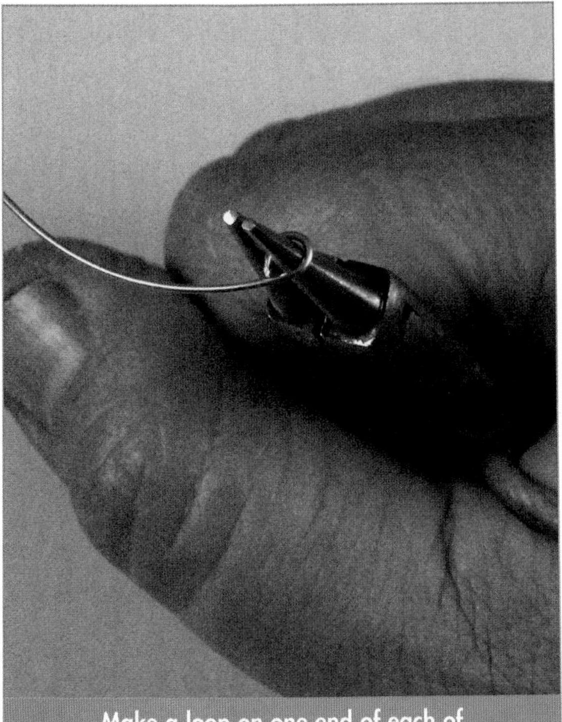

Make a loop on one end of each of your wire "smiles."

5. Using your round nose pliers, create a small loop in one end of the curved wire. Hold the wire so it looks like a smile, and then make your loop inward toward the center of the smile. Repeat with the second wire. You should have only one loop on one end of each wire at this point.
6. Make all your dangles. You'll need 14 in all, with beads threaded on in this order:

   1 (6mm) Light Colorado AB

   1 (5mm) Indian Red

   1 (4mm) Light Colorado AB

   You'll also need 2 dangles with loops at either end. These will have the following, in order:

   1 (4mm) Light Colorado AB

   1 (5mm) Indian Red

   1 (4mm) Light Colorado AB

Now you have all your dangles completed and ready to go on both earrings.

7. Now add your beads and dangles to one of your curved wires, in this order:

   1 (4mm) crystal

   1 (5mm) crystal

   1 dangle

   1 (5mm) crystal

   Repeat alternating 5mm crystals and dangles until you have 6 dangles. End with a 5mm crystal and then a 4mm crystal.

With all the crystals and dangles assembled and in order, you're ready to make a loop in the other end.

Pearls

Now is a good time to straighten any dangles that might have gotten bent as you worked.

8. Cut the end of your curved wire so only ¼ inch of wire remains (remember the 10mm bead trick?). Be careful to hold the beads on with one hand as you cut with the other. Using your round nose pliers, make a loop to keep the beads on. Repeat steps 6 and 7 with the second curved wire.

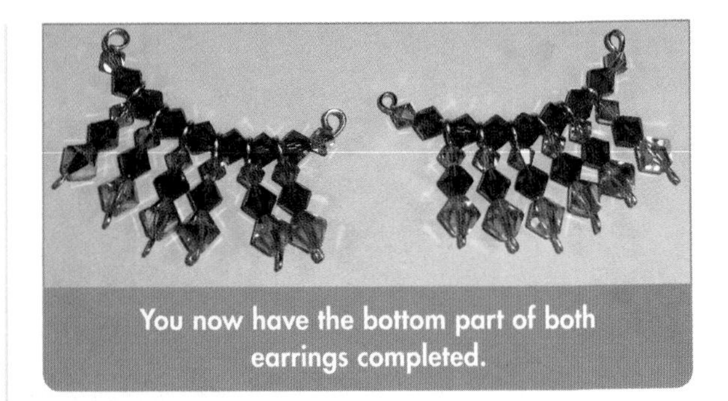

You now have the bottom part of both earrings completed.

9. With your chain nose pliers, twist the loop of one of your jump rings open a bit and add on one of the long lengths of chain, one short length, and then another long one. Put the jump ring on the ear wire, and twist the jump ring closed. Repeat with the second set of chains, the second jump ring, and the remaining ear wire.

Here's what your project should look like with all three chains on your ear wires.

10. With your flat nose pliers, twist open one loop on the crystal-covered "smile," and slide on the bottom link of one of the long chains. Close the loop, making sure it meets and is closed tight. Repeat this on the other side, and do the same with the second earring.

Your earrings are really taking shape now!

11. Twist open one end of the double loop dangle, and add it to the short chain. Close tightly. Twist open the other end of this double loop dangle, and add the final head pin dangle. Close tightly. Repeat with the other earring, and you're finished!

Crimps!

Don't pull a jump ring apart to open it because you'll distort its shape. Twist to the side with your flat nose pliers to open and then twist back the opposite direction to close. You might find that using two pairs of chain nose pliers works best for you. (To learn more about jump rings, skip ahead to Chapter 3.)

Your set of gypsy earrings should now be complete. Aren't they pretty?

Variations

These earrings can go even more "uptown" or casual, depending on the beads you use and how you use dangles. Try some—or all!—of the variations, coordinating them to your wardrobe and lifestyle.

Turquoise and Silver

Wouldn't these look great with a pair of jeans? Designer Bobbi Wicks ditched the bottom dangles and added one at the top, switching to silver and turquoise for a Southwestern flair.

Chandeliers, Southwestern style.

Using Premade Chandelier Findings

Manufactured findings for chandelier earrings abound, as you'll soon notice with a quick look around your bead shop or local craft store. Using one of these findings is instant gratification at its easiest!

With so many intriguing chandelier findings available for instant glamour, can you have *too* many earrings?

Earrings assembled on ready-made chandelier findings like these are so easy!

Adapting Findings for Chandeliers

Sometimes you can look at a finding intended for a completely different purpose and see an earring. Don't forget to look at old or broken jewelry, too! You might be surprised what you can turn into an earring.

These double-drilled squares evolved into a pair of fabulous chandeliers!

Chain and Dangles

When you start experimenting with chain and wire, all sorts of ideas will pop into your head. Use heavier chain and bigger dangles, and simply go vertical. Use finer chain and very fine wire and crystals, and you have something quite different and lovely.

Start experimenting, and you'll find lots of ways to "pull your chain" and "keep yourself dangling!"

Jigged Chandelier Finding

If you haven't explored the wonders of "jigging" yet, I recommend that you do. Using a system of removable pegs and a base with holes drilled in a grid, the jig and some wire open up a whole new world of design.

A few twists and turns on a jig created the bottom finding for this pair of Swarovski cube chandeliers.

Chandelier earrings just make you want to toss your head and move your body. You'll feel glamorous wearing them, whether you're dressed in an evening gown or jeans. Start now and make some for that special New Year's Eve party. If you make 'em, you'll be sure to get an invite to the party of the year!

Resources

Beads and findings: Fire Mountain Gems (www.firemountaingems.com)

Wire jig: WigJig (www.wigjig.com)

Bead a Little Bead and Glow!

Skill level: Beginner

What you need:

24 (4mm) red crystal bicone beads

4 (5mm) clear crystal AB bicone beads

2 long clear crystal AB Swarovski drop beads

3 feet very fine flexible wire (.010 diameter, 7 strand)

2 small big eye needles

1 pair of earring findings, French wire or post type

8 inches (20-gauge) gold-filled wire (half hard) or 2 each 1½ inch gold head and eye pins

Chain nose pliers

Flush wire cutters

Round nose pliers

Flexible wire cutters

Techniques and skills needed:

Two-needle right angle weave

Basic wirework loops

Never thought of beading a bead? That's what you're going to learn to do in this project. You'll be making two for a pair of earrings, but you'll undoubtedly think of lots of other ways to use them. Change the size of the beads or the shape, and you have something else again.

I chose flexible wire for this project because crystals are very sharp and can cut other stringing media. The fine flexible wires are relatively strong but resist cutting and can be knotted fairly easily.

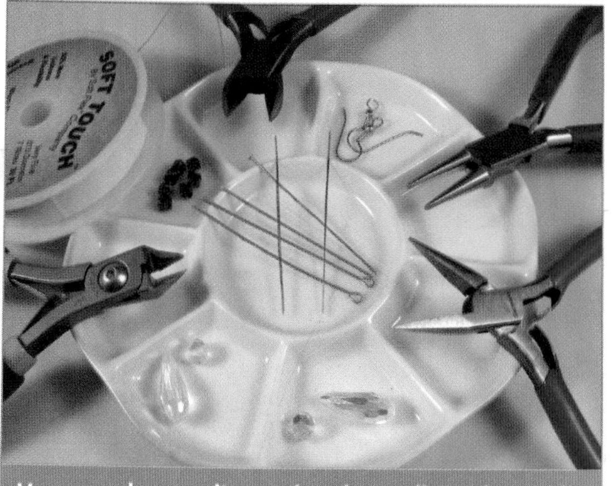

Here are the supplies and tools you'll need to make this beaded bead earring project.

You might not have tried right angle weave (or RAW, for short) before, but it's an extremely versatile technique. (You become more fully acquainted with RAW in Chapter 3.) Beaded beads can also be made from peyote and other off-loom stitches. Consider this a "teaser" for what lies ahead because after make your first beaded bead, you'll want to explore the world of 3-D beading further.

RAW can be done with one needle or two. In this quick and easy beaded bead, you'll use two needles.

Gather your flexible wire, needles, and beads, and let's get started by making your beaded bead first.

Pearls

I never thought I needed special cutters for flexible wire, but after I bought a pair, I wouldn't ever again be without them. They give a clean cut easily on all sizes of flexible wire, and you won't ruin your flush cutters for regular wire.

1. String on one red 4mm bicone, and bring it to the center between the two needles.

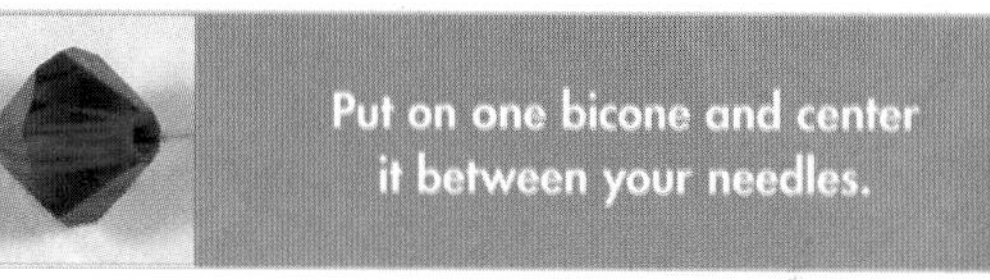

Put on one bicone and center it between your needles.

2. Add one red 4mm bicone to each needle.
3. Add another red bicone (this makes 4 total), and go through it with both needles going in opposite directions.

This is what your work should look like after going through the fourth bicone in opposite directions with each needle.

Pearls

When doing a two-needle RAW row that's this short, you might find it helpful to anchor your first bead circle with a piece of tape on a flat surface and work away from you.

4. Tighten up your work by pulling on both needle and thread ends. You'll end up with a circle or diamond shape.

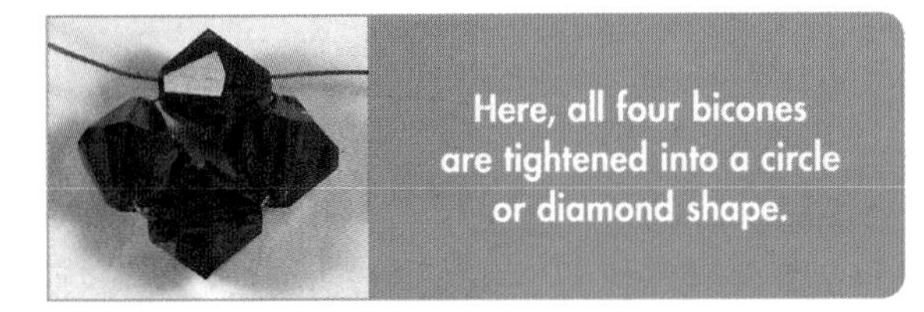
Here, all four bicones are tightened into a circle or diamond shape.

5. Add one bicone to each thread and then go through another bicone with each needle in opposite directions, as you did in step 3. Tighten.

This is what your work should look like after adding three more bicones and making a circle.

6. Repeat step 5. You should now have three loops or diamonds.

You should now have three bicone circles or diamonds.

7. Add one more bicone to each side, and come back down around to the very first bicone you put on. Put your right needle through the bicone going right to left, and your left needle from left to right.

After adding another bicone to each side and coming back around to the first bicone you put on, this is what you should have in front of you.

8. Tighten, and like magic, you'll have a finished bead!

You've now completed your first beaded bead!

9. To secure your beaded bead, grasp the left needle and thread in the palm of your left hand and hold tightly. Holding the bead between your thumb and forefinger, take your right needle through the bead in between the two bicones where your thread is coming out. Make an overhand knot and tighten. Make a second knot. Weave your ends through a bead or two and snip off. Switch hands and do the same on the left side.
10. Put one 5mm clear crystal AB bicone on an eye pin. Put the eye pin with the clear crystal up through one of the "holes" in your bead, and bring it up straight through the other side. If you look at your bead closely, you'll see each side is in a four-bead circle. Go through the center of one of the four-bead circles and straight through to the hole in the opposite four-bead circle.

11. Add a second 5mm clear crystal AB bicone. Make a tight loop at the opposite end (you learned how to do this in the previous project!). Put this unit onto your ear wire or post.
12. Put a head pin through your crystal AB dangle, and make a simple loop at the top. Put this dangle onto the beaded bead unit, and you've completed your first earring!

Crimps!

Crystals are delicate and can crack or chip easily. Be careful when you bend your wire to make the top loop of your dangle. Add a seed bead or small metal bead at the top if you're having trouble.

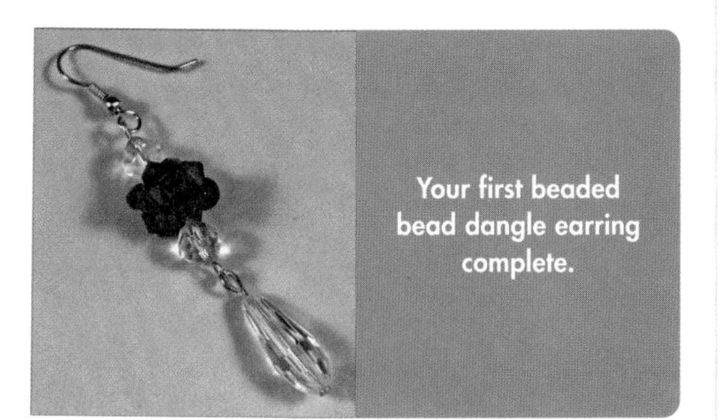

Your first beaded bead dangle earring complete.

Variations

The beaded bead unit you created can be used in any number of ways. You can also surface-embellish it with seed beads. I offer two variations for earrings in the following sections, but you could certainly use it as a focal bead in a Y necklace (see Chapter 2) or make it on a smaller scale and use it as a connector unit.

Beaded Ball and Chain Earring

Go smaller in scale (use 3mm bicones) or bigger (or 5mm bicones, as I did), if you dare! Just use a head pin to go through the bead, make a loop at the top, add chain however long you'd like, and attach the chain to your ear wire or post finding. You've got a retro hit!

A little chain makes a big difference in appearance.

Beaded Ball and Chain Loop Earring

Here's a version that uses chain and your beaded bead unit in a different way. Just use an eye pin, turn it on its side, attach two equal pieces of chain, and add a jump ring at the top. You'll think of still more ways, I'm sure of it!

Now that you've tried a simple beaded bead, challenge yourself to make some more complicated ones. If you remember your geometry, it'll make it even easier. Polyhedrons anyone?

Turn this design on its side for something totally different.

Resources

Beads and findings: Fire Mountain Gems (www.firemountaingems.com)

FireLine: Wal-Mart, Cabela's (www.cabelas.com)

Flexible wire cutters: Soft Flex (www.softflexcompany.com)

All-in-One Together Now!

Skill level: Beginner

What you need:

- 2 of the same beads (or a combination of beads), any size
- 8 inches (20-gauge) beading wire
- Large round nose pliers
- Chain nose pliers
- Side cutters
- Fine file or emery board

Techniques and skills needed:

Basic wirework

These simple earrings have a clean, modern look. All you need is a couple of beads and some wire—use up those stray beads you have hanging around. They're so fast you can even whip up a pair to match your outfit just before you go out.

A few odd beads, some wire, and a couple of tools are all you need for these fun earrings.

Got 15 minutes? That's all it takes for this earring that's really just a series of bends. It's so simple and fun, you can't make just one pair. Dress it up or down by choosing different beads. You'll learn one way to bend the wire, but as you'll see from the variations, there are lots of other ways to go.

1. Cut 4 inches of wire. With the small end of your round nose pliers, make a tight loop at one end.

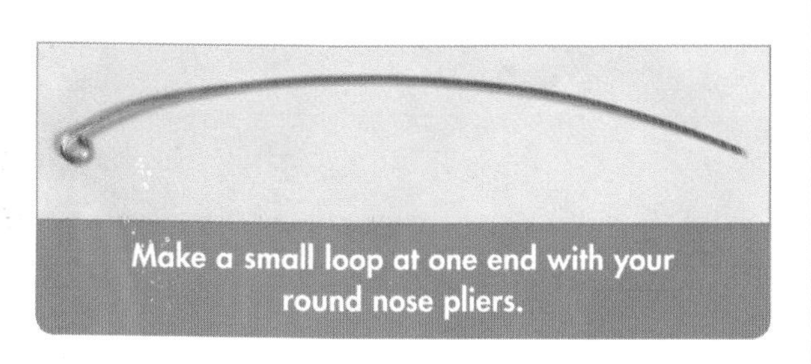

Make a small loop at one end with your round nose pliers.

2. Come down approximately ½ inch from the loop you just made, and with the largest part of the round nose pliers, make a U-shape bend coming up alongside the back of the little loop.

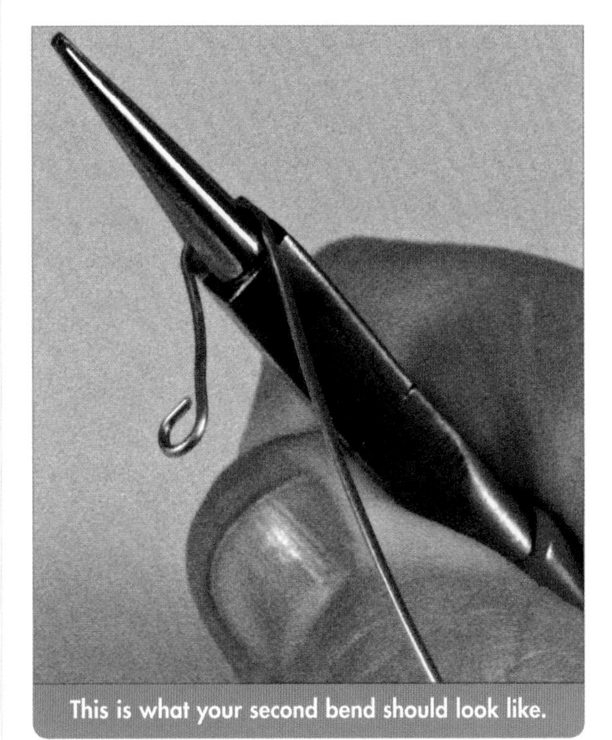

This is what your second bend should look like.

3. Slide your beads onto the straight edge of the wire. You'll want to put a larger bead on the bottom, or it might slip off unless you secure it with a dab of *Hypo Cement*.

Beadwise

Hypo Cement, or G-S Hypo Cement, is manufactured by Germanow-Simon Corporation and available from most jewelry supply outlets. The cement is clear and becomes tacky in 10 to 15 seconds, allowing parts to be readjusted, and dries in 10 to 15 minutes. It's ideal for jewelry and beadwork, plastic, glass, metal, ceramics, painted or sealed woods, and other nonporous materials.

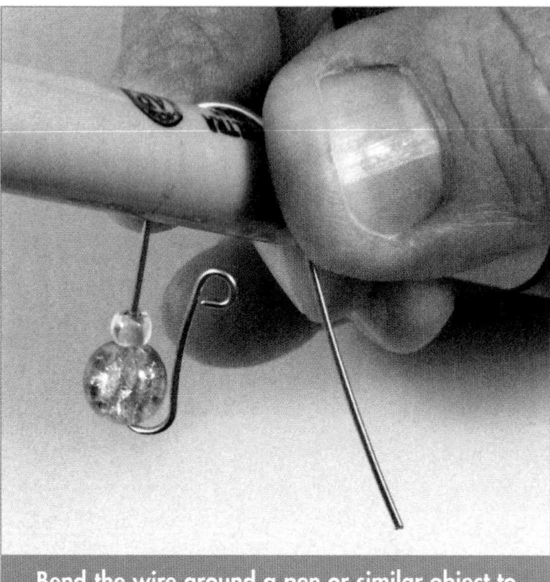

Bend the wire around a pen or similar object to get the bigger loop.

4. Using any cylindrical object such as a pen to bend the wire around, make another U-shape bend about a 1¼ inches from the last one you made, going back down toward the original loop.
5. Cut the end of the wire even with the bottom bend of the earring, and bend the bottom of the straight part out slightly.
6. File the end of the wire so no sharp edges remain, and you're done. It's that easy!

Crimps!

Be careful about filing the end of the earring wire that will go through your ear. Burrs or sharp edges can scratch your ear as it goes through, and your ear could get infected. Also, be sure you use wire that you can wear without an allergic reaction.

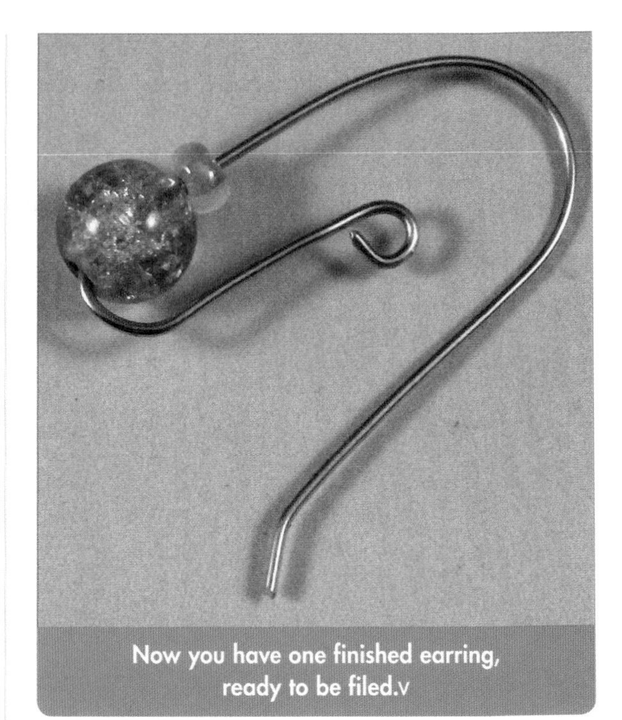

Now you have one finished earring, ready to be filed.v

Variations

You can vary the look of these earrings with the size of the loops, the beads you used, and how you make the original loop. You can also bend the wire in different directions for different effects. Instead of curves, how about trying some geometric shapes as well? Just look at the following photograph for some additional ideas, and you're sure to come up with some of your own.

Resources

Beads and wire: Your bead stash, your local bead shop, or your favorite bead catalog

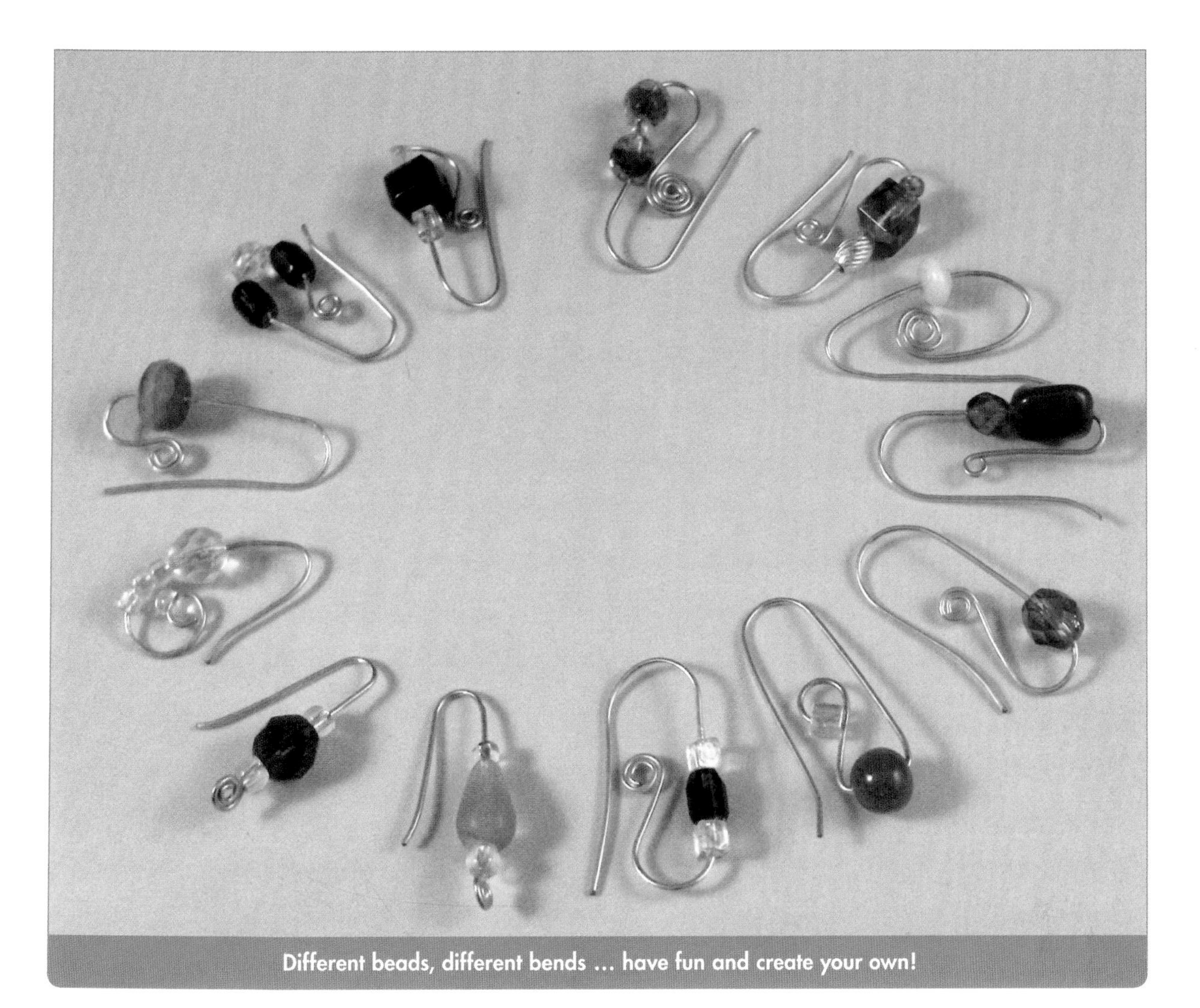

Different beads, different bends ... have fun and create your own!

Neckline Trends

In This Chapter

- Making easy Y necklaces
- Creating a variety of necklaces with semi-precious chips
- Weaving a choker with netting stitch

Some of the most provocative and intriguing women have learned the value of a beautiful necklace to frame their face. A look at the portraits from the masters will attest to that.

Grace your neck with the perfect bauble you've made yourself using just the right colors and lines to suit your style by choosing a project (or two or three) from this chapter.

Y Not a Necklace?

Skill level: Intermediate

What you need:

- 1 amethyst pendant
- 2 size small Swarovski Baroque pendant crystals
- 44 assorted 3mm and 4mm Light Amethyst bicones, oval faceted crystals, and other amethyst crystals in different shapes and sizes
- 2 crystal rondelles in Light Amethyst
- 20 seed pearls
- 4 rice pearls
- 8 (¼-inch-long) lavender-colored oval pearls (also known as potato pearls)
- 9 (1mm × .5mm) "cathedral" (also called "window" or "window pane") Czech crystals in Light Amethyst
- 4 (.5mm × .5mm) "cathedral" Czech crystals in Light Amethyst
- 2 strands (size 10) seed beads (I used Czech seed beads in a champagne color.)
- 12 (3mm) round gold beads
- 6 feet .015-inch (.038mm) satin gold Beadalon wire
- 4 (size 1) Beadalon crimp beads
- 2 gold jump rings
- Y necklace finding in gold finish
- 4 inches (20-gauge) gold-filled wire (half hard) or 1 gold eye pin
- 1 gold filigree double connector box clasp
- Chain nose pliers
- Flush wire cutters
- Round nose pliers
- Flexible wire cutters
- Crimping pliers (standard)
- Set of bead reamers
- 2 small alligator clips (1¼ inches)

Techniques and skills needed:

- Stringing with flexible wire and crimping
- Making simple wirework loops

The Y necklace takes its name from its obvious shape. The "arms" of the Y go around your neck, and the "leg" of the Y dangles in front. This classic design was very popular in the Victorian era, and this version is going to pay homage to its heyday. In this project, you use some vintage findings and beads, as well as some Czech and Austrian crystals and pearls.

The expensive look of this necklace is deceiving. I've designed it to make use of inexpensive seed beads, which offset only a few individual units made up of the more expensive components.

An assortment of pearls, crystals, and seed beads, plus a few findings and supplies, are what you need for this Victorian Y necklace.

And here are the tools you need for this project.

Crimps!

Working with pearls can pose a few challenges. Sometimes the holes aren't drilled all the way through; sometimes they're irregular in size. The holes are also usually too small to accommodate larger gauges of wire, and often you can't fit two strands of wire through the hole at all. If you decide to work with pearls, have a set of bead reamers to help open the holes. By carefully twisting the reamer through the pearl (or other beads, for that matter), you can make the hole more uniform and larger.

1. Cut 2 (3-foot) pieces of gold wire. Fold one piece loosely in half, and put it through one of the two "arm" loops of the Y finding.
2. Slip the ends of both halves of the wire through a crimp bead, and using a standard size crimp pliers, crimp the crimp bead around the two wires. Be sure you use the correct size crimp pliers for the size crimp you are using to ensure it will hold the wire tightly.

Pearls

You can get some of the most interesting findings and beads on websites like eBay. Some sellers have access to old brass stock from the nineteenth century or are using tooling from that period to create new brass stampings or castings. Keep your eyes open for vintage clasps, beads, and pendants as well. The pendant in this necklace was created from a vintage glass cabochon from Germany, the setting and clasp are vintage brass, and the Y finding is a Victorian reproduction—all purchased from different sellers on eBay.

3. Slip both ends of the wire through two size 10 seed beads, a 4mm oval crystal, a large cathedral bead, and another 4mm oval crystal (or whatever bead unit you decide to create). After this point, you start stringing the two wires separately. Think of them as the top wire and the bottom wire.

To start, you string beads on both wires and then string them separately.

4. String all your beads on the top wire first in a pleasing sequence. I used repeating units in between spacers of seed beads. Keep your design symmetrical, and repeat it exactly on the other side of the Y finding.

   Remember, the top wire determines the length of your necklace. Measure periodically to see whether you're reaching your desired length. I made this necklace approximately 16 inches long, including the clasp. You might want yours shorter or longer, so decide now and make allowances. I had you cut enough wire so you'd have what you needed in case you changed your mind as you began to design your own version.

Crimps!

Be sure not to twist or cross your two wires as you work, or your necklace will twist and won't lay flat. Keep the bottom wire on the bottom.

This is the stringing pattern I used for the top wire. Feel free to use this pattern or come up with your own.

5. Now begin stringing your bottom wire. I added a jump ring to the baroque crystal drops and threaded them on between two beads.

Here's an example of how you might choose to string the bottom wire and add a hanging element.

6. At various points, you'll go up through beads on your top wire. This gives the necklace a scalloped effect.

The next scallop without a hanging element.

7. Attach your clasp using crimp beads. I used a double box clasp and added some seed beads, a small gold bead, and then the crimp. For this type of clasp to work properly, you need position it properly (there's a back and a front). The box usually has a design on the top. Remember to keep the tab to close the clasp facing upward. You also need to decide which half of the clasp you want on the right side and which half you want on the left (depending on whether you're right-handed and left-handed).

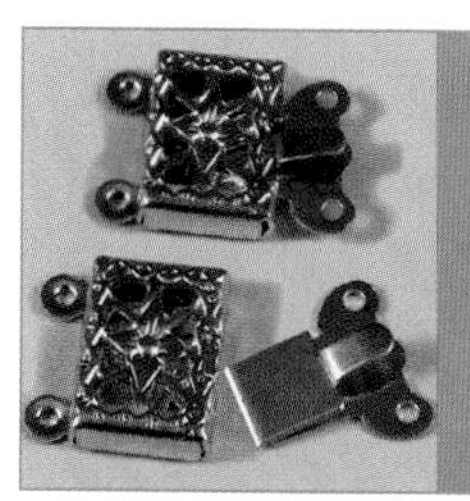

A box clasp has a front and a back and must be positioned correctly.

8. Bring the wire down through a few beads and snip the end close to a bead using flexible wire cutters. Be careful to cut only the end wire.
9. Repeat steps 2 through 8 on the other side of the Y finding, working the pattern as a mirror image of the first side. Count your seed beads to be sure your design is symmetrical and even.
10. Make a wire and bead connector using an eye pin (or making your own), and add it to the bottom of the Y finding. Add your pendant, and you're done!

Here's my version of the Y necklace in amethyst with a distinctly Victorian feel.

Variations

Not into Victorian? That's okay. You can make your Y necklace in any style. Don't have a Y finding? That's okay, too. Following are some variations where the apex of the Y is a bead or the finding is one you make yourself.

Red Spiral Necklace

This necklace, designed by Bobbi Wicks, uses a finding she made by bending wire. The red beads and simple spiral shape make it sassy and modern.

A silver Y finding made with bent wire and spicy red beads gives this Y necklace a modern look.

Wirework and Chain Necklaces

Using completely different design proportions, these delicate Y necklaces use simple wirework units connected by chain and a single bead at the apex of the Y instead of a finding. Silver bead caps and spacers add detail. Although less ornate, these necklaces also have a Victorian look.

These more delicate interpretations of the Y necklace use a bead instead of a Y finding.

Embellishments

Start noticing what your favorite television stars, news anchors, and pop music divas are wearing, and you'll see versions of the Y necklace everywhere. Some have even longer drops to highlight more daring décolleté; others have a double strand, one at choker length and the second a lower Y. Look for variations, and try modifying one to your own style.

Unique Y Findings Necklaces

Unusual Y findings or findings with two loops on the top and one loop on the bottom abound. The following figure shows two more examples.

The silver version is all wrapped wirework loop components, and the gold version is made with wrapped wirework crystal components and chain.

So many different Y findings are available to inspire you in your own designs!

The Chips Are Never Down!

Skill level: Beginner

What you need:

- Quartz chips in stone of your choice (I used approximately 70 chips for this 20-inch necklace.)
- Complementary accent beads (I used 18 vintage Czech faceted glass beads.)
- Side-drilled glass leaves (Mine were vintage reproductions in gold and green—5 in all.)
- 3mm round gold beads (I used 38.)
- 22 (size 6) seed beads in a complementary color
- 3 feet .015-inch (.038mm) satin gold Beadalon wire
- 2 (size 1) Beadalon gold crimp beads
- 1 gold-filled toggle clasp
- Flexible wire cutters
- Crimping pliers

Techniques and skills needed:

- Stringing with flexible wire
- Crimping

Say hello to chips! These irregular pieces of semi-precious stones have a distinctive way with jewelry. Pair them with metal, crystal, matching stone beads, or whatever suits your fancy. I bet you can't use just one!

Some chips and a few accent beads and findings make this necklace a stunning autumn accessory.

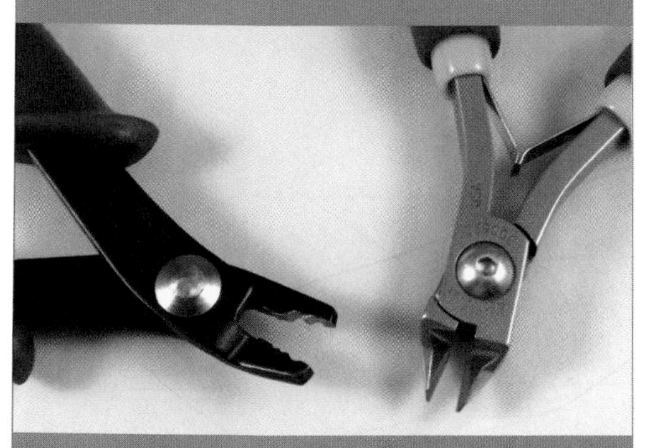

These are the tools you'll need for this project.

Pearls

Stone chips come in all shapes, sizes, and thicknesses. You might want to sort them into groups according to thickness and shape so you can mix them into each group. Also, the holes can be drilled almost anywhere and are sometimes hard to see. Use a contrasting surface underneath to help you see the drill holes, and keep a magnifier handy.

1. Cut a 3-foot length of flexible wire, and put a piece of tape or an alligator clip on the end to keep the strung beads from falling off. Leave a "tail" of about 4 inches below your tape for later, when you'll be attaching your toggle clasp.
2. Begin by stringing a small gold bead and several size 6 seed beads. This is the part that will rest against the back of your neck.

A section of smooth seed beads makes your necklace more comfortable where it hangs from the back of your neck.

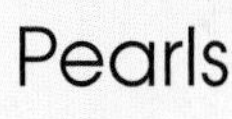

Pearls

If you are absolutely sure of your design, you can begin a stringing project by adding one half of your clasp at the outset. However, by using tape or an alligator clip at the end, you allow yourself some "wiggle room" to change the design without having to cut off the clasp and to add beads at the end for comfort around your neck, if you decide to.

3. String the design elements in groups. My design is made of three different design units: a group of five chips, an accent bead framed by two gold beads, and a glass leaf surrounded by two accent bead with gold bead units on either side.

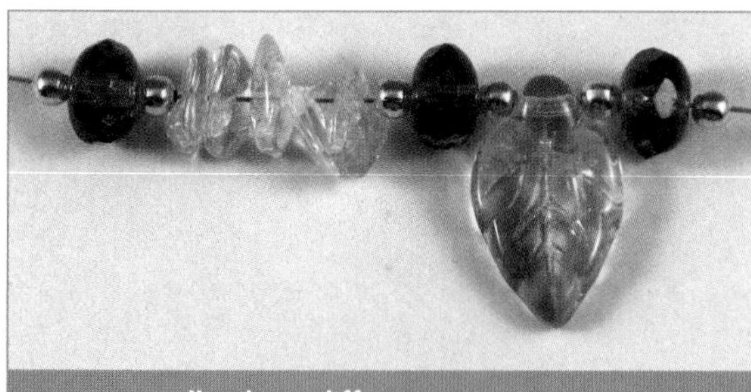

Essentially, three different stringing units are repeated in this design.

I repeated the accent and gold bead units by themselves twice before I added a glass leaf unit so the leaves were highlighted where they would create the most visual interest.

This design uses the special glass leaves sparingly at the front of the piece, for visual impact.

4. Add a toggle clasp at either end using a crimp bead and crimping pliers. Cut off the excess wire, and your necklace is complete!

A toggle clasp with crimps completes this necklace.

Variations

Change colors of beads and chips, and you change moods. From the warm earth tones of the featured necklace to the soft pastels of rose quartz and the rich red of garnet, you can have your chips fall any way you want!

Rose Quartz Necklace

In this variation, a shorter necklace, made with rose quartz chips, size 8 two-cut matte seed beads, silver beads, and matching round rose beads is redesigned to accommodate a matching rose quartz pendant.

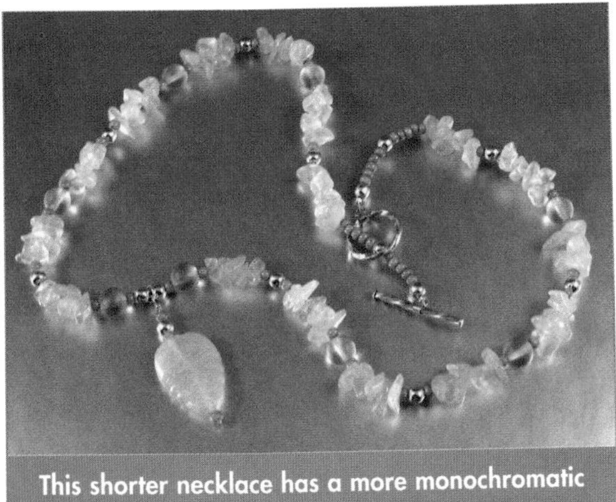

This shorter necklace has a more monochromatic color scheme.

Garnet and Rose Quartz Necklace

Add a darker color of chips (in this case, garnet) to the rose quartz chips for yet another look.

Inexpensive stone chips are full of design possibilities, as you can see. Turquoise chips mixed with silver and red coral beads is another exciting combination. Keep your eyes open for your next bag of chips!

Mixing more than one color of chips is another design idea.

Resources

Glass side-drilled reproduction leaves: Eclectica (www.eclecticabeads.com)

Brown faceted vintage glass accent beads: Rebshans

Wire and crimps: Beadalon (www.beadalon.com)

Flexible wire cutters and crimping pliers: Soft Flex (www.softflexcompany.com)

Bibs Are for You, Too, Baby

Skill level: Beginner

What you need:

Approximately 200 main color E beads
Approximately 31 accent color E beads
Approximately 27 size 11 seed beads in accent color (or complementary color)
1 top-drilled accent bead for dangle, such as a glass leaf
Additional spacer beads for dangle, such as metal novelty spacers and crystals (I used one of each.)
1 yard 8-pound test *FireLine*
1 silver lobster claw clasp
2 (4mm) silver jump rings
2 inches silver medium wide cable chain
1 big eye needle

Techniques and skills needed:

Vertical netting stitch with decreasing

The bib-style necklace has been around for thousands of years. You might have seen the rather spectacular one from Ancient Egypt in the Metropolitan Museum of Art. Technically, a bib necklace (also known as a *collarette*) is a short necklace or choker with some sort of ornamentation hanging in the front, resembling the shape of a baby's bib. Sometimes it takes the form of a collar that extends more deeply in the front and tapers off as it moves toward the back. Or it can be a simple V shape made of woven beads, wire loops, or even metal mesh hanging off a single row of beads that circle the neck.

Bib necklaces tend to be quite dramatic and are especially suitable for lower V necklines, including the plunging necklines associated with evening wear, and strapless dresses. They draw attention to the face and neck, and … other things …, depending on how long they are and how much skin they cover!

This project is easy to make, and afterward, I suggest many variations you can create just by using different sizes of beads or adding rows of vertical netting. Working with E beads (size 6 seed beads) keeps costs down and saves time, but the results are by no means short on "look at me" drama!

These are the beads and supplies you need to make this simple but noteworthy beaded bib choker.

Beadwise

FireLine is a very strong fishing line made from Dynema, a gel-spun polyethylene (GSP), and widely used by beaders as a stringing material. FireLine is sold in strengths and the most commonly used in beading are 6- or 8-pound test.

1. Cut a length of FireLine that's comfortable for you to work with; 2 yards is usually a good length to start, but you might want to work with less. (If you run out of thread, you can simply knot off and then knot on a new thread and continue.) Thread the FireLine through the big eye needle.

Pearls

When you make a knot to end a thread before adding a new one, be sure to double-knot. You can even put a dab of glue on the knot to make it more secure. Do the same with the knot on the thread you're adding.

2. String on 10 size 11 seed beads and, leaving a tail of about 6 inches, make a circle and tie an overhand knot. Go back through the circle with your needle and thread to reinforce it.

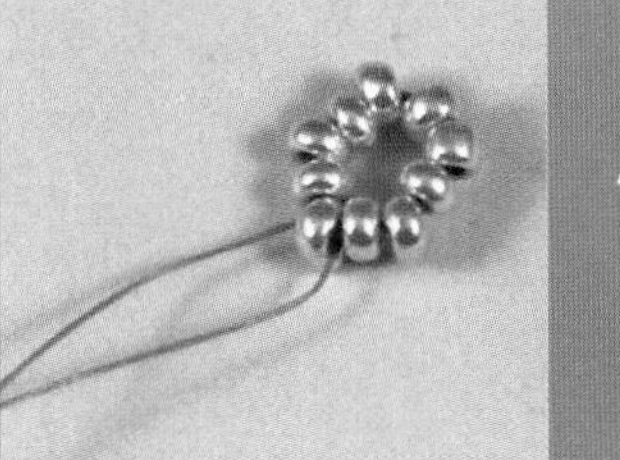

A reinforced circle of size 11 seed beads holds your clasp.

3. String on one accent E bead and 5 main color E beads. Repeat the pattern until your base necklace is the desired length. (My choker ended up being 20 units.) End with an accent E bead.
4. String on 10 size 11 beads and make a loop. Knot and reinforce as you did in the beginning.

Repeat this stringing pattern until you have 20 units of main beads and accent beads.

Pearls

Remember that you'll be adding a chain extender to your necklace, so you can adjust the length to make it looser around your neck. Keep your basic choker fairly snug; you'll have room to adjust the finished necklace.

5. At this point, you probably want to knot off your thread and add thread at the point where you'll start your first row of vertical netting. From the end, I had my thread coming out of the ninth accent bead.

Bring your thread back through the ninth accent bead so you're ready to begin the first row of vertical netting.

6. * String on 4 main color E beads, 1 accent color E bead, and 4 more main color beads, and go through the next accent color bead in the necklace. **

This is the path of your thread for the first stitch of the first row of vertical netting.

7. Repeat from * to ** three more times.
8. From your position coming through the fifth accent bead from where you started your row of netting stitches, come down around the outside of the accent bead and back through the previous 4 main color beads and the middle accent bead.

This is how your work should look after you've completed the first row of vertical netting stitch and are preparing to start the second decreased row.

9. Add 4 main color beads, and go through the next accent bead (at the bottom of the V of the previous row). Repeat twice more, coming up through the last middle accent bead in the row.
10. Come down around the outside of the accent bead and back through the 4 main color beads you just added and the middle accent bead. Continue the vertical netting stitch for two more rows, one made up of two stitches and one a single stitch.
11. Work your needle back around the final "diamond" so you're coming out one side of the very bottom-most accent bead. Add 3 size 11 beads, a crystal, a metal flower bead, your dangle bead (I used a glass leaf), and a size 11 seed bead. Come back up through the leaf, the metal bead, and the crystal. Add 3 more size 11 seed beads and knot off. Trim thread close to a bead. Weave any other threads into your work and trim.

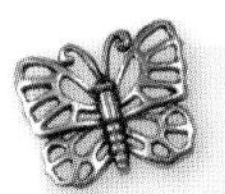

Embellishments

You can choose to make your bib wider than these directions. Begin at an earlier unit, making sure to add an equal number of netting stitches to the other side so your bib is centered. You can also plan to add dangles in other places or other embellishments, depending on your skill level.

This figure shows four rows of netting with decreases completed and dangle added.

Pearls

You can make a wirework dangle instead of the threaded one I used here. Add it to the accent bead with a jump ring.

12. Using jump rings, attach the lobster claw clasp on one end and the chain on the other. You might want to put a small dangle at the end of the chain as a finishing touch.

This is what your finished piece will look like after adding a clasp and chain.

Variations

The size of the beads you choose makes a big difference in the total effect of a netted design. You can also make a more elaborate choker to add interest to the piece.

Turquoise and Copper Necklace

This necklace uses size 11 seed beads throughout the netted part of the work. The base choker was done in two-needle right angle weave, and the netting doesn't come to a complete point.

This delicate version of the bib necklace features netting created entirely with size 11 seed beads.

Faceted Pearl and Gold Necklace

For a truly glamorous bib that would be perfect for a plunging neckline, try making longer netted stitches. I used two-needle right angle weave for the base choker with size 9 three-cut seed beads in gold and faceted gold-dyed pearls. Slightly smaller pearls were used for the netting, and a drop of vintage amber crystal and rhinestone ball bead says "evening" and "black tie" without shouting.

When you've mastered the bib design and practiced doing vertical netting, you'll have added some very useful skills and concepts to your bag of design tricks.

Resources

Size 9 three-cut seed beads: Shipwreck Beads (www.shipwreckbeads.com)

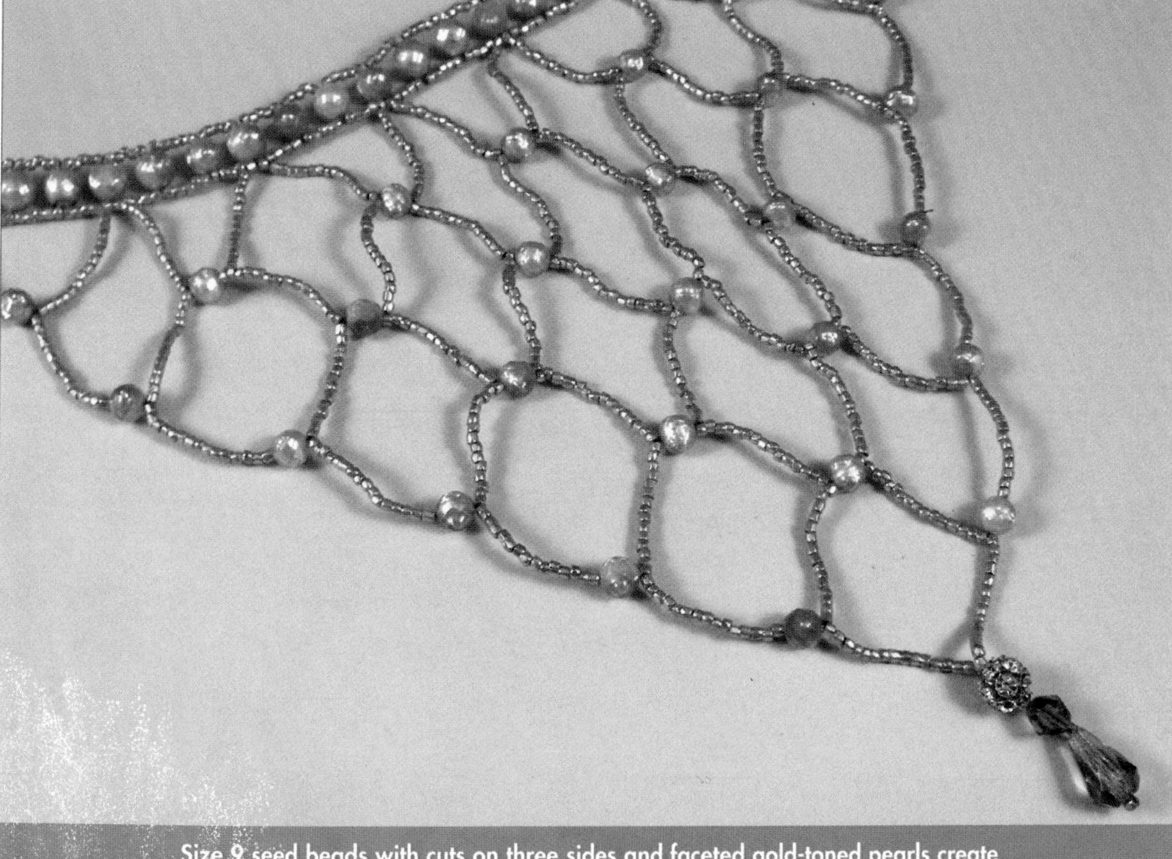

Size 9 seed beads with cuts on three sides and faceted gold-toned pearls create a necklace perfect for evening wear.

It's All in the Wrist

In This Chapter

- Crafting a wardrobe of beaded watchbands
- Making a beaded charm bracelet that's uniquely yours
- Using right angle weave to make a stunning embellished bracelet

You can never have too many bracelets. They can complement a pair of earrings or a necklace as part of a set, or they can be a show all their own. In this chapter, we create three bracelets using three different techniques, each with countless variations. And one even helps you get to appointments on time!

Time Passages

Skill level: Beginner

What you need:

- 6 (9mm) pink and gold main beads
- 7 (7mm) silver spacer beads
- 2 (4mm) silver end beads
- 2 medium silver lobster claw clasps
- 2 (3mm) silver Twisted Tornado Crimps
- 1 silver watch face with end loops
- 10 inches size .24 flexible wire
- Chain nose pliers
- Wire cutters (heavy duty)

Techniques and skills needed:

- Stringing with flexible wire
- Crimping

Using the simplest stringing technique with flexible wire and crimps, you can have an endless selection of mix-and-match watch bracelets and watch faces to suit your mood, your style, and your wardrobe. Take "time" and dress it up or tone it down.

I used these three beads for my watch bracelet.

These lobster claw, crimp, and watch face findings complete the project.

Only two commonly used tools are needed for this project: chain nose pliers and heavy-duty wire cutters.

This watch bracelet project uses flexible wire for its strength and ease of stringing, and a lobster claw clasp on each end makes the bracelets easy to change. Watch faces are readily available in a variety of styles, finishes, and sizes, both with and without loops to attach to your bracelet. In some cases, you might be able to create loops on the ends of a watch face by adding a split ring. (You'll need a pair of split ring pliers for this.) Choose one with loops for this project.

A typical bracelet/watchband length is approximately 7 inches, but you might need to adjust the size for your wrist and depending on whether you like your bracelet snug or a little loose. Don't forget to include the watch face, the watch bracelet connector loops, your beads, the two clasps, and the crimps in your measurements. You'll also need enough room to get your fingers in to attach the clasp. Use a favorite bracelet to get your measurement, or get someone to help you measure with a tape measure or a piece of string fit around your wrist and cut at the right length.

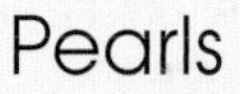

Pearls

A good way to premeasure a bracelet or necklace is to lay out everything on a bead board. These usually have measurements built right in so you can get an approximation of the length, plus see how your design is going to look. It's always a good idea to check again, though, before you do your second crimp.

Understanding Flexible Wire

You'll notice I listed flexible wire in the needed-materials list. Flexible beading wire is actually more than one wire; it's a number of micro-wires braided together and covered with a nylon sheath. It is strong, drapes nicely, and is hypoallergenic. Several brands of flexible beading wire are available, but the best known and, in my experience, the most reliable and easy to work with are Soft Flex and Beadalon. Both come in a variety of sizes (diameter/number of strands in the braid), in silver and gold color, and even in a variety of colors in some diameters.

When working with flexible wire, you need to match the wire diameter to the task and the correct size crimp. For charts to help you determine which wire and crimps are best for a project—along with a host of tips, product information, and projects to try—go to www.softflexcompany.com and www.beadalon.com.

Crimping Like a Pro

To add findings to flexible wire, you need to know how to use a *crimp* bead or tube. Crimps come in different diameters and lengths and are made from different materials, including base metal, sterling silver, and gold filled. You must be sure to match the size of your flexible wire with the size of your crimps. (As with wire, crimp manufacturers' websites often offer charts giving the correct sizes for each.)

Beadwise

A **crimp** is a small metal tube or bead that, when flattened, secures flexible beading wire to findings and beads in a beading design. Crimps come in a variety of sizes, which must be matched to the diameter of the wire you're using.

Some crimps work best when a crimping tool is used. This tool has two functions: it serves to put a crease down the center of the crimp (to latch on to the wire), and it also tightens and flattens it (to secure the wire in place). The higher-quality crimp you use, the better the results. I've found that sterling silver works much better than base metal and that thicker crimps also give better results.

A relative newcomer to the beading world is a crimp called the Twisted Tornado Crimp. This nifty invention alleviates the need for a crimping tool and can be flattened with a pair of chain nose pliers. It's even pretty enough to be part of the final design. You can find these crimps at better bead stores and online at www.viamurano.com. I used Twisted Tornado Crimps for this project because of their effectiveness and contribution to the design.

Here's a shot of the Twisted Tornado Crimp close up.

To use a crimp, thread your wire through the crimp tube, add your finding, and then come back around to re-enter the crimp tube with the wire from the opposite direction.

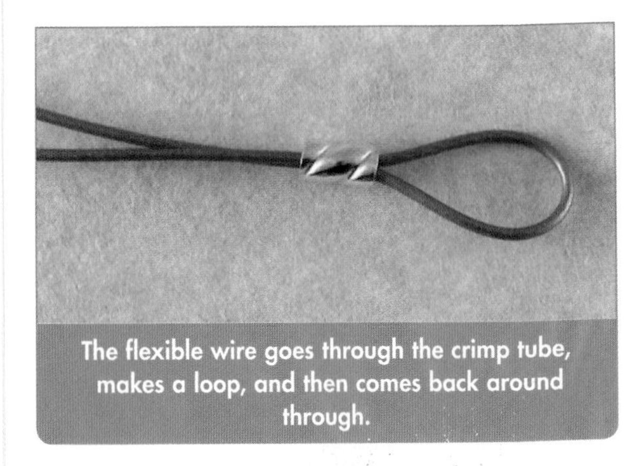

The flexible wire goes through the crimp tube, makes a loop, and then comes back around through.

When you have everything assembled, simply tighten up your flexible wire loop and flatten the crimp with a pair of chain nose pliers.

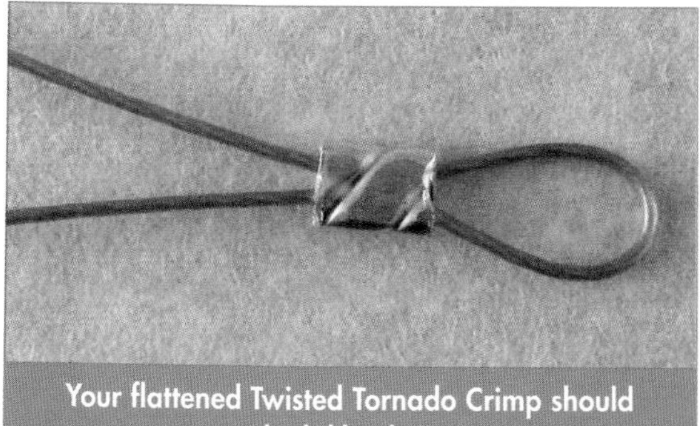

Your flattened Twisted Tornado Crimp should look like this.

Pearls

In the resource section at the end of this project, I share some great places where you can get quality crimps, flexible wire, tools, and watch faces. Or turn to Appendix A, where I give you complete listings for all the resources used in this book.

Assembling Your Watch Bracelet

Now that you know all about flexible wire and crimping, let's begin our first project.

1. Cut 10 inches of flexible wire with heavy-duty cutters.

Crimps!

Don't use your best beading side cutters for cutting flexible wire, or they'll become dull in a hurry. Get a pair of heavy-duty cutters and keep them just for cutting flexible wire, or use an old pair that are on their way out. They need to be sharp enough to make a clean cut, though! If you want to, check the wire manufacturer's website for recommendations on wire cutters specifically for flexible wire.

2. Thread one crimp tube and one lobster claw clasp on one end of the wire. Thread the wire back through the crimp tube, and crimp close to the clasp by pulling the wire snug. You want it tight, but not so tight that the clasp can't move freely.

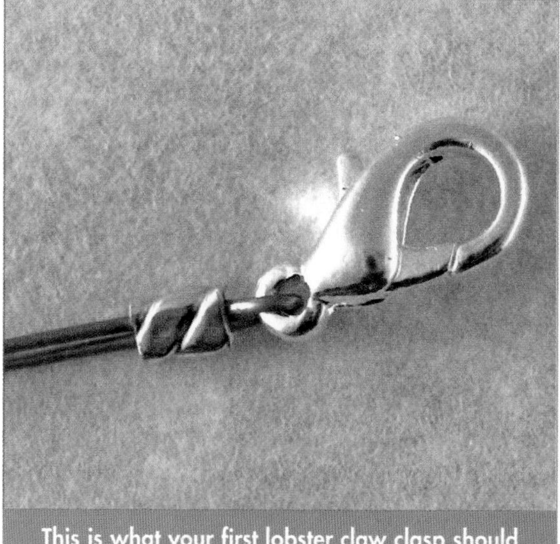

This is what your first lobster claw clasp should look like after you've crimped it tight.

3. Thread the beads on the flexible beading wire in this order:

   1 end bead

   1 spacer bead

   1 main bead

   Alternate spacer beads and main beads until the bracelet measures approximately 5½ inches in length, ending with a spacer bead.
4. Add an end bead, a crimp, and the second clasp on the end of your wire. Thread the wire end back through the crimp tube and tighten.

Your watch bracelet should look like this just before finishing, when all the beads, the second crimp, and the clasp are threaded on.

5. Now's a good time to take a final measurement. Adjust the length to fit your wrist by adding or removing beads.

Measure to see if you need to add or remove beads before you crimp.

Pearls

If the measurement you have now is not right for your wrist, you might have to take off all your beads and restring them. You can add small end beads to add a little bit of length or take some away to make the bracelet smaller. Remember to add or subtract the same number on each end.

6. Crimp and cut any excess wire and then attach the ends with the clasps to the watch face loops. Your watch bracelet is done!

Your watchband is now ready to wear!

Variations

Now that you've got the basics down, let's have a little more fun. In the following sections, I offer several variations for you to try using multiple strands of beads and conventional watches to spruce up with a beaded bracelet instead of a ho-hum watchband. Who knows—these might just jump-start your imagination to come up with your own variations!

Two-Strand Bracelet

This bracelet is made the same way as the featured project, except two strands of beads are used. Two-hole spacers help keep everything lined up nicely and add some glitter and sparkle. Crimp both wires separately at each end, just as you did with the single length of wire.

Pretty spacer findings and crystals make this sparkling two-strand watch bracelet.

Permanent Bracelet with Toggle Clasp

Some watch faces for beading do not have large loops for attaching a clasp. Instead, they have a hole for inserting wire or thread through and require that you add a clasp at the center of the bracelet rather than on the ends like the featured project. To work with these watches, you can either add your own loops with wire, a jump ring, or a split ring, or you can simply make a permanent, nonremovable bracelet.

Some watch faces have holes rather than large loops at each end.

This watch bracelet uses one strand of flexible wire for each side, and both ends of the single strand are crimped onto the clasp at either end. The two strands come together at regular intervals and go through a single larger bead to add interest. You will, of course, need to have the two strands coincide and be of equal length. You'll also need to center the clasp, and each side of the bracelet needs to be of equal length as well.

Colorful and slightly irregular beads make this watch a playful addition to any collection.

In this close-up, you can see how the crimps and clasp ends come together.

Interchangeable Bracelet Using a Conventional Watch

Perhaps you already have a watch that's not specifically designed for beading and you'd like to create a beaded bracelet for it. No problem! All you need is a special metal watch finding.

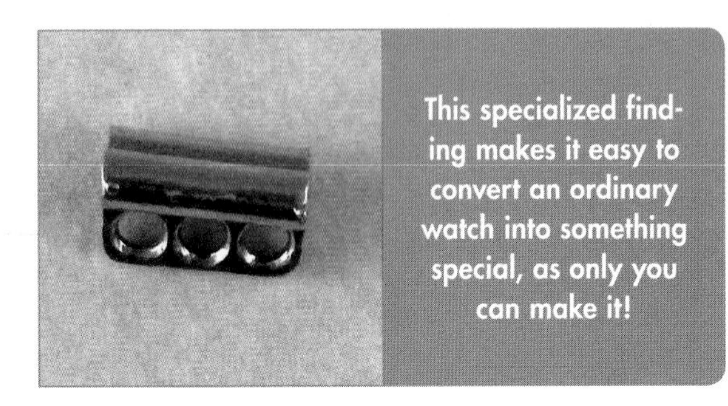
This specialized finding makes it easy to convert an ordinary watch into something special, as only you can make it!

To use this finding, remove the pins that held the original watchband in place (don't lose them!) and slip on the finding. Now you can easily create a three-strand bracelet you can remove just by taking out the pins again and putting on another watch band.

For this watch bracelet, I used cheerful pastel beads along with base metal butterflies and bees for a springtime look.

Pearls

Rings & Things sells a base metal finding that fits over a conventional watch pin and creates three holes for attaching beaded strands. See Appendix A for contact info.

You can also convert a conventional watch into a beaded watch bracelet by adding beads to the watch pin and strands of wire in between. You'll have to find beads with large enough holes to fit over the pin, and they have be the right size to fit between the watch pin bracket and the watch pin. Experiment and see what you can design yourself.

Eyeglass and ID Holders

By making your watch bracelet longer (necklace length) and adding different findings to the ends of your clasps, you can adapt the design used for the feature project to interchangeable holders for eyeglasses, ID or professional passes, or credentials.

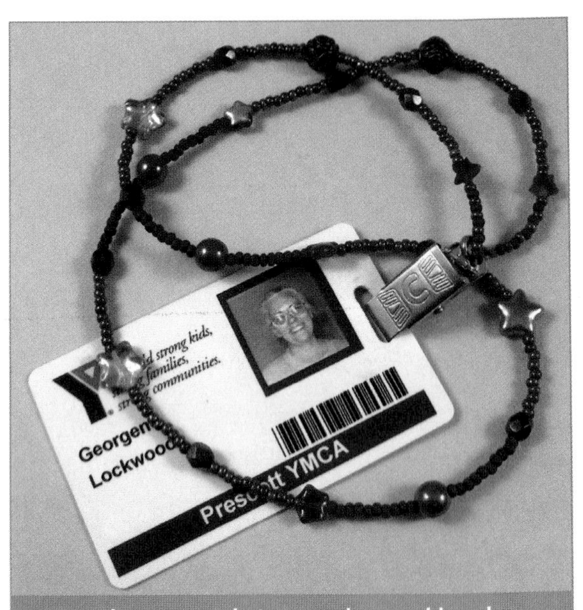

Using the same technique as the watchband, you can string a necklace of beads with a lobster claw clasp on each end and attach them to a clip for an identification card or credentials.

Clip eyeglass holder findings on either end of your necklace and you can keep your specs close at hand. Because you've used lobster claw clasps at the ends you can have a whole wardrobe of holders using the same holder findings.

A small pouch with a zipper can be used to hold your ID safely when traveling. You can tuck it inside a jacket or sweater for extra safety.

If you still need help generating ideas for beaded watch bracelets and bands, look online. Type "beaded watch band" in your favorite search engine, and see what you find! Keep your eyes open when shopping at your favorite stores for ideas, too.

Resources

Flexible wire: Beadalon (www.beadalon.com), Soft Flex Company (www.softflexcompany.com)

Tornado crimps: Via Murano (www.viamurano.com)

Watch adapter finding: Rings & Things (www.rings-things.com)

Beads and findings: Blue Moon Beads (the silver spacer beads used in the main project; ww.bluemoonbeads.com), Fire Mountain Gems (www.firemountaingems.com)

Watch faces: Artgems, Inc. (www.artgemsinc.com); Fire Mountain Gems

Charmed, I'm Sure!

Skill level: Beginner

What you need:

- 1 premade silver or gold charm bracelet for beading
- 6 or 7 silver or gold charms
- 15 or 20 (20- or 22-gauge) silver or gold head pins
- 12 (8mm, 20-gauge) silver or gold jump rings
- Assorted beads for making "charms" (I used 3 to 6 beads and spacers for each charm, adding up to 26 total.)
- Chain nose pliers
- Flush wire cutters
- Round nose pliers

Techniques and skills needed:

- Basic wirework techniques
- Making a simple loop (see Chapter 1 for a review)

Charm bracelets are back! Maybe you remember them from childhood. Well, now they're all grown up and going everywhere! Beading has played no small part in the charm bracelet revival, with precast charms available in every shape, size, and theme, and beadwork incorporated to give a one-of-a-kind look.

All you need to know to create a unique charm bracelet as a gift for yourself or some lucky person is some basic wirework. You can mix and match purchased charms and your own beaded "charms," make a traditional bracelet of all metal charms, or make it all "bead charms." You can even raid the button box, tear apart some old broken jewelry, or borrow from the rubber-stamping and art clay crowds to create charms. The choice is yours.

Embellishments

Don't limit yourself to store-bought charms. Almost anything can be a charm. If it has a hole or if a hole can be drilled through it, maybe it's a charm! Buttons, washers, coins, shells, lockets, game pieces, dice, and pendants from old jewelry all might make interesting charms. There are also kits for making charms with photos and rubber-stamped images. Keep your eyes open!

And if you can think of a theme, you can make a bracelet to portray it. Charms are available for every sport or hobby, organization or society, and occasion. Like hearts, angels, wizards, or dragons—you name it, there are charms out there!

An assortment of metal findings and charms make up the "bones" of this bracelet.

Beads in shades of green and metal beads round out the materials I used in my charm bracelet.

Here are the tools you'll need for this project.

Making a charm bracelet is easy with a premade bracelet created just for adding beads and charms. These are available from a variety of sources, and I've listed some at the end of this project. You can also buy chain by the foot at many bead stores and through catalogs and then just add your own clasp. Be sure the chain you choose is heavy enough to hold up to the weight of the charms and that the links are large enough to fit your jump ring (or several, if you plan on adding more than one charm to a link).

Cast base metal charms are available in a variety of finishes, such as silver, gold, brass, and copper. To make a higher-end bracelet, you can also purchase sterling silver and gold-filled charms. You can find charms embellished with colorful enamel finishes as well. The more you look, the more interesting choices you'll see.

Some charms come with their own jump rings attached; some don't. You can buy jump rings in a variety of gauges and sizes, or use split rings if your charms are heavy and you're concerned about the jump rings coming apart. If you're using sterling silver jump rings, you can also solder them closed.

Embellishments

Another way to personalize your charm bracelet is to create a wire connector for your charms so you can add a bead or two above the charm in that way. You reviewed how to make simple loops and wrapped loops with wire in Chapter 1, as well as how to make beaded connectors and dangles. Consider how you might incorporate these into your bracelet.

Making Your Own Jump Rings

It's handy to have an assortment of jump rings in various gauges and sizes, but sometimes no matter how many supplies you have on hand, sometimes you just don't have exactly what you need when you start a project.

No jump rings on hand? You can make your own. It's easy! All you need is the right wire for the job, something to use to wrap the wire around to create the desired diameter ring, and a good pair of flush wire cutters.

Pearls

If you think you'll be making lots of jump rings, you might want to buy wooden dowels in a variety of diameters and cut them to a manageable length such as 18 inches. Label each with its size, and drill a small hole all the way through at one end using a $\frac{1}{16}$-inch drill bit. Then just insert your wire into the hole to start your coil and wrap the desired number of times. Remove the coil from the "starter stick," and cut your jump rings using your flush wire cutters.

To begin, hold the wire against your stick or whatever you might be using (I used a knitting needle), and begin to twist it in your hand, wrapping wire around it with the other hand. You can keep the wire connected to the spool if you're using spool wire. Keep your coil tight around the stick and close together.

Twist the wire around your stick to make the desired number of jump rings.

Then slide the coil off the stick, and using your flush cutters, snip them through in a straight line. They'll just fall off!

Make your own jump rings by cutting them from the coil with a pair of flush cutters.

With your jump rings and all your materials assembled, you're ready to make your charm bracelet.

Making Your Bracelet Bloom

For the "Garden Flowers" bracelet, I used seven garden-themed charms made out of cast base metal. Some were fairly large and some smaller, so I placed them in a way that seemed balanced, alternating larger and smaller ones. You can lay yours out on a bead board or cloth to see what pleases you.

1. Open a jump ring, and put it through the loop at the top of your charm. (If your charm already has a jump ring attached, simply open the jump ring.)

Crimps!

Remember, twist the loop open. Don't pull it apart.

2. Put the open jump ring through one of the links in your charm bracelet and close. Take care to put your charms on all in one direction if they're not the same on the back and the front. You'll also want to keep the links in your bracelet chain flat so you're attaching your charms all on the same part of the chain links.

Putting on your first charm.

3. Put on the rest of the charms as in step 2, spacing them as equally apart as possible. You can do this by eye or by counting the number of links between them.

This is my charm bracelet with all the charms fastened on with jump rings.

4. Next, you need to make your bead dangles or "charms." You can vary their length and put on as many or as few as you like. In the version shown here, I added a few in between the cast charms, but you can put something in every link (or even several in a link) for a fuller look, if you like. To make your "charm," stack your beads on a head pin and cut off the top so you have approximately 10mm of wire left (use a 10mm bead as a gauge if you like, cut off at the top of the bead, and then remove it). Bend the wire over to make a right angle, and using your round nose pliers, make a simple wire loop.

These dangles will form charms for my bracelet.

5. Add jump rings, and attach your dangles to the charm bracelet where desired.

Your charm bracelet is complete!

Variations

If you don't have (or can't find) a premade bracelet for adding charms or a chain to create one, no matter. You can create one using some flexible wire. It's a different look, but it's lovely as well.

Flexible Wire Charm Bracelet

Cut about 8½ inches of heavy-gauge flexible wire. I used Soft Flex Gold. Have your charms all ready to go by adding your jump rings and closing them. Then you just have to slide them to the wire. Small spacer beads on either side of the charm's jump ring help it hang nicely. Add a crimp bead and clasp on one end and a crimp bead and clasp end on the other, crimp, and you're done!

No chain or charm bracelet? No problem. This one uses flexible wire and crimps instead.

Pearls

Don't be afraid to add small dangles in the jump rings above the store-bought charms you added to your bracelet. This adds still more interest!

Jeans Jewelry

A new place to put charms is on your jeans! Or you can decorate any pair of pants with belt loops, for that matter. The concept is the same as a charm bracelet, except you need a large clasp at either end to attach to the belt loops and you have to cut your own chain to get the right length.

Add some pizzazz with jeans charm jewelry.

Measure the length you want. I used 7 inches of chain. Cut the chain to fit and add a large clasp on either end. Don't forget to add the clasps in as part of your measurement! I found the hardware I needed for this project at my local Wal-Mart.

Hearts Bracelet

Another idea is to look for charms that are variations on a single object. This one is "all heart"—with just a few tiny hematite stars thrown in, for good measure.

In your travels, keep your eyes open for your favorites. You might collect angels, fairies, owls, or hats. I've even seen some absolutely adorable monkeys!

A charm bracelet that's "all heart."

To express yourself, to celebrate any occasion, or for a truly unique gift, a charm bracelet is where it's at. How about a bracelet with baby-themed charms for a new mom? There are charms for just about every sport; make one for your favorite cheerleader or tennis player. If you have a friend in the Red Hat Society, you'll find charms for her, too!

Resources

Charms: Shipwreck Beads (www.shipwreckbeads.com), Fire Mountain Gems (www.firemountaingems.com), Wal-Mart, Jo-Ann Fabric and Crafts (www.joann.com)

Charm bracelets: Rings & Things (www.rings-things.com)

Beads, jump rings, head pins, and wire: your local bead or craft store, Fire Mountain Gems

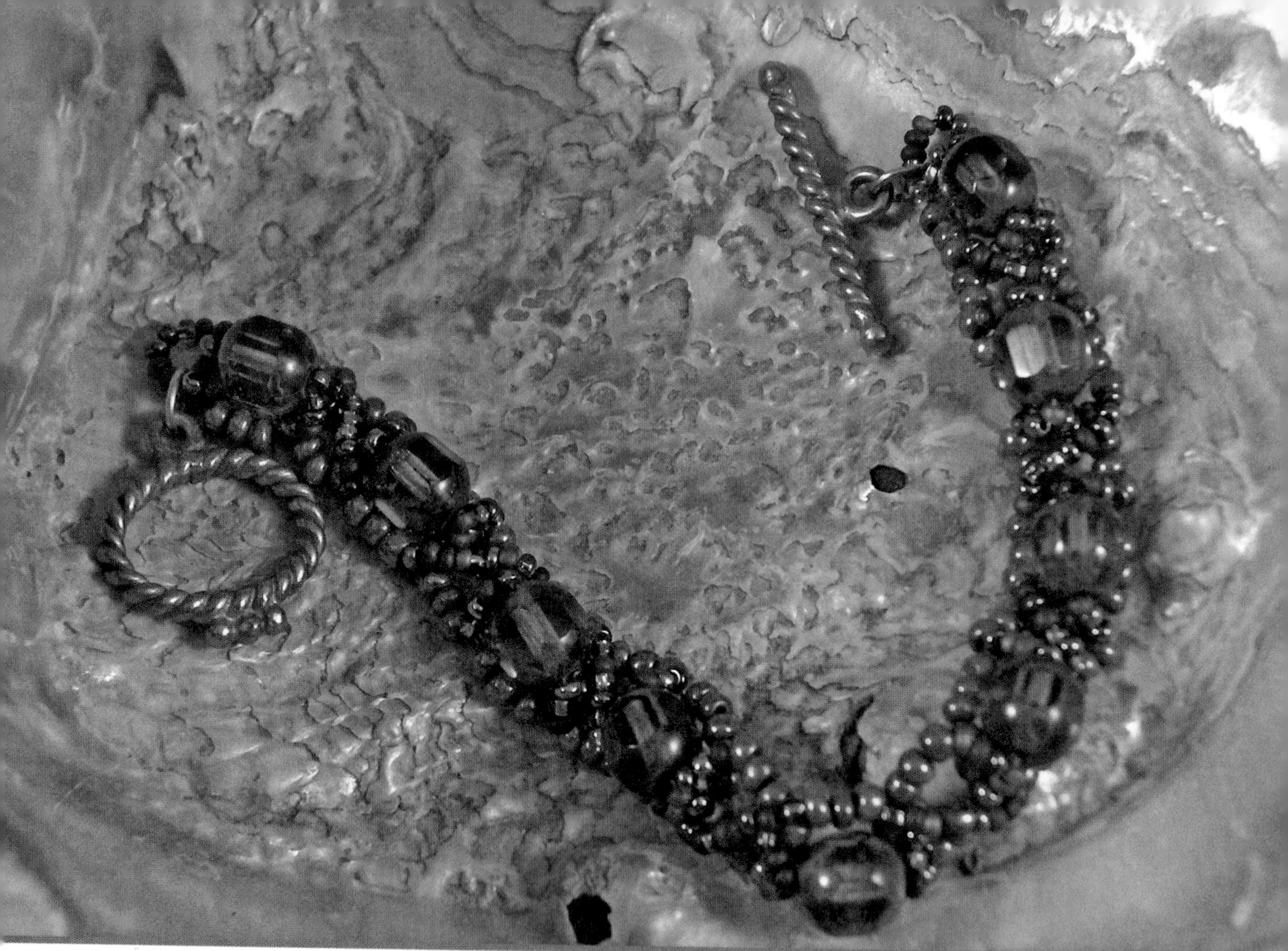

Bracelets in the RAW

Skill level: Intermediate

What you need:

- 2 strands (size 8) seed beads in color of your choice
- 2 strands (size 11) seed beads in complementary color of your choice
- 9 (8mm) beads in a complementary color
- 2 (5mm, 20-gauge) jump rings in metal finish to match toggle clasp
- 1 toggle clasp
- 6-pound FireLine
- 1 (size 10) beading needle or big eye needle
- Chain nose pliers

Techniques and skills needed:

Right angle weaving

As I mentioned in Chapter 1, *RAW* is shorthand in the beading world for an off-loom weaving stitch called *right angle weave*. It's a very versatile stitch you can do flat, tubular, and even 3-D to create a wide variety of forms and shapes.

In this project, you use a single row to create a base over which you weave additional beads to make a texturally interesting bracelet. Vary the size of the beads you use in the base bracelet, and your finished bracelet will have a whole different look.

Two kinds of seed beads, some 8mm beads, FireLine and a needle comprise the materials needed for this unique bracelet design.

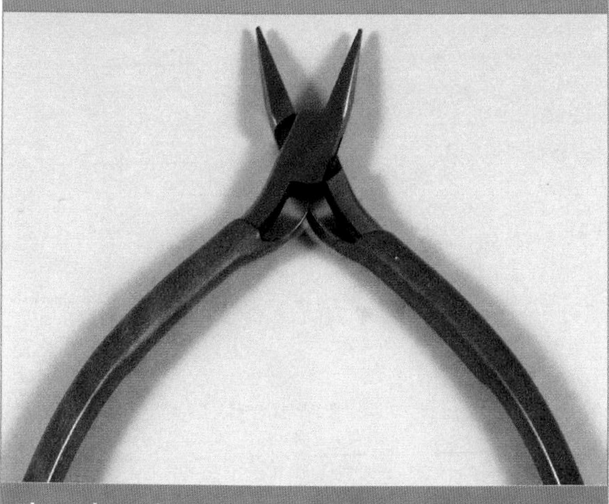

The only tool you'll need for this project is a pair of chain nose pliers.

Pearls

FireLine is actually a high-tech fishing line! Beaders discovered it as a strong and supple "thread" for beadwork. It comes in three colors: Smoke, Flame Green, and more recently, clear Crystal. So check out the fishing department of your local department store or your favorite sporting goods catalog. You'll be surprised at what you might find—including great tackle boxes and storage containers for toting and organizing your beads!

The most important thing to remember about RAW is to be mindful of the path of your thread and to double-check that you've come up through the correct number of beads to ensure you're in the right position to make your next beaded loop. Read through the instructions and look at the pictures carefully before you start.

This bracelet is built over a base bracelet of a single row of simple RAW. You don't even have to turn any corners to create a second row, which some people find tricky when they're first learning this stitch. The look is complicated, but the pattern is easy, and once you start, you won't want to stop! Let's get started.

1. Cut a length of FireLine about 2½ yards long. If you find it awkward to work with this length of thread, you can add in thread later, simply by knotting it on and weaving back to the point where you left off.

Crimps!

Use sharp cutters for cutting FireLine. Otherwise, you'll mash the end, making it difficult to thread on a beading needle.

2. Thread the FireLine on your beading needle (I found a big eye needle worked best), and string on 12 (size 8) beads.

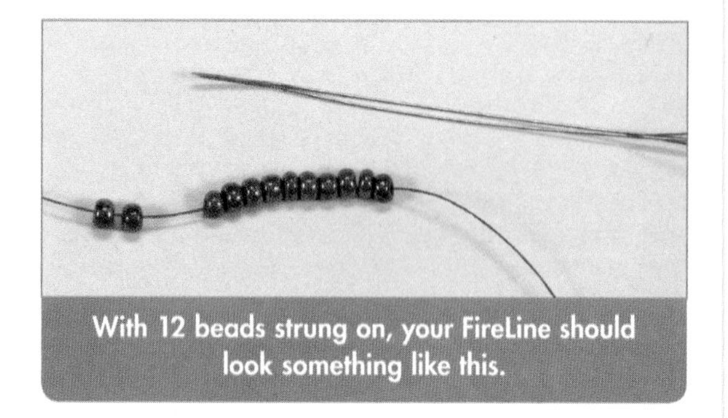

With 12 beads strung on, your FireLine should look something like this.

3. Leaving a tail of about 6 inches, tie the beads in a circle and knot using a simple overhand knot. Knot a second time.

This photo shows the beads tied in a circle and knotted.

4. Bring your needle up through the next 6 beads.

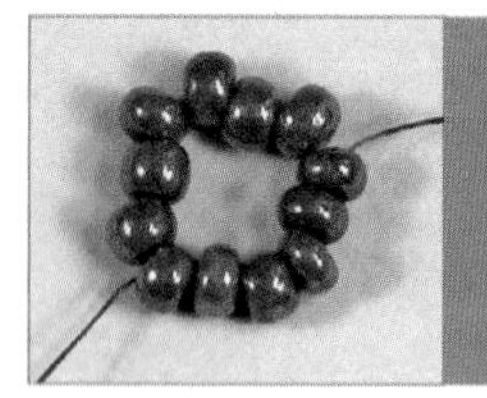

This is what your work should look like as you prepare to make your next beaded circle.

5. String on 9 more size 8 beads. Making a circle, go back around the 3 beads closest to the needle and thread.

Follow the thread path to make your second beaded circle.

6. Turn your work if you want (the instructions from here on assume you have), and bring your needle and thread up through the next 6 beads. You're now ready to create another beaded circle.

This is what your work should look like after step 6.

Pearls

Some people find it easier to turn their work as they do RAW, right after they go backward and make a circle but before they get ready to weave up to the top of the circle they just made to start another one. You decide.

7. String on 9 more size 8 beads, and repeat steps 4 and 5 until your bracelet is the desired length.

   To create a bracelet that fits you comfortably if you have an average-size wrist, it needs to measure approximately 7¼ inches, including the clasp and the beaded loop and jump rings used to attach the clasp. If your wrist is larger or smaller, adjust the pattern to fit. My finished bracelet ended up having 17 beaded RAW loops.

Crimps!

Keep your tension even as you work, and don't allow your thread to get loose. It's difficult to tighten things up later and much easier to watch your tension as you go along.

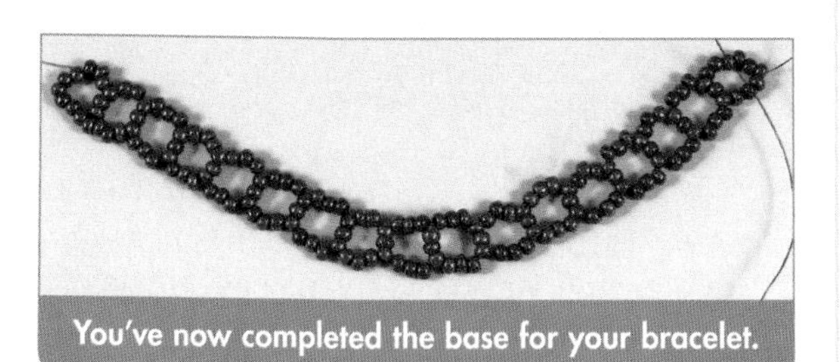

You've now completed the base for your bracelet.

8. Thread on 9 (size 11) seed beads and make a circle, coming back through the last 3 beads in your base bracelet. Reinforce the loop by going over this circular thread path one more time. This loop will be used to attach the toggle clasp using a jump ring.

Make a 9-bead loop with size 11 seed beads for your clasp.

9. Now we'll be working right to left. With your needle and thread at the bottom of your work, coming out of the last 3 beads of your base bracelet (to the right and perpendicular), * thread on 3 (size 11) seed beads, your 8mm bead, and 3 more size 11 seed beads. Skip the 3 (size 8) seed beads at the bottom of the circle you're currently working next to, and go through the next group of 3 (size 9) seed beads. (In other words, skip every other circle.) **

After step 9, your first focal bead should be attached like this.

10. Repeat the instructions from * to ** in step 9 eight more times. String on 3 (size 11) seed beads, your last 8mm bead, and 3 more size 11 seed beads. Skip 3 (size 8) beads, and go up through the next 3 (size 8) seed beads at the other end of your RAW base bracelet (to the left and perpendicular).

11. Add 9 (size 11) seed beads and make a circle, coming back through the same 3 (size 8) seed beads you came out of in step 9. Reinforce by following this thread path one more time. You should now be at the top of your work. You're now ready to anchor your first focal bead over the base bracelet.

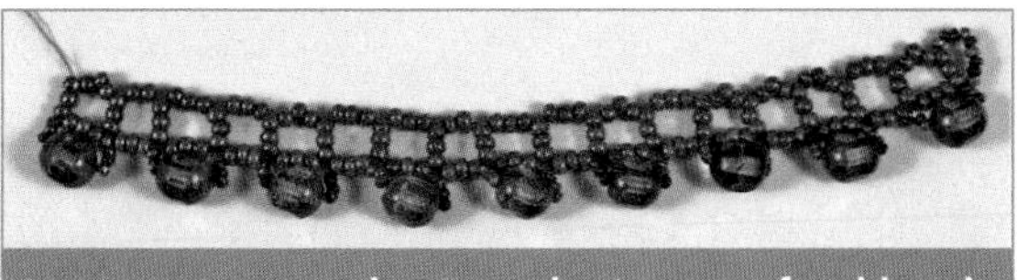

Now you're set to begin anchoring your focal beads to your base bracelet.

Pearls

At this point, you might want to flip your work so your needle and thread are at the bottom-right corner and you'll be working from right to left again (assuming you're a "rightie," this might be easier for you). My instructions from here on assume you have done this.

12. String on 3 (size 11) seed beads, and go through the last 8mm bead you strung on. Add another 3 (size 11) seed beads, and go through the bottom 3 (size 8) seed beads of the very next circle of your RAW base bracelet. The 8mm focal bead should now be "anchored" on top of the first size 8–bead circle.

You have now anchored your first focal bead onto your base bracelet.

13. Repeat this process until all your 8mm beads are "anchored" over every other circle of your RAW base bracelet.

Your bracelet should look like this after you've anchored on all the 8mm focal beads.

14. When you reach the opposite end, come back up through the last 3 (size 8) seed beads and over to the right through the top 3 (size 8) seed beads. String on 9 (size 11) seed beads, and cross diagonally to the lower right of the in-between circle. Go through the bottom 3 (size 8) seed beads from left to right. (You'll be going over the beads at the bottom of the next 8mm bead.)

This is what your work should look like after you've made the first diagonal pattern between the 8mm focal beads.

15. String on another 9 (size 11) seed beads, and repeat this diagonal pattern, this time going from the lower left across diagonally to the upper right and the through the 3 (size 8) seed beads at the top of the next 8mm bead circle.
16. Continue weaving across the surface of your bracelet in this way until you reach the opposite end, alternating the diagonal. You'll end up at the top of your work to the right of the last 8mm bead coming out of the last group of 3 (size 8) beads at the bottom of your base bracelet.
17. Tie an overhand knot twice in between the beads and around the thread going through them, bringing your needle up through the last three beads at the end your bracelet. Snip off the thread.

The surface embellishment of your bracelet is now complete.

18. Weave the tail left from where you began into your work, and snip close to a bead.

19. Open a jump ring with your chain nose pliers (twist it; don't pull!), add one end of your toggle clasp, and attach it to the small loop at one end of your bracelet. Close the jump ring using the same twisting motion. Repeat with the other part of your toggle clasp on the other end of the bracelet. You're finished!

Your embellished right angle weave bracelet is now complete!

Variations

The look of this bracelet changes dramatically when you use different sizes of beads for the base bracelet. You can go smaller or larger, but be sure to adjust the size of your focal beads and the number of size 11 seed beads you use to make your end loops and surface embellishments. You might have to experiment a bit to find the right pattern.

Turquoise and Gold Bracelet

For this bracelet, I used larger beads (size 6) to make the RAW base. This necessitated using 15 (size 11) beads at each end to make the loops for the clasp and 15 beads for the diagonal sections between the larger focal beads. I still used only three beads on either side of the focal beads. I needed only 14 RAW circles for the base bracelet, and because of the even number, I ended up with a slightly different placement of the focal beads.

Using a larger bead for the base bracelet creates a whole different look.

Pink and Green Bracelet

Here I used the same size beads for the base bracelet as I did for the featured project (size 8), but I used a smaller bead as the focal bead (6mm). A more delicate color scheme gives it yet another look.

What a great gift this bracelet would make! Honestly, once you get the pattern down, you can make a bracelet like this in a couple of hours. Get started now, and have a stash in different colors for yourself and all the other lucky women in your life!

Resources

Seed beads: Shipwreck Beads (www.shipwreckbeads.com), Scottsdale Bead Supply (www.scottsdalebead.com)

Clasps: Fire Mountain Gems (www.firemountaingems.com, your local bead shop

A smaller focal bead changes the look.

Pin-Pourri

In This Chapter

- Combining beads and wire to make a spectacular flower pin
- Updating an old-fashioned kilt pin with charms and beads
- Using bead embroidery to frame a cabochon for a one-of-a-kind brooch

Pins are back in a big way. They show up on shoulders, securing a scarf and adding interest to a hat or accenting a collar. Antique pins are in especially high demand. Why not create a pin that speaks of more romantic, feminine times that will bloom on nobody else but *you?*

Garden Variety Pin

Skill level: Intermediate

What you need:

1 hank dark purple size 11 seed beads
1 hank light purple size 11 seed beads
1 hank white size 11 seed beads
1 spool (24-gauge) light purple wire
1 spool (24-gauge) dark purple wire
1 spool (24-gauge) white wire
1 (1-inch) perforated disc pin finding assembly
1 (8mm) crystal bead for center
Nylon jaw pliers
Wire cutters
Bead spinner (optional)

Techniques and skills needed:

French beaded flowers
Simple loop method

The centuries-old technique of French flower beading can be highly complex, but it all begins with some surprisingly simple basics. With some wire and beads and a little practice, you, too, can plant your own beaded garden to wear.

A perforated disc pin finding, some beads and wire, and just a few tools are all you need for this project. I highly recommend a bead spinner if you plan to do more French flower beading.

Beadwise

A **hank** is a strand of beads tied together and sold as a unit. A hank of size 11 seed beads is usually made up of 12 (16-inch) strands, for a total of approximately 4,000 beads.

If you've never done French beaded flowers before, don't be intimidated, because you're in for a treat. Once you make your first flower, you'll begin to see endless possibilities. You can easily adapt these beaded blossoms to hair ornaments and even necklaces and earrings.

But how to get the beads on the wire? If you don't have a bead spinner, there are two possibilities—you can pick them up one at a time (slow) or you can thread them onto the wire directly from the hank of beads (somewhat faster). To do the latter, pick out one thread from the hank and, starting at the top, thread the wire along with the string. Cut the string and carefully pull it out.

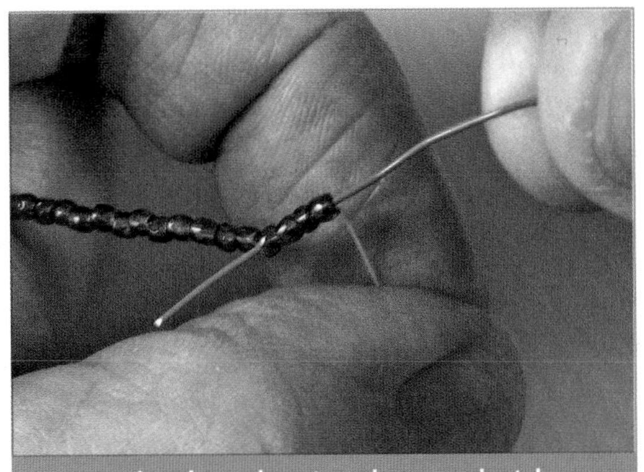

To get beads on the wire when you don't have a bead spinner, slide on several beads at a time directly from the hank.

Pearls

A bead spinner is something of a luxury, but if you plan on doing beaded flowers on a regular basis, you'll be unable to live without one (or two or three). It's so much easier to spin the beads on the wire than it is to either put them on one at a time by hand or try to slip them on from the hank.

Let's get started:

1. Do *not* cut your wire, but keep it attached to the spool. Using your bead spinner, the one-at-a-time method, or the "sliding on from the hank" method, get 3½ feet of the dark purple beads on your wire. To keep the wire from unraveling on your spool, cut a slit in the spool and slide the wire in the slit. Some spools come with this slit already cut.

Crimps!

To avoid having the wire show through the beads and maybe even change the overall effect of your flowers, as best you can, match the wire to the color of your beads. Both Artistic and ColourCraft wire have a wide selection of colors to choose from.

2. Make a small loop at the end of your wire to keep the beads from falling off. Then, grasping the end of the wire firmly in your hand and leaving approximately 3 inches of bare wire above it, count out 25 beads with the other hand and slide them up from the spool end. Always working from the same direction (either right to left or left to right), make a loop with your beads and wire, and twist one *full* turn at the bottom.

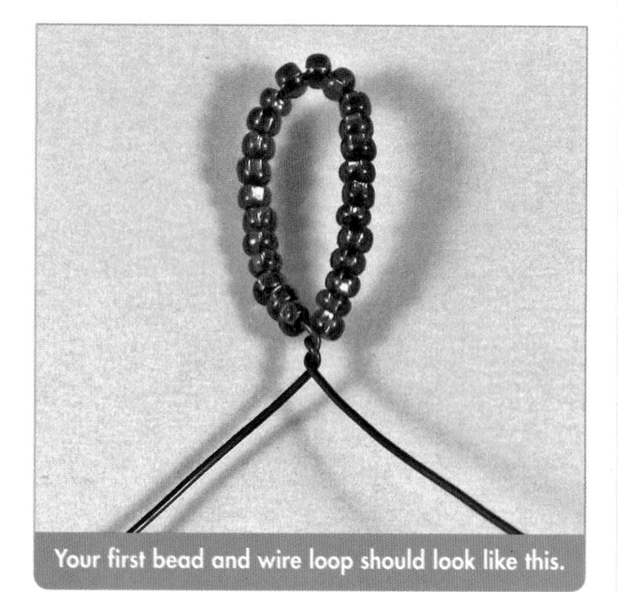

Your first bead and wire loop should look like this.

3. Count out 35 beads, make another loop above the one you just made, and twist.

The second loop follows around the first, and you twist right below it.

4. Allow approximately ¼ inch and make another pair of loops. You leave the space between to create room for the next petal.

A second pair of loops makes a second petal.

5. Repeat step 4 until you have 10 double-loop petals. Cut the wire off the spool, leaving a tail of about 2 or 3 inches.

Your first round of 10 petals should look something like this.

6. Join together the two wires (your starting "tail" and the end you just cut) by twisting just a couple of times.

This is what the back of your first round of petals yshould look like.

7. Put 4 feet of light purple beads on the light purple wire.
8. With this round of petals, you'll be using 3 rows of beads for each petal. The first loop is 15 beads, then 25, then 35.

The 3-loop petal of your second flower layer.

Leave ¾ inch between each petal to accommodate the 3 loops. Make 10 triple row petals and join, as you did in step 6.

The second layer of petals looks like this.

9. Put 2 feet of white beads on the white wire. Draw up 30 beads, make a loop, and twist at the bottom as before, but press it closed and continue twisting with the beads themselves. Be careful not to twist too hard, or you could break the beads.

By twisting the beads and wire together, you get this interesting feature for the next round.

Leave approximately ¼ inch between these twisted loops. Make 10 and join as before.

The third layer of your flower will look like this when it's joined.

10. Cut a piece of wire 5 inches long that matches your center crystal bead. Place the bead on the wire, fold the wire in half, and twist under the bead to secure it.

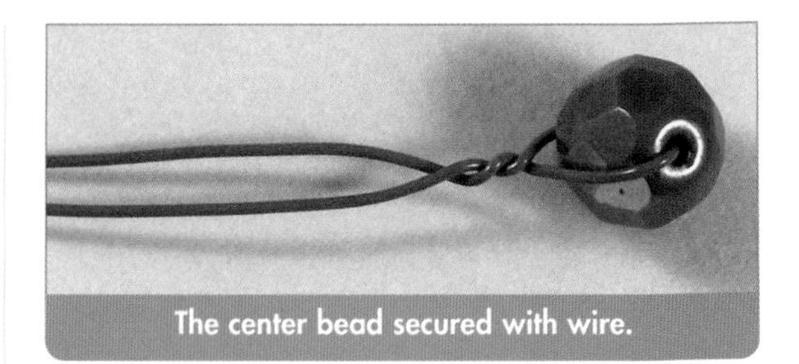

The center bead secured with wire.

11. Cut a 3-inch piece from each color wire, and bend each in half in a U shape. They will look something like hairpins.

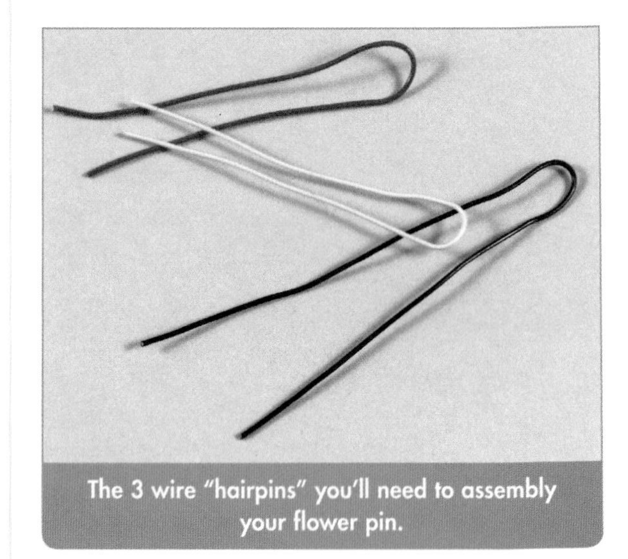

The 3 wire "hairpins" you'll need to assembly your flower pin.

12. Now we're ready to assemble the pin! Take the perforated disc part of your pin assembly and insert the wire from the dark purple petal ring through a hole that allows you to center the ring on the disc. You might have to try a few different holes before you find the best one.

    Now, insert the dark purple wire "hairpin" it over the wire ring in between one of the petals directly opposite to the one you just inserted. You want the wire to straddle the wire and secure the ring to the disc. Turn it over and twist once as close to the back of the disc as you can.

This is what the perforated disc looks like from the back after you've secured the first round of petals to it.

13. Next, insert the wire of the light purple ring in the same way, finding a hole that lets you position the ring in the center of the disc and on top of the dark purple ring you just secured. Use the light purple wire "hairpin" to secure the opposite side of this ring as you did in step 12.
14. Repeat this procedure with the white center ring.
15. Insert the crystal center bead in a single hole in the center of the three layers you've already attached.
16. Twist all the wires tightly together (you can use chain nose pliers to help you) and trim the wires close to the disc, leaving about ½ inch. You might need to spread the ends a little to be able to cut through all the wires. Push the remaining wire nub close to the center of the perforated disc.

The back of the disc looks like this just before you attach the pin back.

17. Position the pin back over the back of the perforated disc, and push down the fasteners with your nylon jaw pliers or chain nose pliers.
18. Rearrange the petals so that they're even and cover the pin assembly as well as possible. Your pin is finished!

After you've repositioned the petals and spread everything out evenly, your finished pin looks something like this.

Variations

By changing colors and/or sizes of beads, or by using a different shaped perforated form, you can create an infinite variety of flowered pins. Check out the fun beauties I made shown on the next page.

The fan-shaped pin (bottom center) was made using a kidney-shaped disc from an old earring that was taken apart and salvaged for beads and findings.

The orange pin (top right) has two rounds of 12 petals each and a different center.

The pink and red pin (top center) uses size 10 seed beads for the outer round and size 11 for the second round. The center is made the same way as our featured project, but the loops were made shorter and gathered up.

The last pin (bottom left) is made from three separate flowers, each made complete before adding to the disc. The centers are tiny buttons instead of beads.

Embellishments

As you begin to make more beaded flowers, you'll also notice a lot more about the way flowers are constructed. Look through garden catalogs and books about flowers to get ideas and imagine how these might be translated into beads on wire.

Resources

Wire: Artistic Wire (www.artisticwire.com), Parawire (www.parawire.com/craftstore.html), Beadalon ColourCraft Wire (www.beadalon.com)

Bead spinner: The Beadspinner Lady (www.beadspinnerlady.com), "Bead Spinner with a Twist" made by Hand-Made N Beads, available from Studio Baboo (www.studiobaboo.com)

Change one thing or a few, and you can have a bountiful garden of pins to wear or give away.

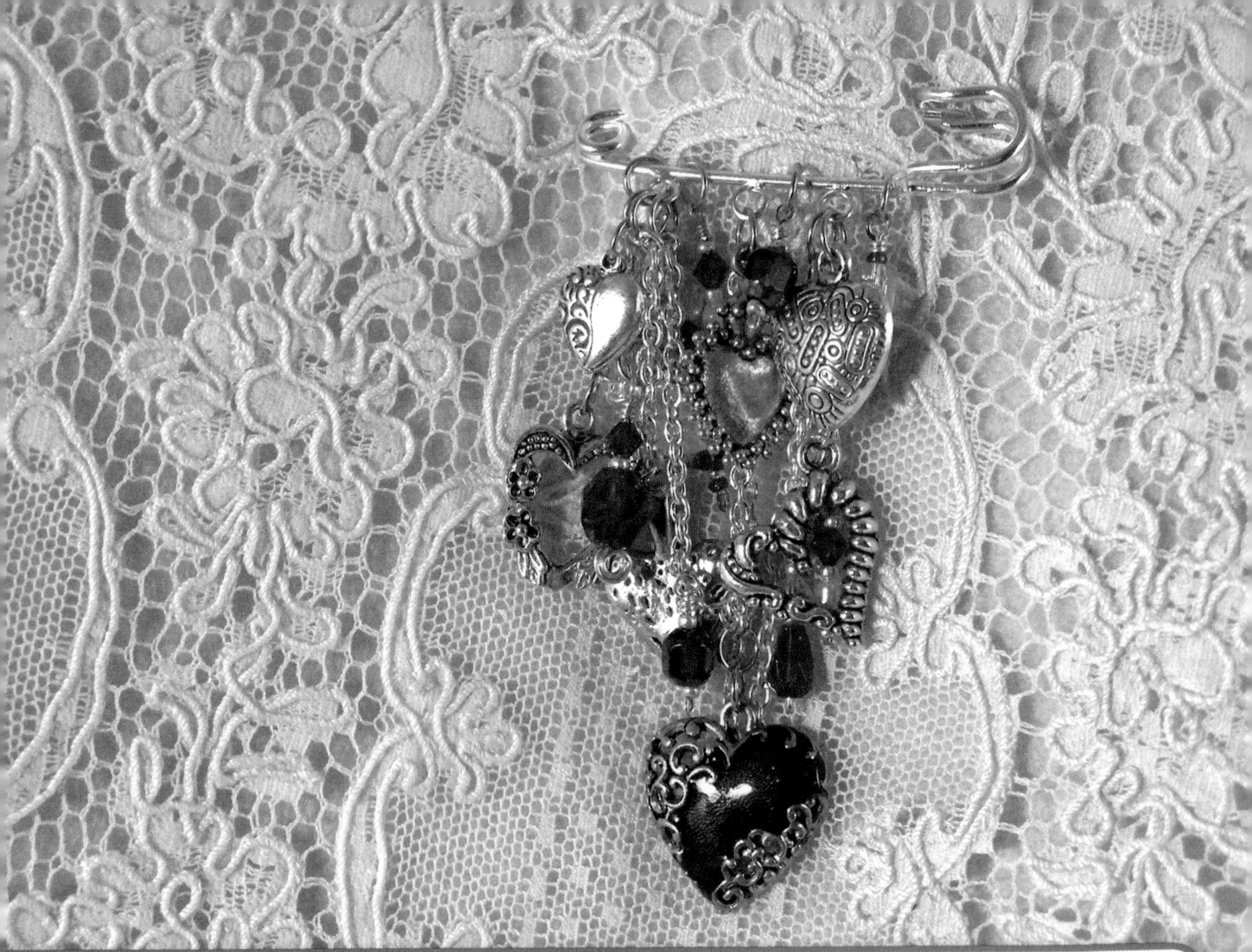

Hearts Aplenty Charm Pin

Skill level: Beginner

What you need:

- 7 assorted charms in desired theme, different sizes
- 26-gauge silver wire (If using pearls, you'll need to use 28-gauge wire for those dangles.)
- Assorted beads to complement charms (I used crystals and rice pearls.)
- 13 (size 11) silver accent beads
- 4 (size 11) red accent beads
- Kilt pin with loops
- 14 inches fine cable chain
- 4 (4mm) jump rings
- 17 (6mm) jump rings
- Wire cutters
- Chain nose pliers
- Round nose pliers

Techniques and skills needed:

- Basic wirework

This is a quick project that's fun and creative. Don't limit yourself to store-bought charms, though. Go through your old jewelry and trinkets, and look for things you can make into charms. Perhaps you have an old locket you never wear. Even a Cracker Jack toy can be wire wrapped, or perhaps you can drill a hole in it. Look for the unexpected!

These are some of the beads, findings, and tools you need for this project.

Pearls

On the hunt for new beading supplies? Don't forget to look at scrapbooking supplies. Words and other charms can multitask. Rubber stamps can be used to make unique and personalized charms. An interesting book on the marriage of scrapbooking and beading is *Making Jewelry with Scrapbook Embellishments* by Kristin Detrick (North Light Books, 2005).

Let's get right to it:

1. Lay out your charms in a pleasing pattern. Try different arrangements and see what looks most pleasing.
2. Attach the chain to the pin finding using 6mm jump rings. The loops of the chain don't have to be equal; just go for good proportions. The chain ends on either side can hang down, or you can attach them to the end loops with jump rings as well.

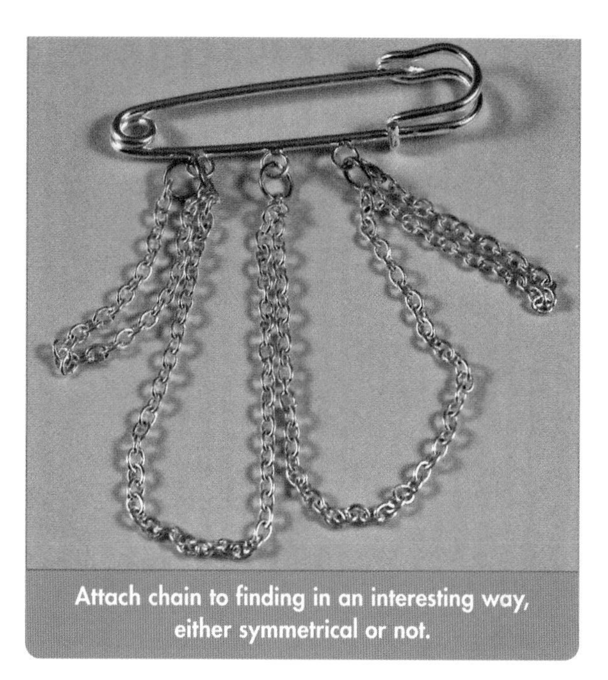

Attach chain to finding in an interesting way, either symmetrical or not.

3. Using jump rings (whichever size works best), attach charms at various places along the chain and in the loops of the pin finding.

Space out your charms when attaching them to your pin and chain.

4. Make as many dangles as you like, and attach them with jump rings. Remember, you can put more than one element in a loop on the pin or even over the pin between the loops.

When you've added all your charms and dangles, you can step back and admire your work!

Embellishments

When looking at a design, try moving back and getting a different vantage point. Sometimes what looks good to you up close just doesn't hold up to the "distance test." Sometimes the reverse is true. Also remember that when you're laying something out flat that will eventually be hanging, it will look different as well.

Variations

Charm pins really lend themselves to themes, as do charm bracelets like the one we made in Chapter 3. You'll even find packages of like-themed charms sold together at your local bead store or in supply catalogs.

Pearls

To help you place your charms, once you've found a layout you like on a flat surface, lay out your charms in order, from left to right, and mark the links with a washable fine pen or marker so you can remember where you wanted them.

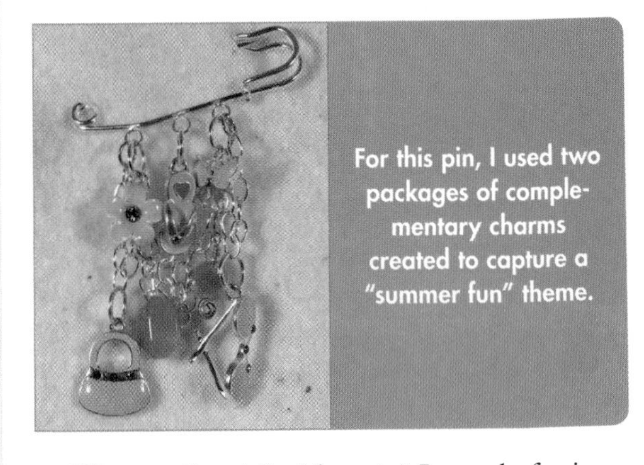

For this pin, I used two packages of complementary charms created to capture a "summer fun" theme.

Why not "say it" with a pin? Instead of using figurine charms, make larger dangles and use one or more of the many word charms available, both for beading and scrapbooking.

How about making a pin that shares an encouraging word with all you meet, like this one designed by Bobbi Wicks?

No charms in the house? Make some elegant dangles in a favorite color or to go with a special outfit.

(Note that this one also uses seed beads wrapped around the pin finding itself. Designer Bobbi Wicks used 26-gauge wire to wrap the smaller beads around the pin before she added the wireworked dangles.)

What to do if you can't find a charm pin finding? Don't let that stop you! If you like working with wire and have even a little skill, you can make your own. Complete instructions for making wire findings should come with a jig if you buy one—including a variety of pins, too. You can learn about cutting and hardening wire for these applications and get all the supplies you'll need in one place. WigJig sells such jigs (www.wigjig.com).

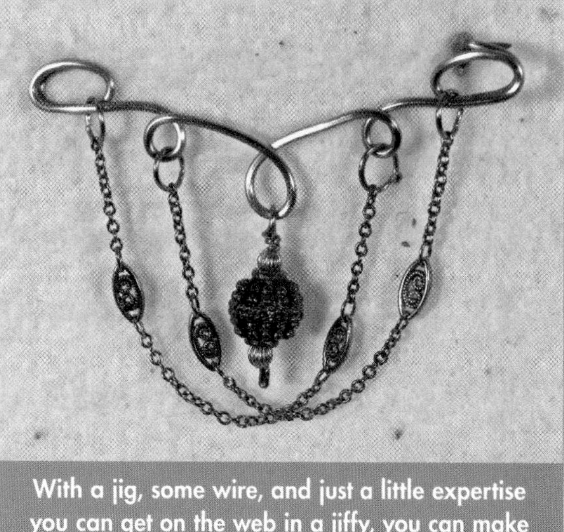

With a jig, some wire, and just a little expertise you can get on the web in a jiffy, you can make your own exquisite pin like this one designed by Bobbi Wicks.

So whenever the spirit strikes you or you sense a special occasion calls for a little trinket that makes a statement, just whip up a charm pin. You might even want to keep some of these inexpensive pin findings on hand and start collecting charms as you find them so everything you need is there at a moment's notice. For an extra-special occasion, considering bringing your gift "up a notch" by working it in sterling silver.

Resources

Charms: Michaels (www.michaels.com), Jo-Ann Fabric and Crafts (www.joann.com), Wal-Mart

Chain: Blue Moon Beads (www.bluemoonbeads.com)

Pin finding: Your local bead or craft store, Silver Charms, Inc. (find a lovely selection of sterling silver charms and charm pin findings here; www.silvercharmsinc.com), Rings & Things (sterling silver and gold vermeil charms and holders; www.rings-things.com)

Moon Maiden Bead Embroidered Pin

Skill level: Beginner

What you need:

- Seed beads in a variety of colors to suit your design
- 1 *cabochon* (or more)
- An assortment of smaller and larger beads in colors to complement your design (I used some *bugles* as well.)
- Lacy's Stiff Stuff or other foundation material for bead embroidery
- Nymo size D thread
- Size 10 bead embroidery needle
- Pin back
- Thin plastic (optional)
- Ultrasuede in a complementary color
- E-6000 or similar glue

Techniques and skills needed:

Basic bead embroidery

For this pin, I want you to "break out" artistically. Don't consider yourself an "artist"? Well, never you mind. Bead embroidery is sure to bring out the artist in you!

Start looking for a design you'd like to recreate in beads. Bead embroidery, as with thread embroidery, gives you amazing freedom to translate a two-dimensional design into a three-dimensional textured piece that reflects your personal vision and style. If you want to see what can be done with bead embroidery, just take a look at some of the many books or websites that showcase pieces with a real "wow!" factor. Believe it or not, these eye-popping creations actually begin with some simple stitches.

The pin I'm going to guide you through in this chapter was made primarily with two easy-to-master steps: couching and back stitch.

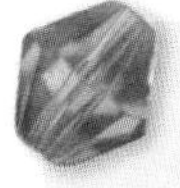

Beadwise

A **cabochon** is a highly polished convex-cut gem, that's usually flat on the back side. A **bugle bead** is tubular in shape and can vary in length.

Unleash your inner artist, and let's begin:

1. Find or create a pattern or design you'd like to translate into a beaded pin.

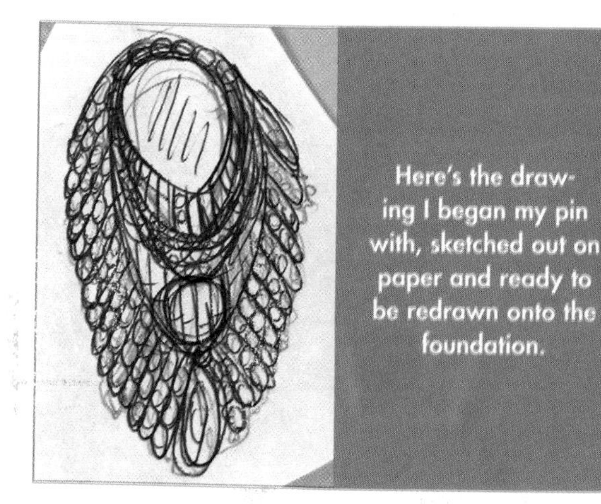

Here's the drawing I began my pin with, sketched out on paper and ready to be redrawn onto the foundation.

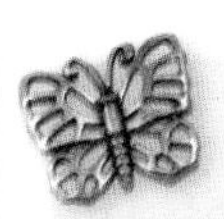

Embellishments

You can find design ideas everywhere. Some very inexpensive design books are available from Dover Publications (www.doverpublications.com). Or look to architectural details, fabric, and nature for inspiration.

2. Draw or trace your design onto a piece of Lacy's Stiff Stuff or other foundation. Using E-6000 or similar glue, affix any cabochons you'll be beading around to complete your design. Let the glue dry as recommended on the product label.

Transfer your design to the foundation, and glue down your cabochons.

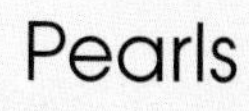

Pearls

If you can't find Lacy's Stiff Stuff, often crafts stores stock a type of stiffened felt sold under the names Easy Felt and Friendly Felt that you can use in much the same way. It comes in a variety of colors and is quite inexpensive.

3. Outline the main elements of your design using the backstitch. This stitch is created by making a knot and coming up through the back of your foundation. String on 4 beads and come back down through the foundation so your beads sit snugly on top.

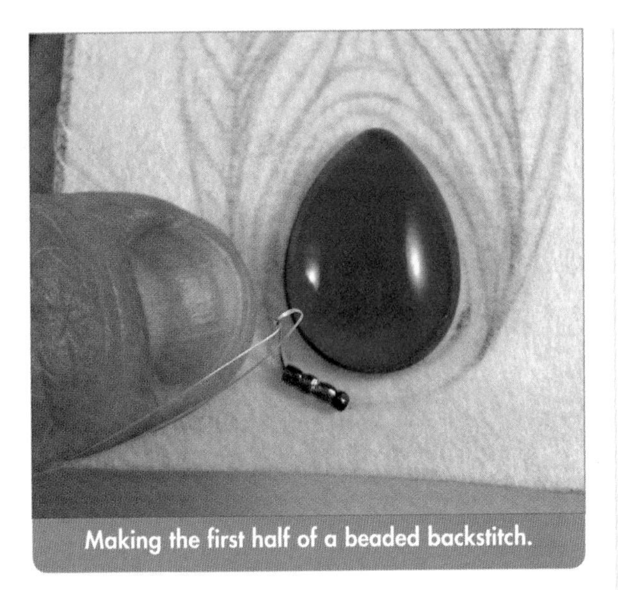

Making the first half of a beaded backstitch.

When making your 4-bead initial stitch, be sure you don't go back down into the foundation too short so your beads buckle or go too far so your thread shows. Take the 4 beads on your thread, lay them down with your thread hand on the line you're trying to outline, and hold the thread taught with the opposite hand. Place your needle right in front of the 4-bead row, holding it straight up and down, and push through the foundation. This should give you a stitch that lays flat and is neither bunched up nor too loose.

Pearls

Many times in beading, you're told to condition your thread to help keep it from tangling, with either beeswax or Thread Heaven. In bead embroidery, you do *not* need to condition your thread. I sometimes just pull the very end of my thread through beeswax to make it easier to put through the eye of the needle, but otherwise, conditioning the thread is unnecessary for bead embroidery.

4. Come back up through the foundation from the back to the front so your needle comes up between the first 2 beads and the last 2 beads of your 4-bead stitch.

This is where your needle should be as you prepare to complete the first backstitch.

5. Go back through the last 2 beads.

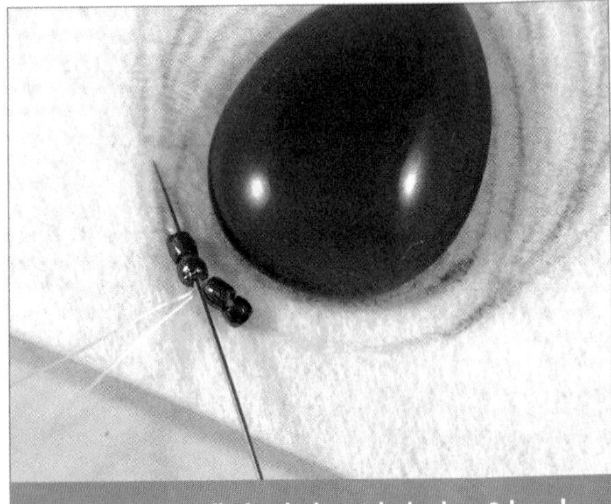

Bring your needle back through the last 2 beads.

6. Add 4 more beads and repeat. Continue outlining until you're satisfied with the results.
7. Begin to fill in with additional stitches and three-dimensional beading. You can create "stacks" of beads by adding several beads to your needle, skipping the one closest to

your needle, and going back down through the rest. This is the stitch I used to create my maiden's "hair."

You can use bead "stacks" or fringe to add lots of texture and dimension to an embroidered project. Here's how I created my maiden's "hair."

8. Experiment with using bugle beads and seed beads together in other ways. You can also create color and play with light using various bead combinations.

Bugle beads add a lot of interest to your embroidery stitches.

Crimps!

When you use bugles in your design, put a seed bead on either end. Bugles tend to be sharp and can cut your thread.

9. Scatter beading is a simple way to fill in spaces and looks more freestyle. To do it, simply take 1 bead and make a stitch, and then randomly make single bead stitches throughout an area in the design. I added dimension to the section around the smaller cabochon by coming up between scatter stitches and adding a bead to create a raised look.

Scatter beading and adding beads on top give the next section some added interest.

Pearls

As you're beading, you might find that your thread keeps catching on the corners of your foundation. Using scissors, round the corners so they'll be less likely to snag.

10. To fill in the bottom of the pin, I used couching. This stitch is also an easy one, done by placing enough beads on the thread to fill the stitch you want to make and then coming down through the fabric in front of the last bead you put on. Then come up beside the beads every few beads, and make a small tacking stitch over the thread between the beads, anchoring the string of beads in place.

Here you can see I brought up the needle beside a row of beads and am getting ready to bring it through the foundation to anchor the beads.

In this photo, you can see the needle and thread being brought over the beads and down through the other side.

11. To add a little more texture and interest, I added 3 larger beads in a row at the bottom of the pin by stringing on the larger bead, adding a seed bead, and coming back through the larger bead with the needle and thread.

Adding larger beads gives the pin yet more texture and dimension.

12. Now to finishing the pin. Even though the directions that come with Lacy's Stiff Stuff say you don't need to add plastic to make the pin stiffer before you add the backing, I decided to use the plastic anyway because of the size of the pin and the weight of the beads. You can decide for yourself based on your own design.

    Trace an outline of your finished pin on both the plastic (I used template plastic intended for quilting, but you can use a lid from a margarine tub or the flat part of an empty milk jug) and the backing material. Ultrasuede makes a nice backing, but you can also use soft leather or a variety of other materials.

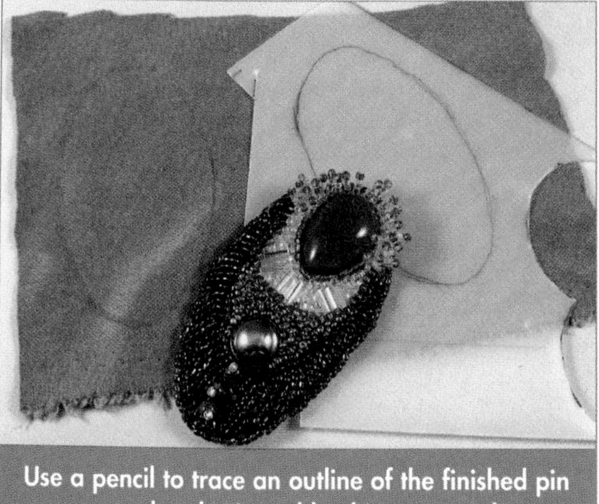
Use a pencil to trace an outline of the finished pin onto the plastic and backing material.

13. Cut out the plastic within the lines you traced, and cut the backing material along the lines. Your plastic should be a little smaller than the edge of your pin so when you finish the edges, you're not trying to push your needle through the foundation, the backing, and the plastic.
14. Lay the pin back on the plastic where you want to attach it, and mark the location of the catch and the hinge. Use a small hole-punch or a sharp knife to make two holes, and fit the pin through the holes. Glue the pin back and plastic to the back of the embroidered pin, being careful not to get glue on the finished beadwork. Let this all dry the recommended amount of time. You can trim back the plastic a little, if necessary, but be sure not to clip your beadwork.

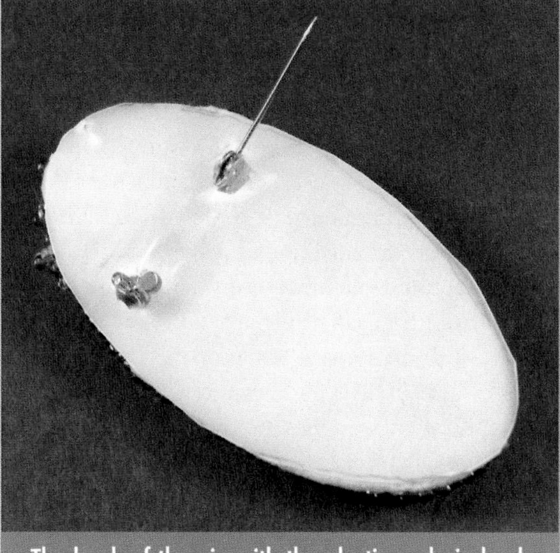
The back of the pin with the plastic and pin back glued on.

15. Repeat step 14 with the Ultrasuede backing (or whatever backing material you chose). Trim the Ultrasuede so it's flush with the edge of your pin, being very careful not to clip any of the threads on your beadwork.
16. Now you can add an edging. I simply added beads along the sides using a simple whip stitch, adding beads (I needed 3 to cover the thickness) and going down through the top, coming up with the needle near to the stitch I just made, and repeating it all the way around the pin.

This is what your whip-stitched edging should look like.

Variations

You can stitch around a cabochon in myriad ways, as you can see in the photo on the next page. The procedure is basically the same as with our featured pin. Just glue it down onto your foundation material and decide how you want to frame your cabochon. Cabochons come in all shapes and sizes, so the design possibilities are endless. You can also make an embroidered piece and add a beaded chain or necklace to it, making it a pendant. And you can combine bead embroidery with other stitches, such as peyote stitch (see Chapter 6), to create a bezel and other surface embellishments.

Now that you've explored various ways of "getting pinned," it's time to move on from jewelry to other types of accessories in Part 2. There you get another chance to try your hand at bead embroidery in our next project!

Resources

Lacy's Stiff Stuff: www.lacysstiffstff.com

Ultrasuede: Jo-Ann Fabric and Crafts (www.joann.com)

Here are several examples of ways to frame cabochons using bead embroidery.
These could be finished as pins or used as pendants in a necklace.
You could even work further embellishment, such as fringe and edgings, into the design.

In This Part

Accessories … to Fun!

You've seen all those wonderful beaded accessories in magazines, in movies, and on TV. But when you go to your local mall or boutique, you find these items are *so expensive!* What drives up the price tag is all the details—fringe, bead embroidery, dangles, and trims.

In Part 2, I show you ways to add dazzle to your days and make your nights a knock-out. All it takes is some ready-made accessories (or handmade accessories, if you're into other crafts, too) and some of your favorite wardrobe items. In the following pages, you learn how to enhance your accessories from "a little" to "wow!"

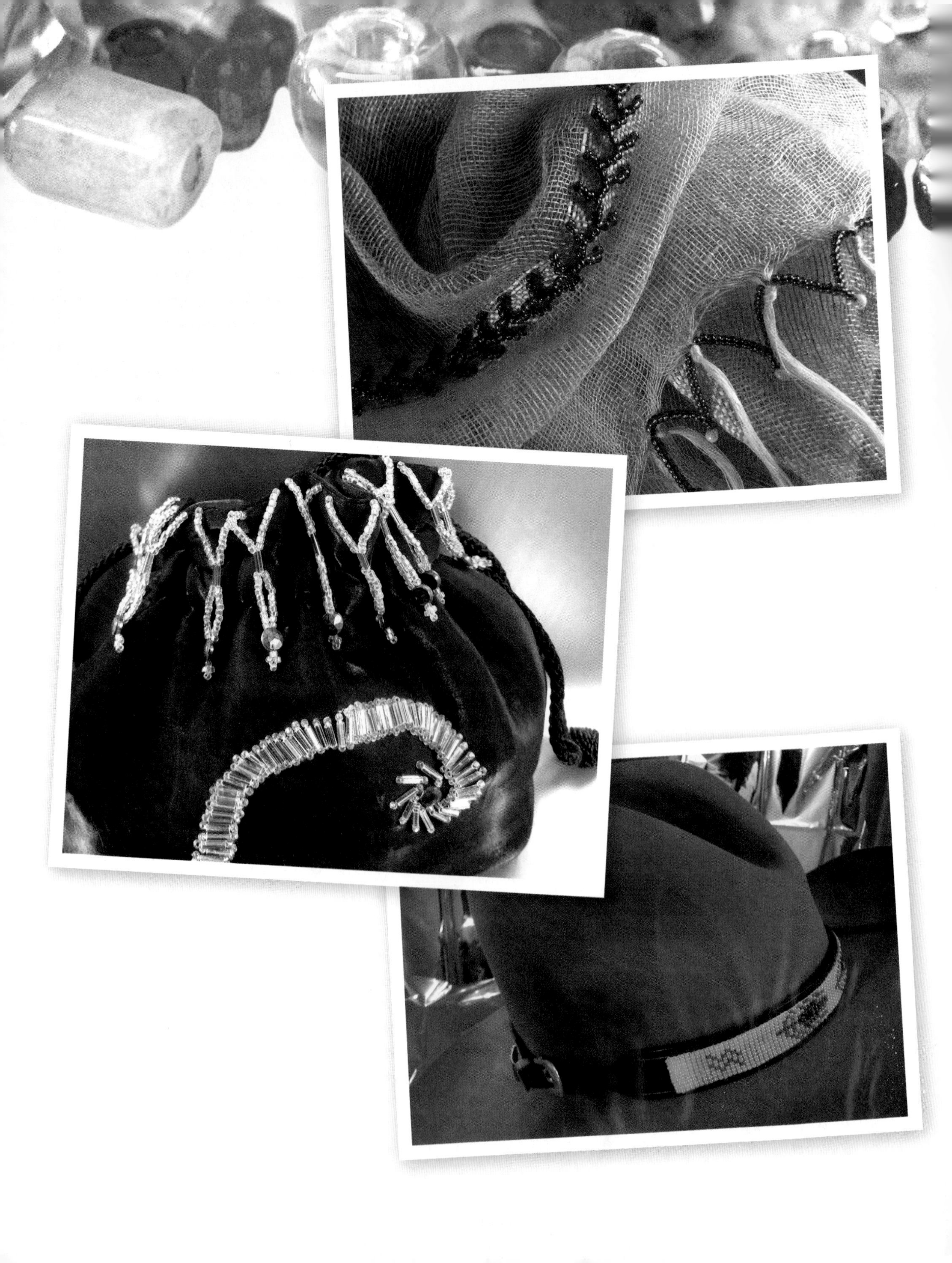

Wardrobe Divas

In This Chapter

- Embellishing store-bought scarves with elegant bead embroidery
- Easy ways of transforming a purchased bag from plain to dazzling
- Dressing up a patterned hat with a beaded band

Simple, everyday items we sometimes take for granted can easily get an upgrade with a few beads and some imagination. I'm not sure who said it, but the quote I remember is "If it doesn't move, bead it. If it moves, tackle it and bead it!" I can't think of many things that couldn't benefit from the embellishment of a few beads!

Those are the projects we tackle in this chapter. You might be surprised by some of the beautiful results!

Scarf Up Some Compliments

Skill level: Beginner

What you need:

- 1 hank size 11 seed beads in a color complementary to your scarf
- Enough small drop beads to add fringe to desired section of your scarf
- Size 10 bead embroidery needle
- Embroidery floss to complement or contrast with beads
- Purchased scarf suitable for bead embroidery
- Scissors
- Adjustable embroidery hoop

Techniques and skills needed:

Basic bead embroidery and embellishment (feather stitch and fringe)

In this first project, we explore the wonderful world of beaded scarves. You can enhance almost any type of scarf with beading, from a light gossamer silk scarf to a heavier scarf or even a shawl. The scarf I chose has a very open weave, which in itself isn't especially easy to bead on. However, it also had several bands of more closely woven fabric that just said "feather stitch!" to me. If you're familiar with regular embroidery, you'll know this stitch. When you bead it, you do it a little or a lot. I decided to go all the way and do the entire stitch in beads.

Pearls

If you're not familiar with embroidery stitches, plenty of books are available to help you. I especially like *Bead Embroidery: The Complete Guide* by Jane Davis because she gives the stitch as it would be done in embroidery floss and then several variations on how to add beads to it, with complete instructions.

Here are the things you'll need for this quick and easy project.

You can really get creative with this project, and more than just with beads. For example, the scarf you choose is an easy opportunity for fun and creativity. A plain scarf lends itself to your own design, or you can bead along the lines of a patterned scarf in colors suggested by the existing design.

The thread you choose depends on a number of factors. First, because beading needles' eyes have to be small enough to fit through a seed bead, some threads may not work with a bead embroidery needle. A "big eye" needle might be a possible choice in that case. If your beads are transparent, the thread will show through and can change the color and effect of the beads when they're sewn on. Experiment with different threads and embroidery flosses to find the best combination.

Crimps!

Be sure you match the weight of your beads and your thread to the fabric of your scarf. Delicate fabrics won't hold up well to the weight of heavy beads and may pucker or, worse, tear.

1. If you're using embroidery floss, separate out 2 or 3 strands (depending on the weight of your fabric) and thread your needle. You can also use good sewing thread or even Nymo for other fabrics. Tie a knot.
2. Begin embroidering with beads across one end of the scarf using the feather stitch. (If there's nothing woven into the fabric that you can use as a guide, you can draw two lines with a straight edge and a washable marker or chalk to help you keep your stitches straight.) The first part of the feather stitch is basically a beaded loop. I added 6 beads to my loop, but you can use any even number. Then insert your needle in the fabric parallel to where your loop begins, come back up, and catch the loop in the middle of the beads (you should have 3 beads on each side). Re-enter the fabric just on the other side.

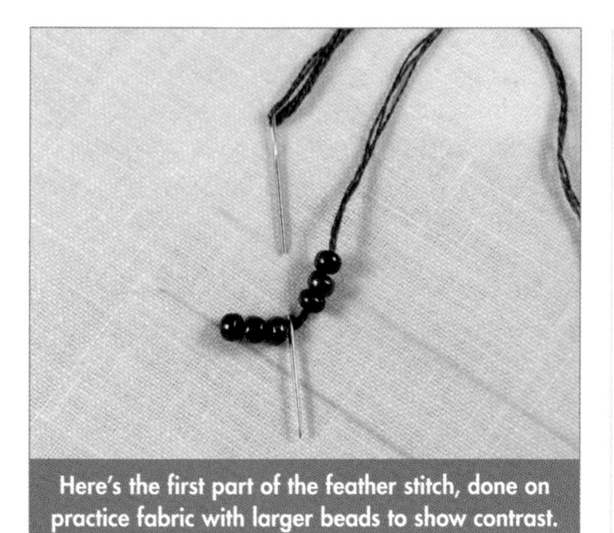

Here's the first part of the feather stitch, done on practice fabric with larger beads to show contrast.

3. For the second part of the feather stitch, simply repeat the previous sequence on the opposite side to create a branching effect. Continue this stitch design as long as you like.

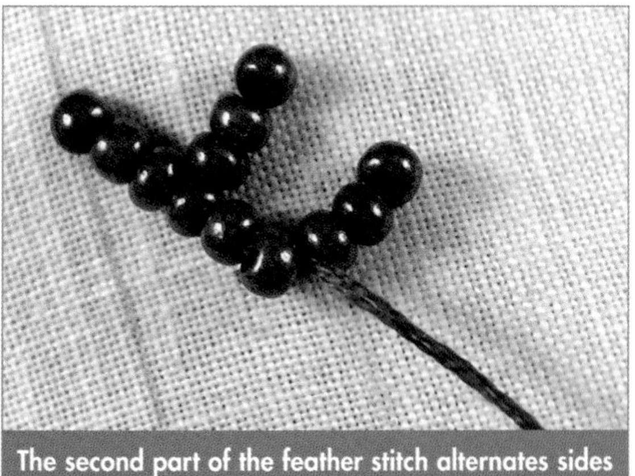

The second part of the feather stitch alternates sides to create a branching effect.

4. Now you're ready to add a beaded border or fringe to the bottom edge of your scarf. My purchased scarf already had a simple knotted fringe, so I decided to make a shorter drop with beads. I used 12 beads, added a drop bead, and then came back up through the twelfth and eleventh beads and added 10 beads.

Bring your thread back through the last 2 seed beads before adding the 10 beads to form the second half of the fringe.

5. In between the beaded fringe, I made a tiny backstitch with embroidery floss over the existing thread fringe to anchor each beaded fringe section.

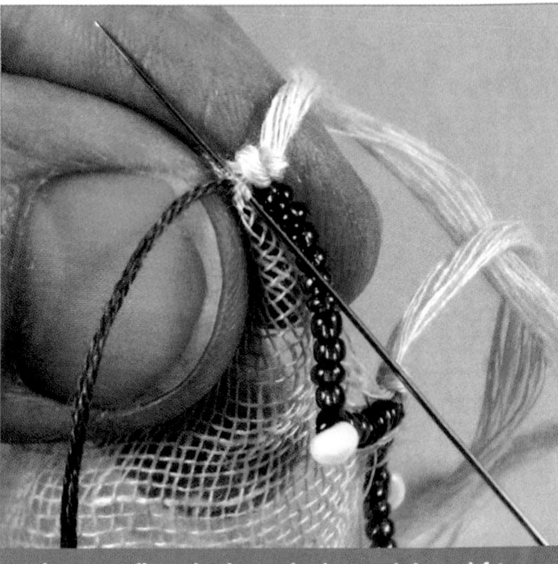

Take a small stitch above the knotted thread fringe to anchor the beaded one.

6. Bead the other end of scarf as you did in steps 1 through 5.

Pearls

Depending on the fabric, you might want to line your scarf to protect your beadwork and prevent snagging the embroidery threads underneath. The scarf I chose was more sheer and didn't lend itself to lining. But when you can, lining is a good way to finish your project.

Variations

You can enhance a prepurchased scarf with beads in countless ways. If you look, you probably can find lots of scarves that have already been embellished with beads. But by choosing a scarf that's not beaded and doing it yourself, you can create exactly what you want for a fraction of the cost, and you know the quality of the workmanship will be top-notch because *you* did it!

Pink Embroidered Appliqué Beauty

Another way to add embroidery to an item is to work up an embroidered motif on a separate piece of fabric and then sew it on as an appliqué. Bobbi Wicks adapted this two-toned pink example, which had an existing embroidery pattern, to beadwork.

Beading on a complementary shade of fabric and sewing the appliqué onto the scarf is a good solution for delicate fabrics.

This method is especially good to use when the fabric the scarf is made of might not handle the weight of the beads well. It's also unnecessary to line the scarf with this method because the back of the beadwork is protected under the appliqué.

Paisley Pizzazz Scarf

Perhaps you have a scarf that has an interesting pattern that would become even more exciting if some beads were used to emphasize the pattern. This is a quick and easy way to add some pizzazz to your accessories wardrobe.

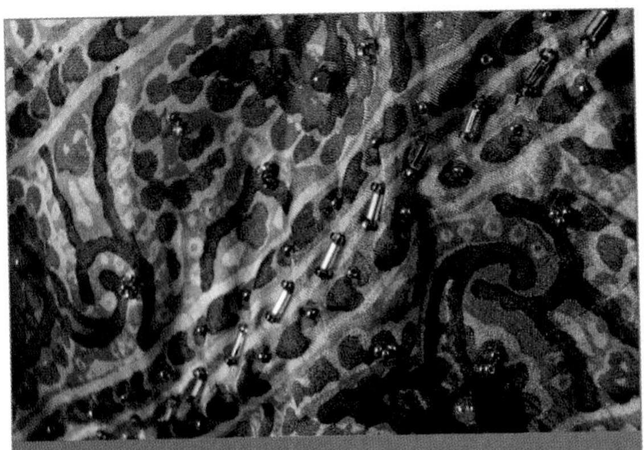

This colorful paisley scarf is lifted above the ordinary with just a few scattered beads enhancing the printed design.

Any of these quick scarf ideas would make a lovely holiday gift or a welcome gift for a special hostess. If you have a lot of time, add a lot of beads! But if you're short on time, a few well-placed and carefully chosen beaded additions will still do the trick. And each one will be a one-of-a-kind, handmade by you.

Resources

Embroidery floss and adjustable hoop: Jo-Ann Fabric and Crafts (www.joann.com)

Scarf: Ross Dress for Less Stores (www.rossstores.com)

Bodacious Bags!

Skill level: Beginner

What you need:

- 1 hank size 11 seed beads in a color complementary to your bag
- 1 hank bugle beads to match your seed beads
- 25 to 30 (4mm) accent beads for fringe
- Size 10 bead embroidery needle
- Thread to complement or contrast with beads
- Nymo thread, size D, for fringe
- Purchased bag suitable for bead embroidery
- Tailor's chalk for marking pattern
- Scissors

Techniques and skills needed:

Basic bead embroidery and embellishment (straight stitch and fringe)

Now that you've got some embroidery experience, let's try another application that's quick, easy, and highly rewarding. The featured project is done on an extremely simple fabric evening bag I picked up at a discount store. This same type of bag was called a *reticule* in times past, and plenty of modern-day sewing patterns are available to make one if you can't find one ready-made. (I've listed some pattern companies in the "Resources" section at the end of this project.)

If you're sewing your own bag, you can do the embroidery on the outer fabric before you add the lining and assemble the bag. This way, you have the advantage of being able to use an embroidery hoop as well, which makes it easier to keep your stitches even. Mine was already constructed, so I worked my stitches between the existing lining and the outer layer—a little tricky, but not that difficult to do.

Here are the things you'll need for this quick and easy project.

1. Using tailor's chalk, draw out your design on the right side of your bag. A very simple design, as you can see from the example, can produce dazzling results. You can try reproducing this classic curve or create your own design.

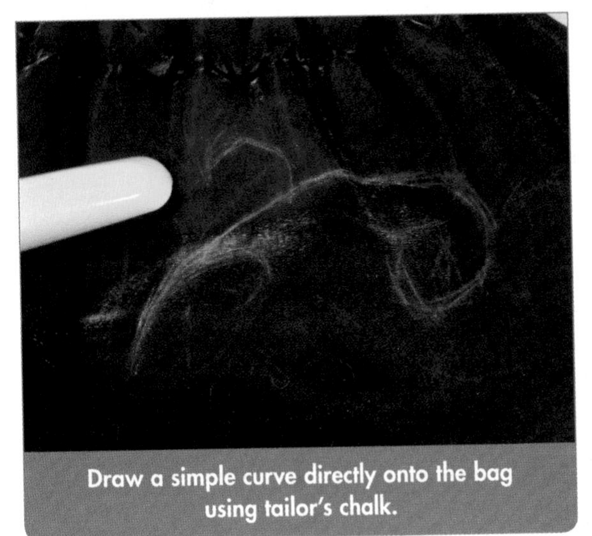

Draw a simple curve directly onto the bag using tailor's chalk.

2. Separate 2 or 3 strands of embroidery floss, and cut a combined thread long enough for you to handle comfortably. Thread your needle and make a knot.
3. Bring your thread up from the inside of your bag to the starting point of your design. Thread on 1 seed bead, 1 bugle, and another seed bead. Go back down through the fabric at an angle at the same distance as the length of the 3 beads you just put on. The angle is important so you can bring your needle between the lining and the top fabric. Don't poke all the way through both layers; you want to hide your stitches in between.

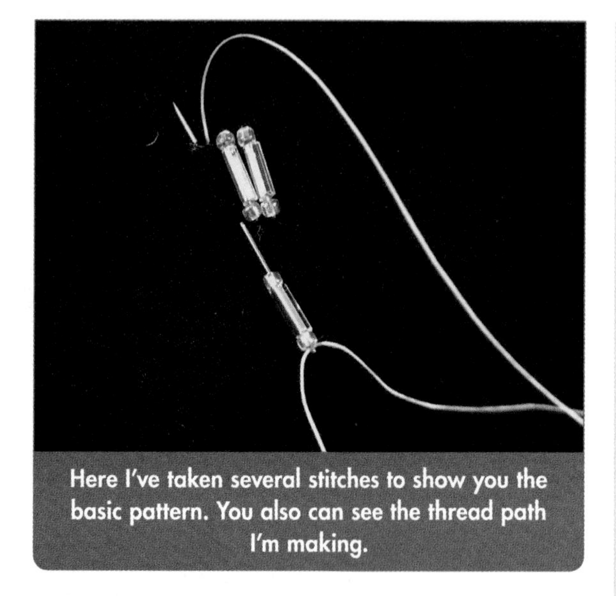
Here I've taken several stitches to show you the basic pattern. You also can see the thread path I'm making.

4. Come up with your needle next to the stitch you just made.

Pearls

Make your stitches close together or leave space between them for a different effect. I chose to put mine close together for a more sparkly effect. If I had spaced them out, the effect would be more understated.

5. Repeat steps 3 and 4, continuing with the bead and bugle zigzag stitches along your design.

Crimps!

If your design has curves, as mine does, adjust your stitches to accommodate the curve. To do this, keep the beads inside the curve close together and gradually increase the space between the outside ones as you go around the curve. Notice in the first photo that at the very end of my curve where it becomes the tightest, I've spaced out the stitches to create the curve's visual lines.

6. Now you're ready to add fringe. You can choose any number of fringe variations; I've given you an easy design here that still has a lot of punch. For some more ideas, turn to any of the many excellent bead embroidery or embellishment books—or just use your own imagination! For this fringe, add on the beads in this sequence: 10 seed beads, 1 bugle bead, 10 more seed beads, 1 (4mm) accent bead, and 4 more seed beads. To hide the stitches, come up between the layers (top and lining) and then add your beads. Start at any convenient place, which on my bag was at a side seam.

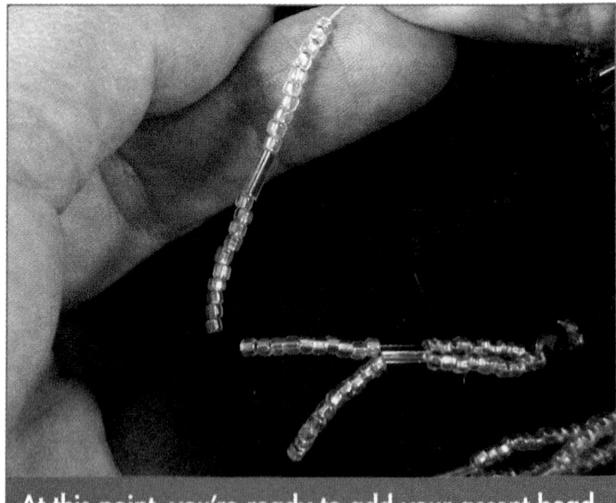
At this point, you're ready to add your accent bead.

7. Go back with the needle through the first 4 seed beads you added after the accent bead. Pull up the thread snugly—but not too tight. This should give you a *picot* under the accent bead.

Beadwise

A **picot** is a series of small embroidered or beaded loops forming an ornamental edging, design, or used at the bottom of a fringe.

Go through the first seed bead below the accent bead to create the 4-bead picot. Notice the finished fringe in the corner of the photo with the picots already completed.

8. Go up through the accent bead and string on 10 seed beads. Pass your needle through the bugle bead and string on 10 more seed beads.

Add the other side of the fringe unit.

9. Choose a pleasing distance between the two top strands of your fringe (I chose ½ inch), go down into the fabric, and come up through with your needle about ⅛ inch away. Repeat around the top of your bag.

Take a small stitch between the fringe units.

10. Take a few tiny stitches in the inside of your bag through the lining to secure your thread, and cut it off with scissors. Your bag is now ready for a night on the town!

Pearls

If you don't feel comfortable "eyeballing" distances, you could make a template for the two measurements you use for your fringe, one for the distance between the two top strands of the beaded fringe unit, and one for the distance between each unit. Simply mark these distances on a small, sturdy piece of paper, and you can use your template each time to be sure.

Variations

The possible variations here are nearly endless. Don't limit yourself to what you can purchase in a department store. Thrift stores, antique shops, and online auction sites are treasure troves for interesting bags to add beading to.

Antique Bag with Netted Fringe

This turn-of-the-century bag has a gorgeous frame and subdued but elegant fabric. By simply outlining the frame in beads and adding a netted beaded fringe in bead colors that have the same antique look as the fabric, the bag looks even more elegant.

Resources

Patterns: For a period reticule pattern, go to Buckaroo Bobbins (www.buckaroobobbins.com). Butterick's pattern #B4411, "Handbags Circa 1890 to 1910," has some bags that would make interesting evening accessories; plus, they have many other handbag patterns to choose from (www.butterick.com). Vogue's pattern #V7354 is just made for beading. In fact, the pattern's picture shows several beaded examples (www.voguepatterns.com). Also check out Simplicity patterns (www.simplicity.com) and McCall's patterns (www.mccallpattern.com).

I enhanced this antique store find with elegant trim and fringe beading.

Tapestry Bag

Be sure to check out catalog sources for interesting bags to bead, too. I found this reproduction of a Victorian tapestry bag that just begged for beading! Again, I simply used the existing pattern to dictate the colors and location of the beading.

So now that you have it "in the bag" and have certainly expanded your bead embroidery horizons, let's move on to a whole new frontier in accessories for beaded accents—hats!

Filling in the pattern with beading lifts the color and adds a whole new dimension to this reproduction tapestry bag.

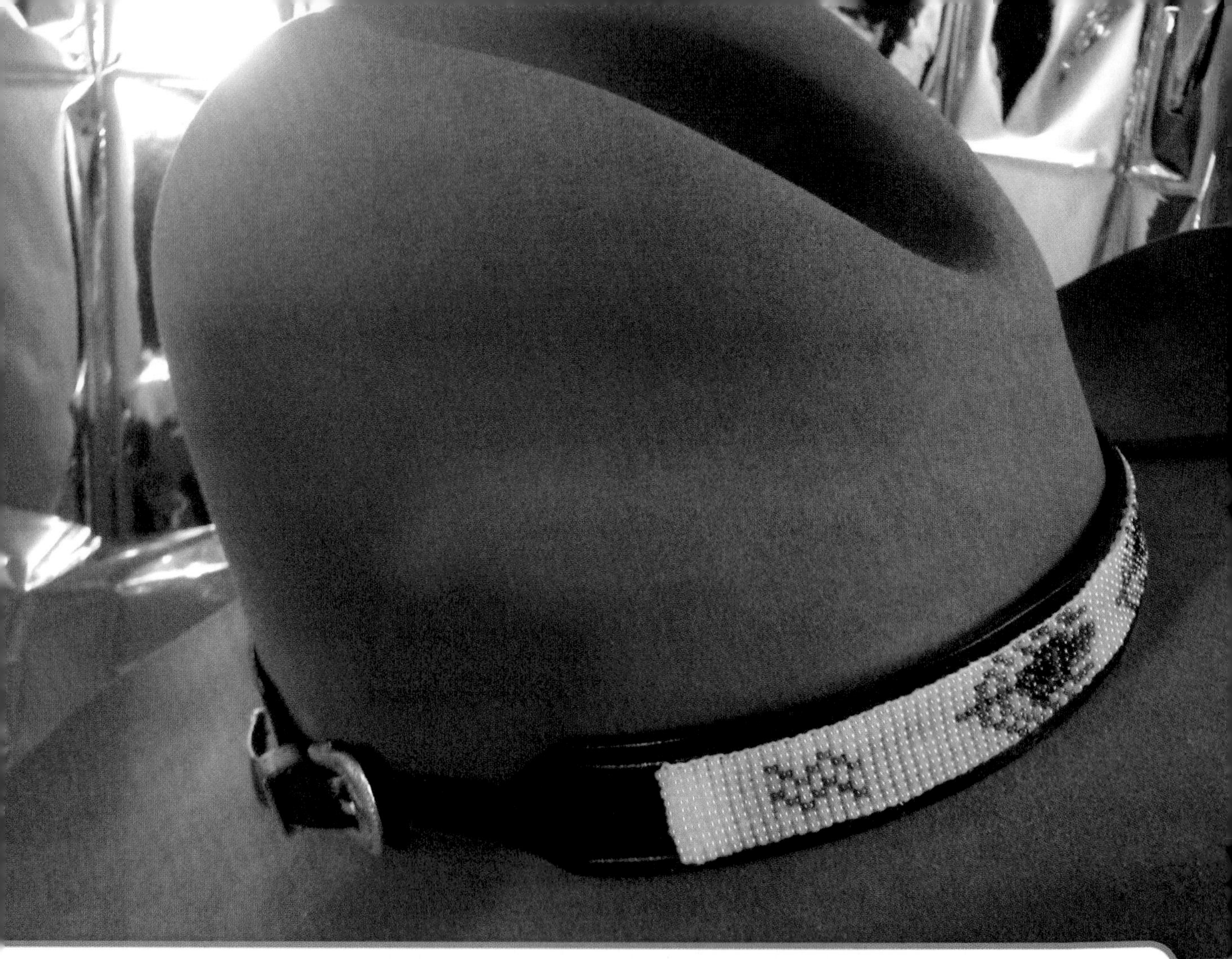

A Feather on Your Cap

Skill level: Intermediate

What you need:

- 3 strands white or off-white size 11 seed beads
- 2 strands dark green size 11 seed beads
- 2 strands light green size 11 seed beads
- 2 strands turquoise size 11 seed beads
- 2 strands bronze or rust size 11 seed beads
- 2 strands cobalt or dark blue size 11 seed beads
- Size 10 beading needle
- Nymo thread, size D
- Material to finish hatband: velvet ribbon, leather, suede, Ultrasuede, or other material of your choice
- Scissors
- Beading loom

Techniques and skills needed:

- Basic loom work or square stitch

How can you wear a hat and not add some beadwork? Not you! Not me! Not now!

The more you learn about beading, the more things you'll see as canvases for adding beadwork. One simple way to do that on a hat is to craft a hatband. This project is designed for the loom, but if you don't have a loom and still want to try it, you can work it in square stitch as well.

Here are some of the supplies you'll need for this and most any loom work project.

1. String your loom according to the manufacturer's directions—or refer to *The Complete Idiot's Guide to Beading Illustrated*, Chapters 8 and 9, for a complete discussion on how to choose and string a loom, plus detailed instruction on basic loom work.

Crimps!

When doing bead weaving, both on and off the loom, you might find that your thread has a tendency to tangle. You can condition your thread to help alleviate that problem using beeswax (available in craft stores) or a thread conditioner made just for beading, called Thread Heaven.

2. Knot on a length of thread, leaving a generous tail (you'll need this to weave a selvage at the end), and begin the first row of the pattern. There are 8 rows of the background white color to work first. To start, put 10 white beads on the thread, bring them up from under the loom, and push them up between threads, 1 bead for each space. Bring the needle from right to left through all 10 beads *over* the warp threads.

The loom strung, the thread knotted on, and the first row ready to weave in place.

Bobbi Wicks designed the pattern used in this project using *Bead Cellar Pattern Designer* software, version 1.6.3.

Embellishments

If you have the kind of loom pictured in these photos, it has rollers that allow you to do longer strips of beadwork. You'll notice that the pattern is basically two motifs, and I've provided mirror-image reverse patterns of each as well. Feel free to repeat the patterns as many times as you want, in whatever sequence you want!

3. Following the pattern diagram, and reading from left to right, complete the first motif.
4. Add the 8 rows of white beads, according to the diagram, and complete the second motif, the peacock feather.

The hatband partially worked with the first and second motifs.

5. Work 4 rows of white beads according to the diagram.
6. Complete the next feather motif according to the diagram. This is a mirror image of the first feather motif.
7. Repeat the double line motif according to the diagram (also a mirror image).

Pearls

To keep track of where you are in the pattern diagram, use a ruler or a piece of paper and move it as you complete each row. Post-its work really well. There's also a handy magnetic board with a stand used for counted cross-stitch that works very well.

8. Following the pattern diagram, add 8 rows of background white.

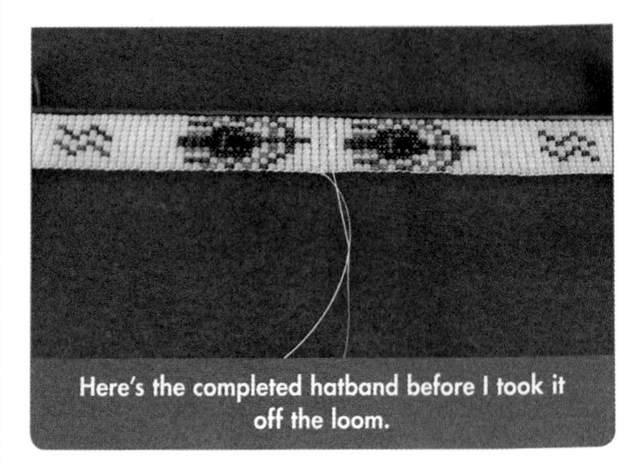

Here's the completed hatband before I took it off the loom.

9. Before removing your work from the loom, weave a selvage with your needle and thread by simply weaving every under and over, alternating each row, to create a kind of fabric you'll use to finish your work.

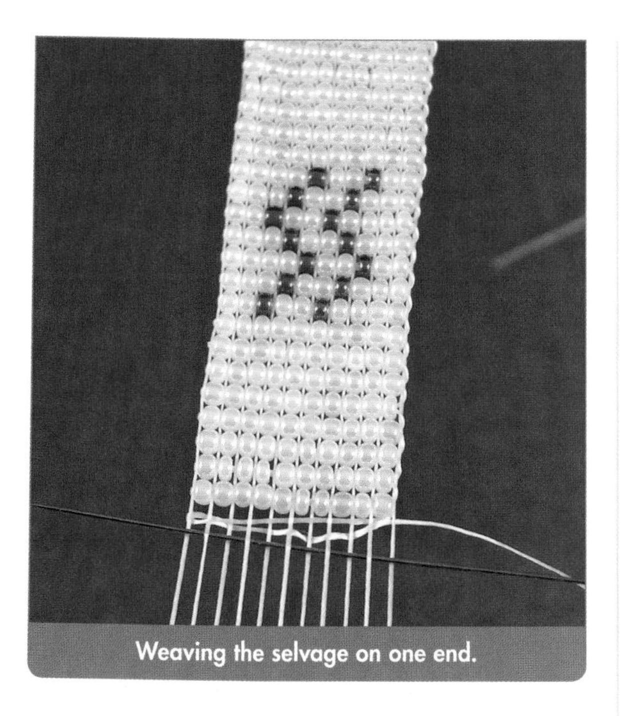

Weaving the selvage on one end.

10. Weave a selvage on the other end of your work with the tail you left when you knotted on your starting thread.
11. Carefully remove your work from the loom.

This is what your woven selvage edge should look like before you glue it and cut the thread ends.

12. Using E-6000 or other craft glue appropriate for the material you're going to glue your bead work to, glue each of the two selvages down to the back of the beaded strip. Let it dry according to the manufacturer's directions and then clip off excess threads. It might be helpful to use clamps or a weight to keep the selvage edges flat until it dries.
13. Glue your beadwork to a leather hatband, or sew it to ribbon, Ultrasuede, or another material of your choice. (I happen to be married to a leather worker, so he helped me make a leather hatband. You might be able to find one already crafted to enhance with your beadwork.) Let your work dry as before, and tie or buckle to your favorite hat.

Variations

Bobbi's lovely peacock pattern is very versatile. It can be used without a loom as a square stitch motif, and if you don't have a hat that needs a band, a bookmark is a nice adaptation. You can probably think of other ways to use a beaded strip with this design.

Creme Square Stitch Hatband

Here Bobbi Wicks used the same motifs as in the featured hatband project, but she didn't use a loom. She worked the design using square stitch with a soft off-white background color and different spacing, and applied it to some matching velvet ribbon for a more feminine look. She also added some individually worked motifs and spaced them out along her ribbon hatband.

Bobbi's pastel hatband is worked in square stitch and has a more feminine look.

The square stitch is also covered in *The Complete Idiot's Guide to Beading Illustrated* in detail. Here is a brief review tailored to this project:

1. Run about 3 inches of thread through Thread Heaven or beeswax to condition it. Thread your needle, and tie a good-size knot or add on a stopper bead, leaving about 4 inches of tail to hold on to. You will have to add more thread before you are finished.

> **Crimps!**
>
> Don't use too much thread at one time, or it can fray.

2. String on 10 white beads and then string on 1 more bead, and bring your needle and thread through the last bead of the first row (bead #10) and then back through the bead you just added (bead #11) in a counterclockwise direction. You are ready to add the next bead.
3. Repeat the process of adding a bead and going back through the bead in the previous row and the one you just strung on in a clockwise direction. Continue to the end of the row.
4. Work the next row back in the opposite direction (you might find it easier to turn your work each time). Add rows for a total of 10 rows of white beads, pulling each row snug but not so tight that your work buckles.
5. Follow the pattern diagram as with loom work, ending with 10 white bead rows. Finish as desired.

Another clever innovation on Bobbi's hatband is a beaded tube she used to secure the hatband in place. By just pulling the two sides apart, the hatband is fully adjustable.

This beaded tube accented with the green and blue beads used in the overall design secures the hatband and makes it easy to adjust.

Now that your accessories wardrobe has experienced the "bead diva" treatment, let's move on to some more unexpected places to add beaded accents to your everyday clothing choices.

Peacock Feather Bookmark

You can use loom work to decorate just about anything, including clothing and accessories, but it's also beautiful all by itself. For this project, I simply worked the motifs in a slightly different way, removed the work from the loom, and braided and tied the ends to create a beaded bookmark.

Resources

Bead software: Bead Cellar Pattern Designer, version 1.6.3 (www.beadcellar.com)

Leather supplies and buckle: Tandy Leather Factory (www.leatherfactory.com)

Ribbon: Jo-Ann Fabric and Crafts (www.joann.com)

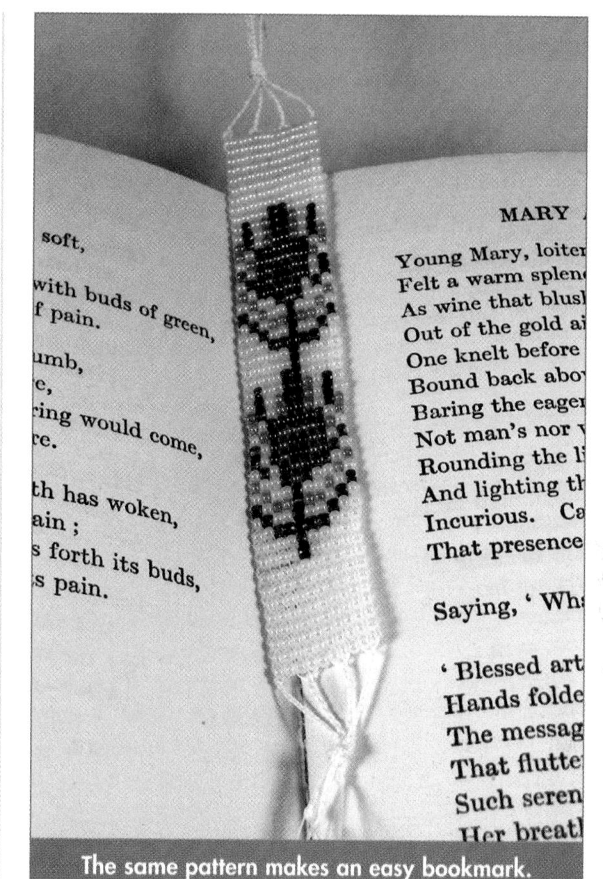

The same pattern makes an easy bookmark.

You could also use the same method as on the hatband, making the selvages and gluing the piece onto a piece of grosgrain or velvet ribbon.

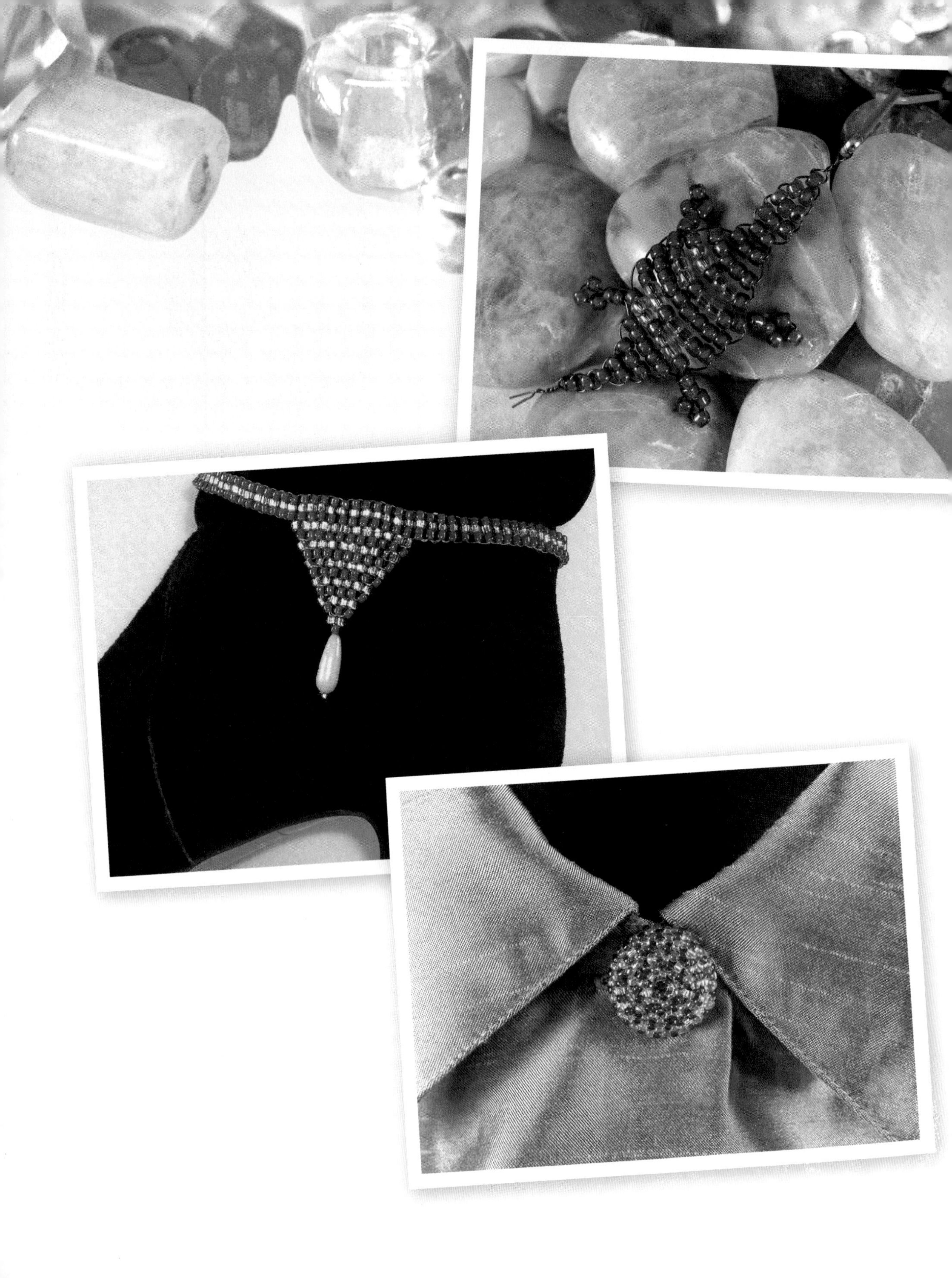

Dazzling Details

In This Chapter

- Add whimsy to everyday items with beaded critters that even a kid will love to make
- Bejewel your boots, and they'll take you everywhere in style!
- Bead some button covers you can change along with your mood

Beads are showing up in the darnedest places! Think of all the little nooks and crannies of your wardrobe (or a lucky kid's) where a beaded detail would please and surprise. This chapter explores some of the more uncommon ways to add beaded delights everywhere.

Turtle Zipper Pull

Skill level: Beginner

What you need:

75 (size 8) brown seed beads
16 (size 8) green seed beads
2 (size 8) gold seed beads
3 feet brown (26-gauge) wire
Lanyard or similar hook finding
Wire cutters
Vise (optional)

Techniques and skills needed:

Basic Victorian technique wirework

If you love critters, you'll love this project. It's so simple a child can do it—or you can simply indulge the child in *you!* After you learn this technique, you'll find lots of ways to use it, and I've provided resources for you to take it as far as you want.

The French beading technique you learned in Chapter 4 is only one way to make beaded flowers, leaves, animals, birds, and insects. Additional methods use thread and various off-loom stitches, but there's also a technique called "Victorian" beading, so named because it was developed in the nineteenth century. The "younger" set today has taken up this technique using large *pony beads* and cord, but it also works quite well with wire and almost any size beads. You can find patterns galore in books and on the Internet. Look for projects called "Beadie Babies."

Beadwise

Pony beads are large, cylindrical beads that come in two sizes, 6mmx9mm and 4mmx7mm (called baby pony beads). They're available in both glass and plastic and a wide range of colors and finishes.

For this project, I've chosen size 8 seed beads, which give you a turtle that's large enough to be noticed but small enough to use as a decorative addition to a zipper pull or key chain without getting in the way. What other critters can you make?

Embellishments

You can easily change the critter with a change in bead size. If you look at the variations later in the chapter, you'll see how the project I've featured changes from bold to delicate with a change in bead size. Size 11 seed beads make a critter small enough to be used for earrings or a charm. Or you can bead the whole animal or just the face!

Just a few supplies and tools are all you need for this quick and easy project.

Pearls

A vise or anything you can hook onto is helpful for this project to give you something to pull against. I like one I found at Arizona Gems and Minerals (see Appendix A), a shop in my neighborhood with an extensive website. My vise has a suction base that enables me to affix it to almost any surface without bolting it down or using a clamp.

1. Fold 3 feet of wire in half. Make the fold a "soft" fold, not a hard crease.

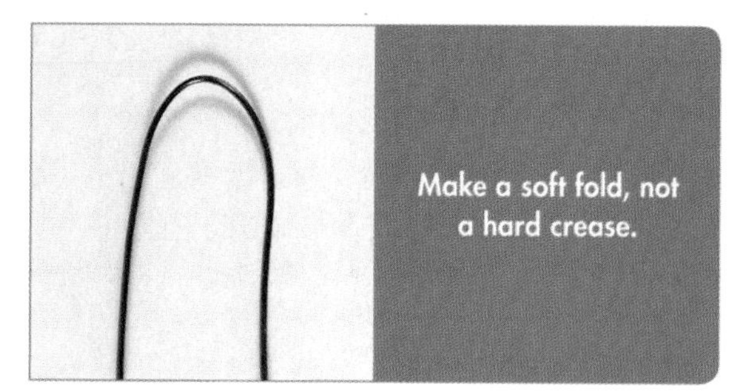

Make a soft fold, not a hard crease.

2. Thread the lanyard hook onto the wire, bring it down to the fold, and twist the wire a couple of times.

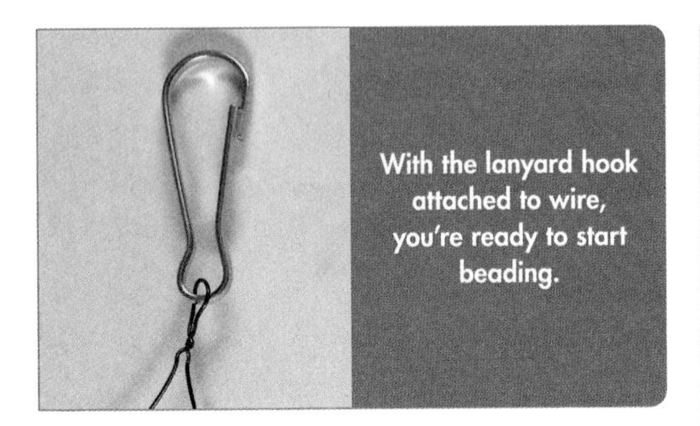
With the lanyard hook attached to wire, you're ready to start beading.

3. Start at the top of the pattern (the nose end, nearest the lanyard) and work down. You might want to put your pattern on a stand and use a guide to follow along each row like I did when I made the loom-worked hatband (see Chapter 5).

This is the pattern I created for the turtle zipper pull.

4. Add the first bead to the right-side wire and cross through from the other side with the left-side wire. (If you're left-handed, you can work this the opposite way.) This may remind you of the right angle weave (RAW) technique from Part 1 using two needles.

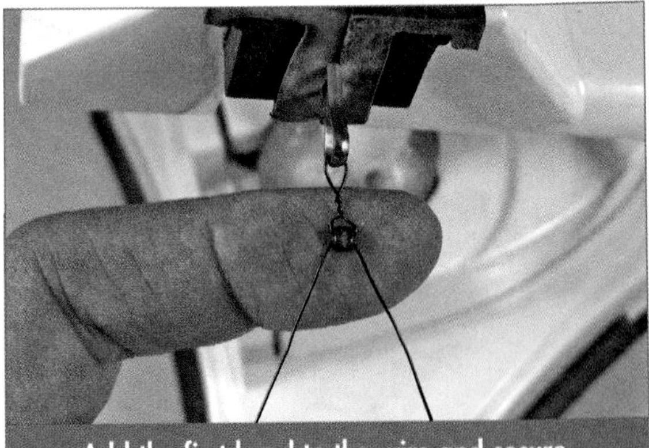
Add the first bead to the wire and secure.

5. Continue working down the pattern from head to tail. To add the legs, between rows 8 and 9 and rows 12 and 13, string 5 beads on the right wire and go back through the second and first beads you strung on. Repeat with the left wire.

Create the legs by bringing the wire back down through the first 2 beads.

6. When you reach the end of the tail, twist the wires together and cut off the excess. You can leave the wire "tails" as is or turn them under.

My finished turtle.

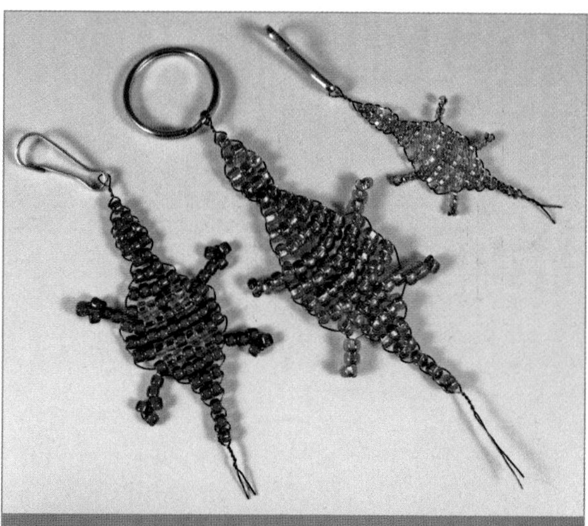

Here you can see the same pattern done in the original size 8 seed beads (left) beside a larger one in size 6 (middle), and a smaller one in size 11 beads (right).

Variations

Now that you've got your first critter under (or hanging from) your belt, you'll probably want to have a whole zoo! Or maybe you want a design for people, flowers, insects, or just about anything you can imagine—you can find them or design them yourself. Or you can simply change to a different size beads and you have something new!

Same Critter, Different Size

I reworked the turtle pattern in size 6 and size 11 seed beads so you can compare the sizes. You could make two of the smallest one (using size 11 beads) and wear them as earrings.

Holy Cats and Dogs!

Find a pattern for your favorite pet and change the colors to match him or her. Or pick your favorite color, even if critters don't come that way!

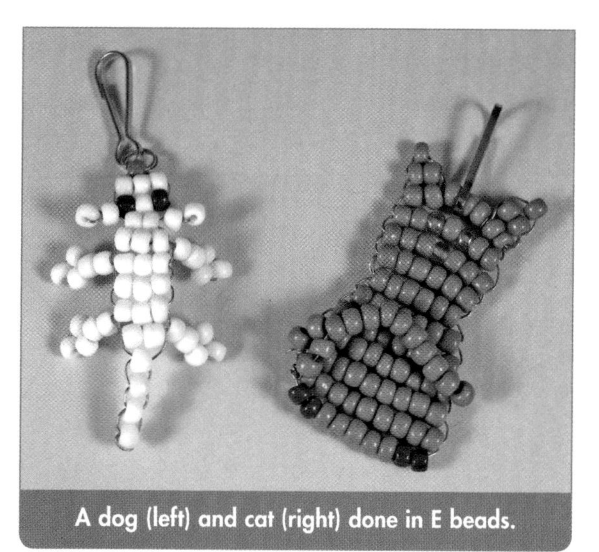

A dog (left) and cat (right) done in E beads.

Flowers Anyone?

Flowers make great subjects for these pulls and charms. Don't limit yourself just to the "Beadie Baby"–type pattern books and websites. Check into beaded flower sources, too. They're often called "Victorian technique" beaded flowers and can be quite intricate and realistic-looking. Look for the flowers that are fairly flat for this application, or just look at your flowerbeds to come up with your own designs!

Beadedy flower charms in two different sizes.

Dangles Work Here, Too!

If you're not into trying this new technique or you're just in a hurry, a beaded dangle works just fine for a zipper pull or backpack charm. You've been making them all along if you've been trying some of the other projects in this book, so you should be a pro by now!

Simple dangles work great as pulls or charms, and nothing could be quicker!

Create a whole world of nature you can wear with the wire technique you just learned. Also experiment with different threads and cords instead of wire. The only difference with those materials is that you need to knot at the beginning and end instead of twisting. Whatever you use, just be sure it's strong enough to hold up to everyday wear and tear.

Resources

Size 8 beads: Whimbeads (www.whimbeads.com)

Books: *Beaded Critters* by Sonal Bhatt, and *Beadin' Critters Fun Faces*, *Beadie Babies*, and *Beadie Babies 2*, all from Suzanne McNeill's Design Originals. I found a good selection of these books at my local crafts shop, and they're widely available online as well.

If you'd like to try some thread techniques for making critters and flowers, you might enjoy the book The Beaded Garden by Diane Fitzgerald.

www.beadiecritters.com is a good resource for finding patterns.

Wire and vise: Arizona Gems and Minerals (www.azgemsandbeads.com)

Boot Booty

Skill level: Beginner

What you need:

- Tube of (size 8) red seed beads
- Tube of (size 8) gold seed beads
- 13 (size 11) gold seed beads
- 1 gold glass dangle
- FireLine 6 lb. test
- Beading needle
- Lobster claw clasp and tab
- Jump ring
- Chain nose pliers

Techniques and skills needed:

- Ladder stitch
- Brick stitch

We've all seen ankle bracelets. Well, now someone's come up with the clever idea of ankle bracelets for boots! For this "small thing–big glamour" project, I used size 8 beads for a bold statement. I used red and gold to really show up royally on a black boot. You can choose your own colors based on your boot collection and wardrobe colors.

Size 8 and 11 seed beads and a dangle are all the beads you need for this project. Add a needle and thread, a clasp, and a jump ring, and what could be simpler?

Make a ladder stitch chain with 2 red beads on either end and a gold bead in the middle of each row, approximately 12¼ inches long. This length will vary depending on the boot you're using and the thickness of your ankle. Start off with 12 inches and add rows as needed, remembering to include about ¾ inch for the addition of the clasp and tab. Leave at least a 6-inch tail.

Ladder Stitch Refresher

If you're not sure (or don't remember) how to do ladder stitch, here's a refresher. This stitch is often used as a foundation stitch for brick stitch. It's usually worked with seed beads (singly or in stacks) or bugle beads.

For the pattern, I've used a base of ladder-stitched size 8 seed beads with 3 beads in each row. Here's how to create the seed bead ladder-stitched base bracelet for this project:

1. Cut approximately 2 yards of thread (or whatever length you can handle easily) and thread on 1 red bead, 1 gold bead, 2 red beads, 1 gold bead, and 1 red bead. Slide them down until they're 6 inches from the end.
2. Bring your needle up through the first 3 beads you strung on, starting with the first bead, and pull up your thread until it feels snug but not tight. You want the beads to lay evenly, side by side. You will have created 2 stacks of 3 beads at this point.

First 2 ladder stitch rows.

3. Go down through the second 3-bead stack, pick up 3 more beads, go through the second 3-bead stack again, and go back through the 3 beads you just added.

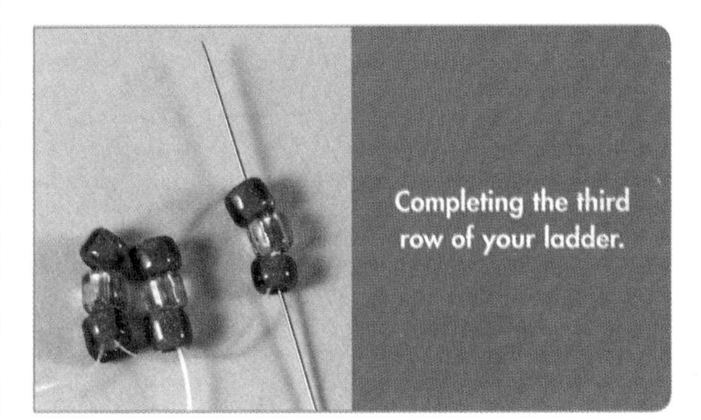

Completing the third row of your ladder.

4. Add 3 more beads and continue this pattern, basically working in a circle and adding beads until you reach the desired length. Mine ended up being approximately 13 inches long.

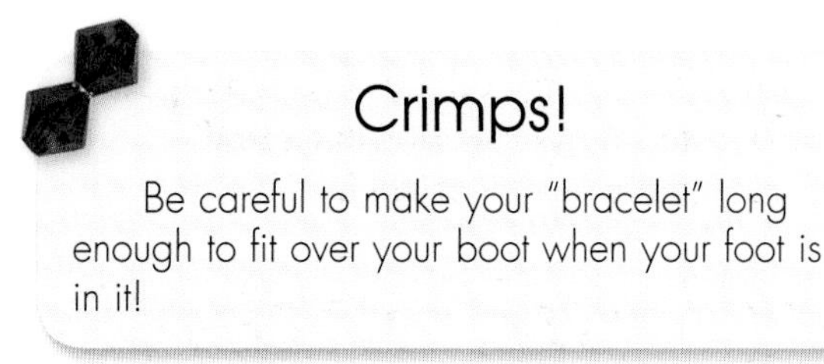

Crimps!

Be careful to make your "bracelet" long enough to fit over your boot when your foot is in it!

5. Check your ladder stitch chain for length, and if you're satisfied, you can now add your clasp.

Here's what my finished ladder stitch bracelet looked like before I added the clasp.

Pearls

Keep your tension even and snug, but not too tight. You want to minimize gaps between the stacks of beads (or bugles). If your ladder isn't even and you have the room, you can go back through the beads and tighten things up.

6. Open the jump ring and put it through the hole of your lobster claw clasp. Close the jump ring using your chain nose pliers, and attach the jump ring with the clasp on the needle end of your bracelet by stringing on 6 (size 11) beads and the clasp. Go back through the last 3-bead row of your ladder to make a loop. Then go back through your clasp loop a couple more times and weave the thread through the bracelet and then knot off. Using the tail on the other end of the bracelet, add the other part of your clasp in the same way.

My finished bracelet with the clasp attached.

Pearls

You might need to use a jump ring when attaching a clasp to make the bracelet lay flat. Sometimes you need to plan ahead or your work will twist when you add the clasp.

7. Add thread if you need to and make the first row of brick stitch. (Need a refresher? I've given you the basic steps in the following section.) I positioned my first row halfway between the two ends of the bracelet so the clasp would be on the inside of the ankle and the design in the middle of the foot on the outside. Twelve beads make up the first row.
8. As you work your brick stitch rows each will naturally decrease to create a triangle. Continue until you have a final row of 2. I chose to alternate rows with each color. You can do the same or create a different pattern.

9. At the bottom of your brick stitch triangle (you should have 2 gold beads at the bottom), add a dangle by using a red size 8 bead, going through the drop bead, adding a size 11 bead, and going back through the dangle and gold size 8 bead. Weave through your work and knot off.

Adding the last bead of the triangle and the drop.

Brick Stitch Refresher

Brick stitch looks essentially like a brick wall, hence the name. Here's how it's done:

1. Come out the top of your foundation ladder and add 2 beads.
2. Go under the threads in between the second and third beads on your base ladder stitch row from back to front.
3. Come up through the second bead you just put on, from bottom to top, then down the first bead, from top to bottom.
4. Bring your needle and thread under the threads between the first and second beads of the foundation row, from back to front. Come up the second bead again, from bottom to top.
5. Add 1 bead and bring your needle and thread under the threads between the next 2 beads in the foundation row, from back to front, then up through the bead you just put on, from top to bottom. Repeat, adding 1 bead at a time to finish the row.
6. Turn your work, add 2 beads, and repeat from step 2. Your work will naturally decrease, creating a triangle.

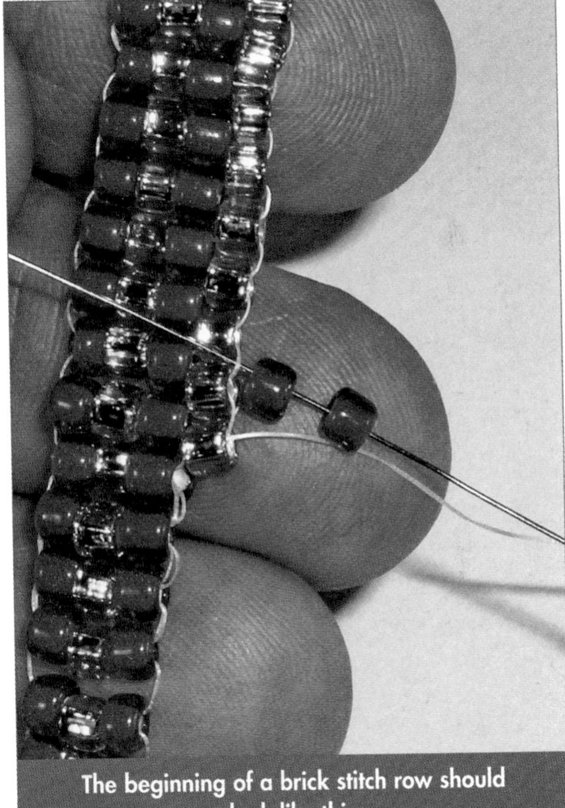

The beginning of a brick stitch row should look like this.

I'm sure you can think of lots of ways to add to this basic design. You could add more drops going up the sides of the triangle, or even add smaller triangles on either side with drops or add loops. If you don't like it, just take it out—that's the great thing about beading!

Variations

Just as with a regular bracelet or ankle bracelet, the different design options you can explore are endless. I've given you three entirely different versions here to get your creative juices flowing.

Silver Heel-Detail Boot Bracelet

Designer Bobbi Wicks used silver-lined bugle beads and seed beads to create this boot jewelry, which picks up the heel interest. She used somewhat heavier FireLine (10 lb. test) and created her ladder foundation bracelet using a seed bead, a bugle, and another seed bead. There are four overlapping loops, two long and two somewhat shorter, with a center dangle. If you're putting your design element at the heel, position your clasp so it ends up on the inside of the boot ankle.

Kick up your heels with this design that'll leave 'em watching you as you go!

Red, White, and Blue Braided Boot Bracelet

A very simple technique adds some patriotic pizzazz to this design. Each strand of size 11 seed beads is strung on flexible wire such as Beadalon or Soft Flex 2 inches at a time. The three strands of beads are braided and then the empty strands are threaded through an E bead and another 2 inches of seed beads are strung. The strands are attached to the clasp using crimp beads.

This patriotic braided boot bracelet lets you show your colors.

Chain and Stone Boot Bracelet

This is a quickie boot bracelet you can put together in a flash. Just cut some chain and attach a clasp, add two chain loops using jump rings, and in the center attach a small stone pendant with another jump ring. Quick and easy—but classy!

You could turn a broken necklace into this classy boot bracelet in less than a hour.

Resources

Size 8 beads: Whimbeads (www.whimbeads.com)

Button Up!

Skill level: Beginner

What you need:

1 hank each, three different colors (size 11) seed beads, to be called colors 1, 2, and 3
Nymo size B thread
Size 10 beading needle
Button cover
Felt in color compatible with color scheme
E-6000 glue
Thread Heaven or beeswax to condition thread

Techniques and skills needed:

Flat round peyote stitch
Tubular peyote stitch

Most buttons are, well, just *buttons!* They just sit there and keep your shirt or pants closed—functional, but not very fun. But with a few beads, you can turn any ordinary button into much more than a button—and you won't want to make just one.

We're going to make a basic button cover you can move from garment to garment. For this project, we explore the wonders of flat round *peyote* (also called flat circular peyote).

Beadwise

Peyote stitch, or Gourd stitch as it's also called, is done by weaving beads together in an off-set row method, with the bead holes lined up end to end.

Three different color seed beads, a needle and thread, a little felt, and a button cover finding are the main ingredients for an easy but striking button cover.

Pearls

Condition your thread using either beeswax or a product called Thread Heaven, a synthetic thread conditioner, to keep it from tangling and make it easier to work with.

1. Trace your button cover on the piece of felt. Measure the side, and cut a piece long enough to cover that, too. Glue the pieces of felt on the top and around the circumference of the cover with the E-6000 glue, and let dry. The felt gives your button cover a nice softness and shape.

Glue felt to the top and sides of the button cover finding.

2. Starting with color 1, put 3 beads on your thread. Leave a tail of 4 to 6 inches and knot to make a circle. This is your first "round."

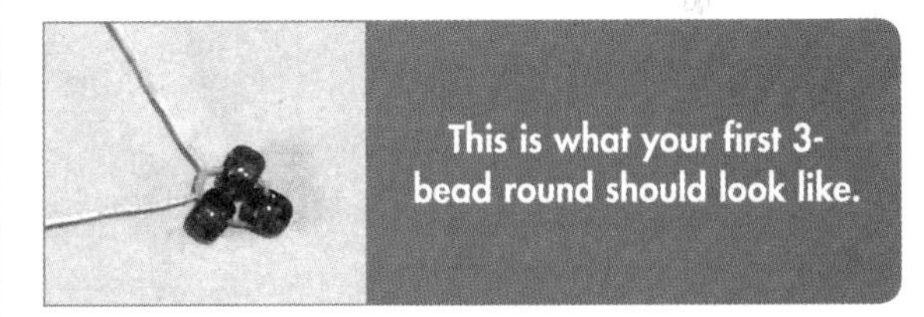

This is what your first 3-bead round should look like.

3. Now go through the first bead after the knot. Add 2 (color 2) beads between each of the single color 1 beads in round 1. This completes your second "round."

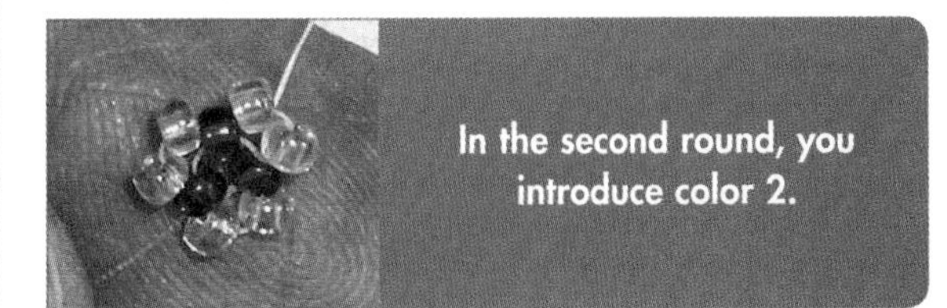

In the second round, you introduce color 2.

Crimps!

Be sure you don't allow your thread to twist as you work the rounds of the pattern. If it twists, your piece won't lay right and it will cause problems on the next round.

4. For round 3, go through the first bead in round 2. This is called a "step up," and you will do this at the end of each round; you will complete the round and then *step up* to the next one by going through the first bead of the previous round. Add 1 (color 3) bead—you'll be between the double beads and dividing them in two like a "split"—and go through the second color 2 bead. Add 1 (color 3) bead in the single bead space and continue in this way through the third round. Alternate between putting a bead over a "split" and a bead on top of a single bead from the previous row.

Round 3 should look like this.

5. For round 4, add 2 (color 1) beads in each space. Don't forget to "step up" to the new round each time!
6. For round 5, add 1 (color 2) bead between each set of double beads and in each space.
7. For round 6, add 1 (color 3) bead in each space.

Crimps!

Pay close attention on round 7 and remember to alternate 2 beads and then 1. It's easy to forget because on all the other rounds, you add 1 bead or 2 beads all the way around.

8. For round 7, add 2 (color 1) beads in the first space and 1 bead in the next space. Continue in this way, alternating 2 beads and then 1 bead, all the way around.
9. For round 8, add 1 (color 2) bead between each set of double beads and in each space.
10. For round 9, continue alternating colors 1, 2, and 3, putting 1 bead in each space for all the remaining rows. You'll start to see the button cover "turn" and curve down the sides as you go around—this is tubular peyote! I suggest you glue the beaded cover to the top part of your felt-covered finding at round 9, let it dry, and then continue beading around the sides until you reach the bottom. Mine took 13 rounds total to complete. Pull your thread snug as you do the sides, and knot off your thread when you reach the end.

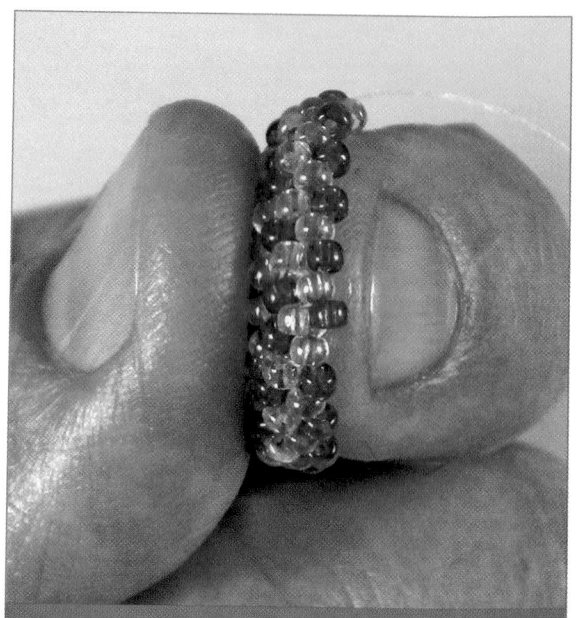

This side view of the button cover shows how your work curves once you stop increasing and continue doing tubular peyote.

You can make a whole set of matching button covers or just one for a little something extra on a shirt that buttons at the collar. This is great for blouses and shirts made of fabrics that don't take kindly to being pierced with a pin back. You can just remove your button cover when you need to launder the garment.

Variations

Beads and buttons just seem to go together. Here are a variety of ways to add beads to buttons. Some are simply glued, and some are conventional buttons sewn on in the usual way with some beads added on top. Some are vintage buttons, and some I purchased at my corner fabric store. Hopefully, I've inspired you to begin making the connection between beads and buttons!

Now that we've had fun playing with our wardrobes, it's about time we turned to dressing up the house. Beads shine here, too. Just keep turning the pages and you'll see!

Resources

Button cover finding: Arizona Gems and Minerals (www.azgemsandbeads.com)

Note the many ways beads can embellish buttons. And they're not all sewn or woven—sometimes glue is a beautiful thing!

In This Part

Beading for Your Home

Living the lush life is easier when you know how to bring along your own sparkle. Everyday items you take for granted around your home can go from so-so to spectacular when you add some beads. From the bath to the breakfast nook, beads are invited guests!

And if your house shines, why not spread it around? These projects make great gifts!

Bling for the Boudoir

In This Chapter

- A decorative bottle collar sure to brighten up your bath
- Light up your nights with a fire-and-jewels votive holder
- Craft a soothing—and beautiful—sleep pillow

It seems only fitting that the places you go to relax and unwind should be enhanced by beadwork. Add romance and sparkle, light and luxury in your bed and bath. Even your sleep can be filled with "bead dreams"!

"Memorable" Bottle Collar

Skill level: Beginner

What you need:

A mixture of beads in your color of choice
Size 11 beads in complementary colors
Size 6 seed beads in complementary colors
Size 14 seed beads in gold, silver, or other metallic color
2 gold (size 8) beads for ends
Memory wire for bracelets (You can do ring size, too, for bottles with narrow necks.)
Heavy-duty cutters
Round nose pliers
FireLine crystal 6 lb. test
Beading needle

Techniques and skills needed:

Basic bead stringing
Fringe

I always love it when I can get two for the price of one, and that's what this project is all about. What better to decorate a pretty bottle filled with your favorite bubble bath or bath oil than a smashing beaded collar? Plus, it's adjustable, so when you tire of it on one bottle (or you run out of bubble bath), you can move it to another bottle, even if it's a different size. (Memory wire makes all the difference.)

This project is a great way to use up all those odds-and-ends beads you have. You probably want to have some beads that are top- and side-drilled for added interest.

You'll need a variety of beads to do this project, plus some memory wire and a few tools and supplies.

If you don't have enough "bead soup" or odds and ends of similar size beads in a color family, you can buy bead mixes by color in bead stores, through catalogs, or online. I've given you a couple of sources at the end of this project.

To make your own mix, choose a variety of beads in a color family and add some metallic accent beads or a bright complementary color. You'll be making lots of fringe for this project, so look for beads that lend themselves to fringe, like drops and leaves that are drilled from top to bottom as well as side-drilled through the top. You can also combine beads to make interesting fringe drops, adding spacers and seed beads to make tiny "lanterns" or fun combinations.

This is a project where you can exercise your imagination. If you try something and you don't like it, simply take the beads off and try again! There is no "right way," and there are no rules. Whatever you like goes.

1. Cut your memory wire so it makes at least one round and overlaps. You can decide how many times. Just remember that the longer you make the bracelet, the more fringe you need to make and the more beads you need.
2. Make a loop at one end with your round nose pliers.

Use your round nose pliers to make a loop at one end of the memory wire coil.

3. Thread on 1 (size 8) gold bead and then enough size 6 beads to cover the bracelet. End with the second size 8 gold bead, and make a loop.

The beaded bracelet base for your bottle collar should look something like this.

Pearls

It helps to hold the memory wire in your nondominant hand and stretch it out a bit, picking up the beads with other end of the wire in your dominant hand. As you put on a few beads, let them fall toward the end with the loop and move your nondominant hand up to keep the beads from moving back up to the other end.

4. Thread 3 yards of FireLine on your needle (or less, if that's too much for you to handle without getting tangled up). Go through the last 3 beads toward the loop (2 [size 6] beads and the size 8 gold end bead), around the end gold bead, and back through it. Come up between the gold bead and the first size 6 bead. Make a knot around between the beads and around the wire to secure.

Crimps!

Don't keep your thread tension too tight or too loose. You want fringe to flow, not stick out stiffly, but you also don't want to see thread gaps between the beads. Bending your needle so it's a little curved can help get in between the beads on the bracelet.

5. Make a fringe between each size 6 bead by stringing on between 3 and 6 (size 11) seed beads, put on your accent bead or beads, and add a size 14 bead. Go around the size 14 bead (not through it) to secure your fringe. Then go back through all the beads you strung on and through the next size 6 bead on the wire.

This is how you make a fringe.

6. Continue in this manner all the way to the end, through the gold bead, around the gold bead, and back through the first size 6 bead.
7. Make another fringe in each space. You can even go back through again if you want so there are three fringes in each space. You're limited only by time and patience and whether the thread will fit through the number of times you envision. Vary the beads you use. If you have a top, side-drilled bead, put on 6 (size 11) seed beads, go through the bead, add 3 more (size 11) seed beads, and go through the first 3 (size 11) beads you put on.

Pearls

Fringe uses up a lot of thread, so try to work with as long a thread as you're comfortable with. You'll have to add thread less often.

8. When you're finished with all your fringes, knot off and clip the thread ends.

You can add a dangle at each loop if you want. (I didn't on mine.) Adding charms gives the collar additional interest.

Variations

The fringe between beads technique is extremely adaptable. These variations show how you can make more fitted bracelets using it.

Bottles also lend themselves to different beading techniques. The second variation employs simple wirework.

Fringe Bracelets

These bracelets use exactly the same technique, only they're not worked on the memory wire. Here I used size 8 seed beads for the base bracelet, instead of 6s, and added a gold toggle clasp. I used FireLine here, too, and used two fringes between each bead of the base bracelet. Notice the different colors and sizes of beads in the mix.

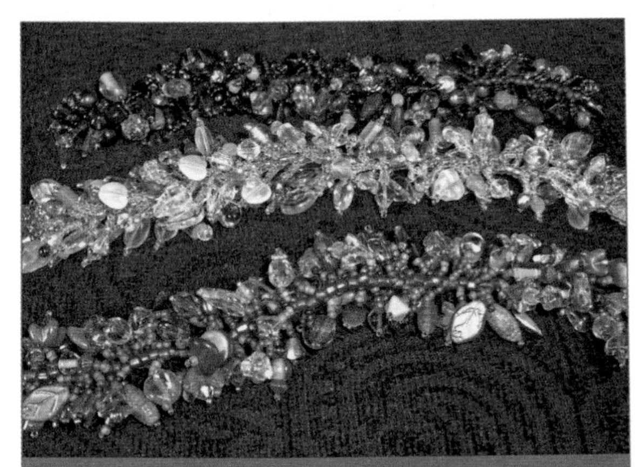

These fringe bracelets are fun mixes of color and texture, and use the same technique as the bottle collar.

Resources

Memory wire: Beadalon Remembrance Stainless Steel Memory Wire (www.beadalon.com)

Wire and Found Jewelry Collar

You can make bottle collars in a variety of ways. This is a very simple variation using copper wire and a shell necklace that had broken. What a nice addition in a bath that was decorated in a sea theme.

Copper wire and a broken shell necklace on an ocean-colored bottle make for a "sea-worthy" bath accessory.

So don't just settle for plain bottles in your boudoir! Cover them with beads, and you'll see stars—and when you're lounging in your bubble bath, you'll feel like one, too!

Fairy Lantern

Skill level: Intermediate

What you need:

- 20- and 18-gauge wire
- Assorted mixture of beads
- Votive holder
- Chain
- Wire cutters
- Round nose pliers
- Chain nose pliers
- Nylon jaw pliers
- Wire jig

Techniques and skills needed:

- Basic wirework

Tinker Bell would be right at home in these hanging votive cups. Pink beads and gold wire surround a pale pink votive holder you can hang just about anywhere. These are so easy to make, you can make several and create a fairy wonderland around your bath. They also make great outdoor accents.

The only somewhat unusual tool you'll need for this project is a wire jig, which you'll want to have anyway, as it can open up a world of possibilities for creating accents and findings for your jewelry and home accessory pieces. (See the "Resources" box for information on where to get jigs that'll make your projects dance.)

This is what you need to make your hanging votive holder

1. Make 4 jig elements: cut 4 pieces of 18-gauge wire, each 8 inches long. Using your round nose pliers, make a loop on one end of the first piece of wire and put the loop over the smaller peg on the left of the jig. Come up over the top peg and then cross diagonally and under the bottom peg. Repeat this figure-eight design two more times, come up to the left of the right peg, and make a loop around it.

My jig is a stationary one. If you're using a removable jig, set up your pegs as shown here.

2. Remove your wire element from the jig and spread it out slightly so the loops lay flat. Harden the wire by hammering it slightly with a metal or plastic block placed over the piece. Continue with the remaining 3 pieces.

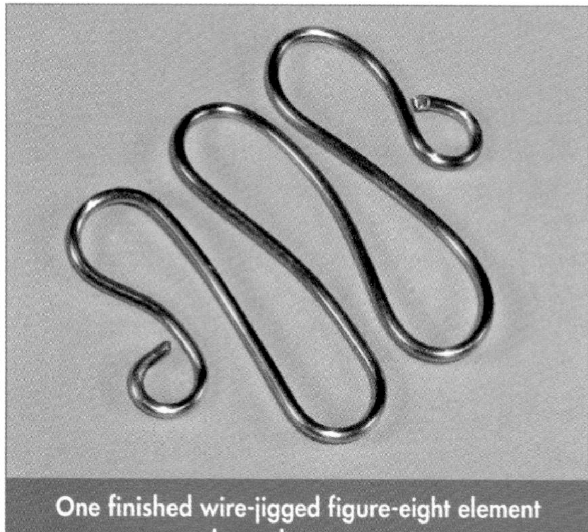

One finished wire-jigged figure-eight element done; three to go.

3. For the "dangle element," cut 3 (4- to 5-inch) pieces of 20-gauge wire. Just as you did in step 1, make a loop on one end of the wire and slide it over the left peg of the jig. Bring your wire between the left peg and the top peg, up over the top of the top peg, diagonally across from right to left, and around the bottom peg. Then bring your wire up to the left of the right peg, over the top, and around to make a loop.
4. Harden your wire element as you did in step 2, and continue with the remaining 2 pieces.

Three finished wire-jigged dangle elements.

5. Cut 3 (8-inch) lengths of chain. Attach all 3 to 1 figure-eight element at the top and then attach each length of chain to one of the 3 elements at the bottom using the small loop.

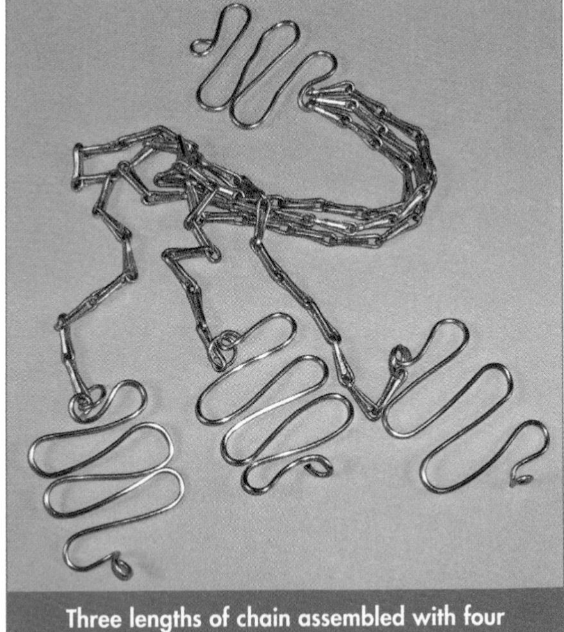

Three lengths of chain assembled with four figure-eight elements.

6. Turn the bottom loops of each of the figure-eight elements hanging from the chain to a 90-degree angle. Later, you'll attach these to the beaded collar you'll make to go around the votive holder.

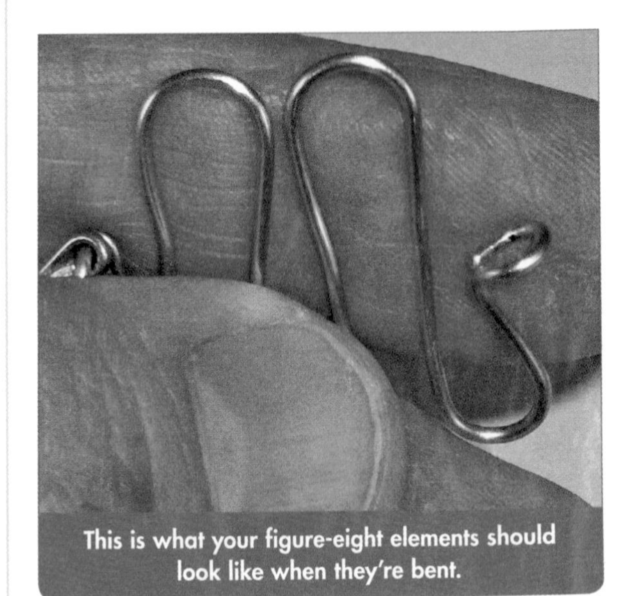

This is what your figure-eight elements should look like when they're bent.

7. Now for the beaded collar: cut 10 inches of 20-gauge wire and make a loop at one end with your round nose pliers. Thread on your beads, the 3 dangle elements, and 3 figure-eight elements at the ends of each of the chain, evenly spacing the elements.
8. Put the remaining wire through the end loop of your collar, and fit the collar around your votive holder. Make a loop at the end of the remaining wire, and using your chain nose pliers and holding the loop flat, make a spiral around the loop. Remove your votive holder while you finish the hanger.
9. Add dangles to 3 dangle elements. I made spirals first and then added the beads to make a more interesting dangle and to match the spiral I made to finish the collar.
10. Now place your votive holder back in the collar, suspend it from the top element, and hang it up!

This project lends itself to any number of variations, as wire, chain, and beads offer limitless possibilities. Now that you understand the basic construction, try some different versions for different effects.

Pearls

Don't worry if you have to put on and remove your beads, dangles, and figure eights several times to get them evenly spaced. You're looking for balance when you hang your votive holder, so either use your eye (which is how I did it) or measure the distances to get things even.

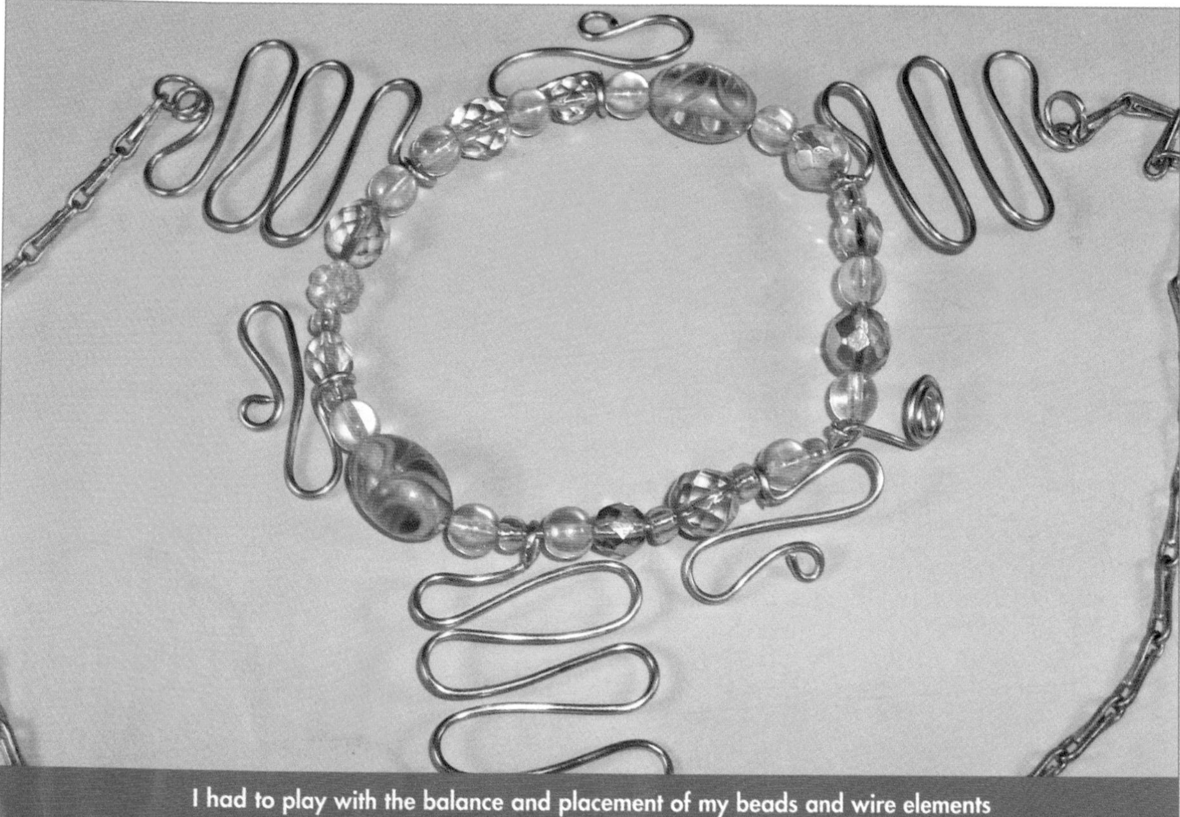

I had to play with the balance and placement of my beads and wire elements a couple of times until they were even.

Variations

Wirework accessories are quick and easy. Found objects are fun to incorporate and keep costs down to practically nothing. Start frequenting your local thrift shops!

Wild Wire!

You don't necessarily have to make a hanging candle holder, and you don't need a jig. Designer Bobbi Wicks found this standing candle holder at a thrift store and hung pendants from broken necklaces and bracelets from the wire loops she created free-form.

The collar attaches over the lip of the holder using U-shaped wire sections that she then bent over to form a kind of clip or hook. She used 18-gauge copper wire.

Bobbi Wicks designed this free-form collar to suspend from the top of a standing candle holder.

Coils and Spirals

This version uses a collar design, similar to the featured project, but picks up on the spiral theme. I made coils by wrapping wire around a pencil and then pulling them apart slightly. This could also be converted into a hanging candle holder by simply adding chain and a hanger at the top.

Coils and spirals give this candleholder a playful, modern look.y

Resources

Wire jigs: WigJig (www.wigjig.com) offers lots of instructions, tips, and projects on its website, as well as a wide variety of available jigs. There are even videos to help you learn additional jig-making skills.

Thing-A-Ma-Jig (www.beadalon.com)

Wire: ColourCraft wire (www.beadalon.com)

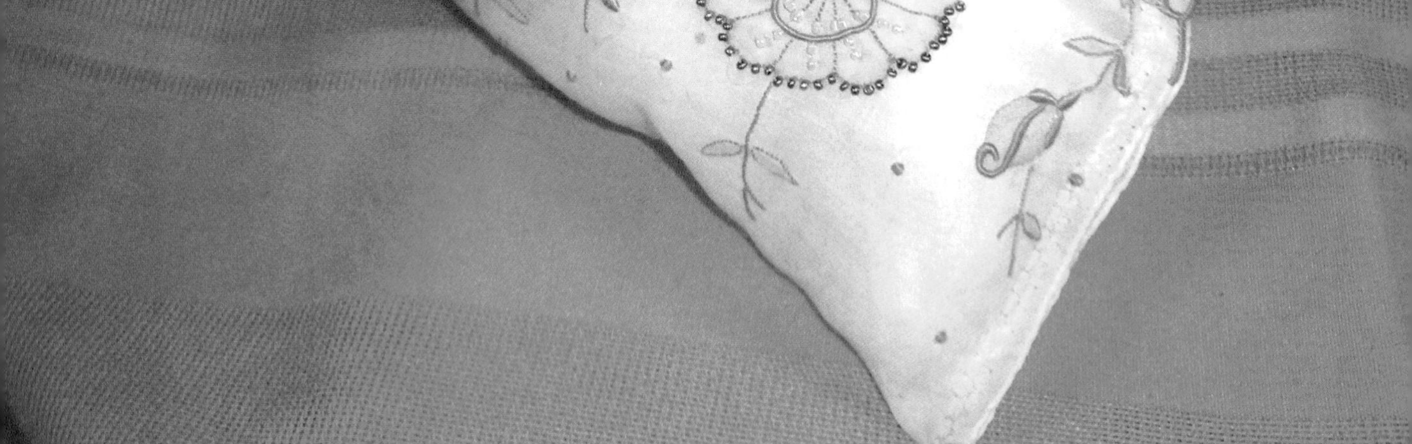

Sleep Sweet … Hankie?

Skill level: Beginner

What you need:

Vintage handkerchief with embroidery
Needle and thread
Size 11 seed beads in colors to complement handkerchief
Hops or lavender flowers for filling
Ribbon to complement handkerchief
Fiberfill (optional)
Essential oil (optional)
Muslin bag (optional)
Rubber band

Techniques and skills needed:

Bead embroidery

Most of us have some fancy handkerchiefs forgotten in a drawer or stuffed away in a trunk (or maybe Grandma's bureau drawer!). If not, they abound in thrift and antique stores. Put them to new (and restful) use in your bedroom with this next project.

Try to find a handkerchief that has some fairly elaborate embroidery, usually on one corner, or an overall design you can work with. You can always add more of your own embroidery design, but this project goes more quickly if the design is already there for you to embellish.

Here are some examples of handkerchiefs you're likely to find in your own stash or in thrift stores that will work well for this project.

All you need for this project are some beads to complement your hankie design and a needle and thread.

1. Using simple outlining embroidery and scatter stitch, which you learned in Chapter 4, embellish your handkerchief as much or as little as you like!

This handkerchief has a lot of appliqué and embroidery, so I just added some beaded accents to give more depth to the design and add some more sweetness.

Pearls

You can use a small hoop to help you embroider, if you need to. Baste the handkerchief to a larger piece of material so it will fit in the hoop, if necessary.

2. Fold your handkerchief in half so you have a rectangle, with wrong sides together. You will be top stitching. You'll want the most embellished part of the design to appear on the front. Pin and then sew together two sides of your handkerchief, one short side that should be the bottom of the bag you're creating, and one long side. The fold will form the other side. Leave the top open.

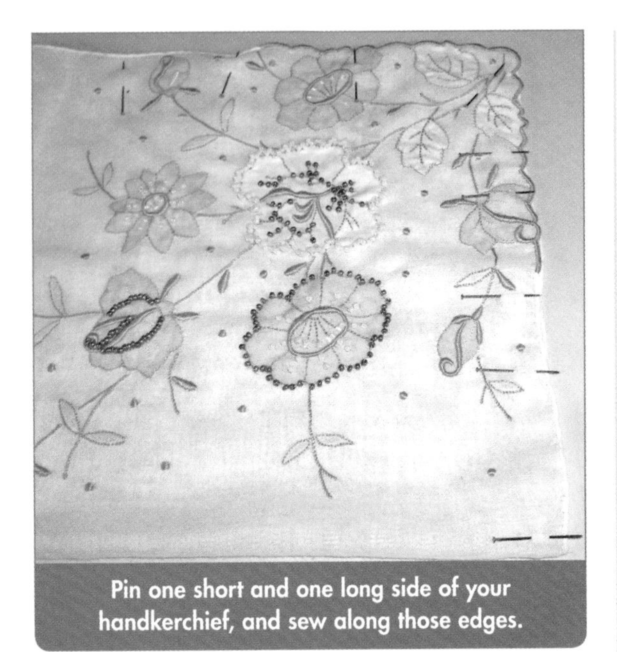
Pin one short and one long side of your handkerchief, and sew along those edges.

3. Fill your pillow with lavender flowers or hops, both of which are said to help induce restful sleep. If you don't want to fill the entire bag with herbs, you can use fiberfill for part of the filling and mix it with the herbs, or you can put the herbs in a muslin bag and insert that into the fiberfill.

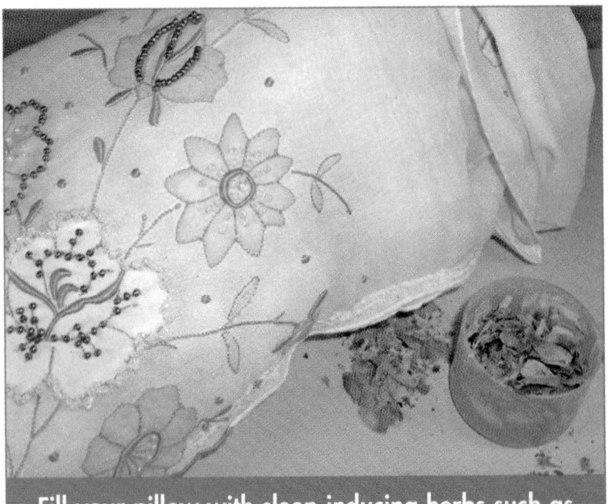
Fill your pillow with sleep-inducing herbs such as lavender or hops.

4. Wrap a rubber band tightly around the top of your pillow. Tie a ribbon over the rubber band, and your pillow is complete.

Embellishments

This is an easy project to "dress up" even more. Add fringe. Add lace or other trim. Add as little or as much as you want to your sleep pillow. Let the handkerchief design and feel guide you to use your imagination.

Variations

If you have still more vintage hankies, why not make some more dainty beaded things? They look sweet in your guest bedroom, and they make great gifts to your favorite people.

Sweet Sachet

I folded this handkerchief in quarters and closed it using a blanket stitch along the edge. Filled with your favorite potpourri, it would make a pretty scented surprise for your own drawers or as a gift. What a nice idea for a bride!

With a little beading, ribbon, and potpourri, instead of a sleep pillow, you have a sachet!

More Pillow Magic

This sleep pillow is more densely embroidered because the embroidered design just begged for it. I added a delicate beaded picot edging along the top.

A more heavily beaded design and edging add up to a pretty variation on the featured project.

Your bedroom is now an oasis of beaded bliss. Let's more on to the rest of the house!

Resources

Herbs for sleep: Lavender flowers, San Francisco Herb Co. (www.sfherb.com); hops, Frontier Natural Products Coop (www.frontiercoop.com)

CHAPTER 8

Living the Beaded Life

In This Chapter

- Beads + light = an elegant bead-trimmed lampshade
- Beautify a simple store-bought frame with beads
- Transform your drapes from "nice" to "gorgeous" with a bead-embellished tassel

Now let's move from the bedroom and bath to the more public areas of your home. Beaded touches add life and sparkle in ways both subtle and bold.

Little Beads of Light

Skill level: Beginner

What you need:

- Purchased lampshade
- Size 11 seed beads, pale pink and medium pink
- 6mm crystals
- 4mm crystals
- Nymo size B beading thread
- Bead embroidery needle

Techniques and skills needed:

- Beaded embellishment
- Fringe

It doesn't take much to bring a pretty store-bought lampshade into the limelight. This one came from a famous decorating diva's line at a well-known discount department store. It had some nice texture and suggested a Victorian decorating theme, so I chose to bead some trim that took it up to another level. The crystals and seed beads turned a pretty shade into custom-made eye candy.

This project uses size 11 seed beads, but you can experiment and mix other sizes according to your shade design and décor. I went for a delicate look, in keeping with the shade and the romantic decorating scheme of the room where it was going. Let your personal taste dictate how

A store-bought lampshade, some beads, and a needle and thread make for a quick and easy project for your home that you can complete in a couple of hours.

you interpret this project for your own home.

There are no set rules for this project. You'll need to decide on an edging pattern that suits your particular lampshade. My shade has a lot of texture and pattern of its own, so I decided that, in this case, less was more, but I certainly could have gone "over the top" if that gave me the desired effect. You decide!

1. My shade had scallops, so I decided my design should make the most of that. The scallops were approximately 2½ inches from end to end, so starting at the beginning, I measured intervals along each scallop of 1 inch, ½ an inch, and 1 inch. I did it by eye, but you can make a light mark

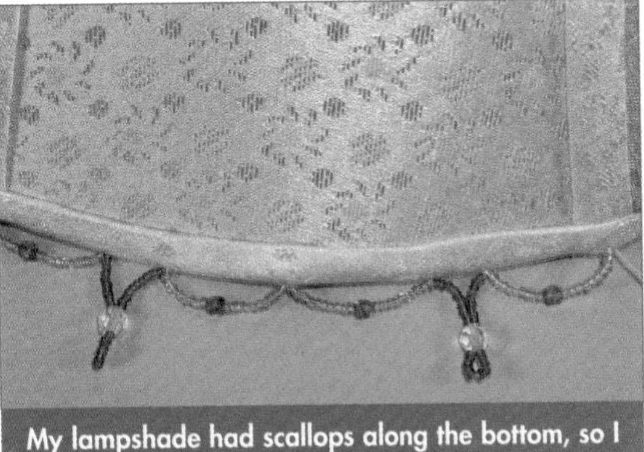

My lampshade had scallops along the bottom, so I used that as a guide creating the edging design.

   with tailor's chalk if you like. That gave me a pattern that put a dangle in the center of each scallop.

2. Thread your needle and get ready to begin the first stitch on the bottom of the shade. I began at the "valley" between 2 scallops. The design for the bottom edge of the shade is made of two sequences. For the first sequence, string on 10 pale pink size 11 seed beads, a 4mm crystal, and 10 pale pink beads. Bring your needle through the

Bring your needle up from behind to prepare for the second sequence of beads.

lampshade from front to back, and come up from back to front right next to the stitch you just made to get ready to make the second sequence of beads.

3. For the second sequence, string on 10 medium pink beads, a 6mm crystal, and 10 more medium pink beads. Loop back through the crystal, and add 10 more medium pink beads to complete the other side of the second element.
4. Repeat the first element (step 2) to finish the scallop.

For the top edge, I decided to do a double swag design, in effect combining the two elements from the bottom. I beaded the entire circumference of the shade using the first sequence and then beaded below it using the second one.

1. Just as I did for the bottom, I came up with my needle and thread to begin adding my beaded trim. My shade has ribs from top to bottom, so I started from the center of one rib to halfway between the center of the other rib to make my first swag. This kept everything even and symmetrical. The first trim sequence consisted of 10 pale pink seed beads, a 4mm crystal, and another 10 pale pink seed beads.
2. I came through with my needle and thread from front to back and then back up right

The design for the top of the shade is a combination of the two used side by side on the bottom—only, this time, they're superimposed on one another.

beside the stitch to make a second identical swag to the middle of the next rib. Then, I repeated this pattern until I had gone completely around the circumference of the shade. The way it worked out there were 2 scallops or swags between each rib of the shade.

3. Using the exact same route as the first embellishment, I now added a fringe. Stringing on 15 medium pink seed beads, a 6mm crystal, and 10 seed beads for a loop, coming up through the 6mm crystal and 15 more medium pink seed beads gave me a nice draped fringe effect. I repeated this around the circumference of the shade.

You can use beading in many ways to embellish just about anything. If you find it easier, you can use ribbon and add your fringe to that, gluing or sewing it onto the lampshade after it's completed. You can also embellish the "ribs" of the shade if you want to add even more glamour.

Variations

You may already have a shade that could use a facelift. Beads will do the trick. You can also strip a shade down to its frame (or buy a shade frame) and bead it from top to bottom. The beads are always pretty, but when the lights go on, look out!

Tailored Chic

This pleated shade was quite plain to start. Its tailored look suggested only touches of beading would be enough to set it off. Designer Bobbi Wicks used beads from old jewelry that had outlived its usefulness. The mother-of-pearl discs have two holes at the top. The white beads are size 6 seed beads.

Found beads and other jewelry components make a plain-Jane shade look like it went to finishing school!

Blueberry Shake

This variation took a little more time and ingenuity. Another thrift store find, the fabric covering this shade had seen better days, so designer Bobbi Wicks removed it and wound wire in both directions, some with beads, some without, around the bare frame, capturing the beads in the wire grid. Then she added dangles for a little more "topping."

A wire grid captures beads for a blueberry "dessert."

Start looking for inexpensive shades at discount stores and thrift shops, and think of their potential, not their current condition. With a little more skill, you can even learn to recover a lampshade to live up to your beading ideas.

Resources

Shade: Martha Stewart for K-Mart (www.kmart.com)

Seed beads: Studio Baboo (www.studiobaboo.com)

Shade frame: Fogg Lighting (www.fogglighting.com)

You've Been Bead-Framed!

Skill level: Beginner

What you need:

Purchased wooden frame, preferably with a wide surface area

Package of upholstery nails

24-gauge wire

Assorted beads in complementary colors

Wire cutters

Hammer

Ruler and pencil

Techniques and skills needed:

Basic wirework

If it's worth a picture and a picture is worth a thousand words, then it's worth at least a *few* beads! Here's another project that uses up those beading odds and ends. But if you don't have any (or need an excuse for buying more beads), don't let that stop you.

Are your frames just, well, frames? Why not add some beads and dress them up in your new bead-found style? A thrift store frame and some spray paint gave us the inspiration for this simple bead-and-wire-embellished frame.

A purchased frame, some decorative nails, wire, and beads, plus a few household tools, are all you need for this project.

You can purchase a frame from a department store, or do as I did and buy one at a thrift store for about 50¢ and paint it. Get one with a wide surface to use as a canvas for your beadwork. My frame is 8 inches square with a 4-inch-square opening. That gives me 2 inches to work with.

The upholstery nails I chose have a hammered silver pattern, but you can also find them in brass, white, and other finishes. Check your local home decorating, fabric, or crafts store for options.

You'll want to space your upholstery nails evenly along the top edge and the inside opening. I spaced mine by eye, but if you want to use a ruler and do the math, go for it. I also chose to bead only two sides of my frame, for an asymmetrical look. You can do whatever you want!

1. When you've determined the intervals for your nails, hammer them in along top and the opening. Be sure not to hammer them all the way down to the wood. Leave them up 1/4 inch. You'll need this space to wrap your beaded wire around in later steps.

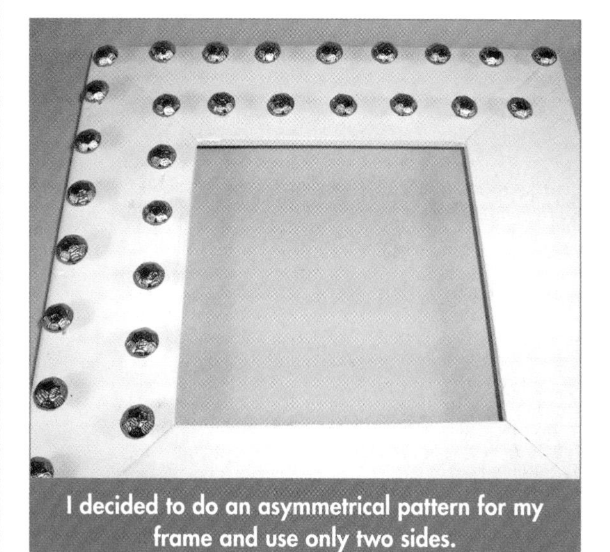

I decided to do an asymmetrical pattern for my frame and use only two sides.

Crimps!

Be careful with the inside edge of your frame. Mine had a lip where the glass and the picture fit, so I had to move the nails back enough that they didn't go through. You might need an awl to make pilot holes for your nails, depending on how hard the wood of your frame is.

2. Cut a length of wire and wrap it several times around the first nail at the top. For my frame I used about 3 feet of wire. If you run out of wire before you finish, not to worry. You can simply add in some more wire by wrapping the new end around a

nail and continuing on. Thread on your beads in a pleasing pattern, making a scallop and then wrap the wire around the next nail. Keep your scallops fairly even.

Make a scallop of beads between the nails using your wire.

3. Continue along the outside of the frame until you reach the end.
4. Now you're ready to wrap the inside of the frame. You can continue where you left off from the outside in, or wrap the wire and cut it starting again on the inside of the frame. I chose to wire wrap and bead continuously.

You can wrap the outside wire around and continue on the inside, as I did, or end and begin again.

5. Finish where you began. Insert a picture and the glass, and you're done!

Any number of wire and bead patterns work with this frame. You could do a lattice design or a more free-form one. If you're not sure what you want to do, sketch out some designs on paper first.

Variations

Frames present a blank canvas for beading and embellishment of all kinds. You might want to combine other hobbies like decoupage or stamping with your beading skills. Paint and glue, even fabric, can all make for an intriguing "frame up" of your favorite characters or scenes.

Fill in the Blanks

This store-bought frame had lots of open areas where I could thread wire through and add beads. This is pretty quick and easy, but it takes a plain frame to a special one!

This rodeo queen gets the royal treatment with just a little effort, wire, and beads.

Pretty, Period!

This father and daughter dressed up in period Civil War garb needed a sweet frame to complement their dress. I painted a simple wooden frame and then glued on strung beads, along with some bead-embellished flowers.

Nothing beats glue and beads for a super-simple embellished frame that perfectly suits the historic re-creation clothing the couple is wearing.

Rustic Reclaimed

For this project, I first converted this photo to black and white on my computer, and then put it into a distressed barn-wood frame and embellished it with barbed wire, an old nail, and Heishi beads. I used a strong glue to affix the heavier elements.

A photo of an old Western barn is paired with a frame that suggests its weathered past, enhanced with small Heishi beads and found objects from the ranch.

Bead-embellished frames make great one-of-a-kind gifts. I bet you can even imagine adapting some of these techniques for the cover of a scrapbook or photo album!

Resources

Upholstery nails: Jo-Ann Fabric and Crafts (www.joann.com)

Wire: ColourCraft (www.beadalon.com)

Tied to Baroque

Skill level: Beginner

What you need:

Pair of store-bought tassel tiebacks

Size 9 (3-cut) seed beads to complement color scheme (I used garnet and gold.)

Bugle beads in a complementary color

Crystal rounds and drops

Nymo size D beading thread

Size 10 beading needle

Techniques and skills needed:

Bead embellishment

Fringe

Now, I'll admit. Some pretty fancy tassels are available these days. Just go into any home décor or fabric store that sells home decorating fabrics, and you'll find them. But sometimes more is more, and these Baroque beaded tassel tiebacks look like a million bucks—because when it comes to richness and glamour, you can never have enough. Why just settle for fancy when you can add beads and have fantastic?

I chose size 9 (3-cut) seed beads for extra sparkle and shine and to suit the scale of the tassel. Bugles and crystals finish the look.

This is a project where you can't overdo it. Imagine the Italian Renaissance, a Baroque palace, or art of the Rococo period when you choose your materials. Rich tones and lots of gold or silver suggest the opulence of an age when nothing is "too much."

1. Use your tassel's own construction and color scheme as a guide, and enhance it using bead embroidery and embellishment techniques.

Beaded loops and a diamond pattern echoed the tassel's fiber embellishment.

2. The top part of my tassel had thread loops, so I added beaded loops over them. I followed the netted section as well.

My tassel had threads that suggested possible patterns for the beads to follow. Let yours do the same.

3. Now add netting and fringe over the lower part of the tassel. I used bugles and seed beads joined in a ladder stitch to add richness. (You learned the ladder stitch in Chapter 6.)

Some netting in gold and garnet with gold bugles added in a ladder stitch complete the elegant embellishment.

Repeat the same patterns with the second tie-back tassel. Add to your drapes, and drool!

Variations

Tassels aren't just for drapes anymore! You can use them as fan or shade pulls, on clothing, on pillows, or even as a Christmas ornament or key chain. You can find them in all sizes, so start shopping and get ready to twirl your tassels anywhere.

Beaded Beauties

These antique tassels are completely beaded—there's no fiber in sight. The one on the left combines 2 beaded beads created by beading around 2 large wooden beads and a long bugle bead fringe is attached at the bottom. The top of the tassel on the right is formed over a wire base, and the beads are wired over it.

Tassels can be completely beaded, as these antique beauties attest.

Red Says Romance

Tassels are available without tiebacks, too. I found a bunch in different colors at a local name-brands-for-less store, and the workmanship was quite lovely. Adding beads just makes them more so. Wouldn't this be a great add-on to a Christmas or Valentine's Day gift?

This plain gold tassel becomes rich with romance with the simple addition of some red beaded embellishment.

A Vision in Blue

This tassel already had a lot of silver thread embellishment, but some additional silver beads and crystal cubes send it "over the top."

Silver threads suggest silver beads and crystals as an appropriate addition.

Now, isn't surrounding yourself with beads a worthy endeavor? Look around. I bet you can find places to enrich your everyday environment with luxury and beauty for pennies. A little thread, a bit of wire, and some imagination are all you need to live the beaded life!

Resources

Tiebacks and other tassels: Tuesday Morning (www.tuesdaymorning.com)

Beads: Studio Baboo (www.studiobaboo.com), Shipwreck Beads (www.shipwreckbeads.com)

In This Part

Celebrate With Beads!

Changing seasons bring beading opportunities. There's not a holiday or special occasion that wouldn't benefit from some beaded elegance or whimsy. Start with December and work your way through the year. You'll find plenty of projects and ideas you can adapt for all your holidays.

And if you have a bride-to-be in your life, give her some dynamite accessories she'll never forget. For other milestones, like births, graduations, or religious celebrations, bead the perfect memento to light up the day. Part 4 shows you how.

CHAPTER

9

Holiday Enchantment

In This Chapter

- Brew an old-fashioned metal tea ball into a terrific Christmas ornament
- Ring in the new year with beaded snowflake champagne glass charms
- Help out the Easter Bunny with beautiful beaded eggs

Ah, the holidays—they mark the seasons of our lives with celebration and mirth. Why not take our beading passion to new heights and make all your occasions sparkling ones? This chapter is just the tip of the iceberg. You'll find ideas abound in magazines, online, and in your wildest imagination.

Christmas Tea

Skill level: Intermediate

What you need:

1 metal tea ball, new or vintage
6mm pale blue crystal beads
Size 9 (3-cut) crystal AB seed beads
Size 11 seed beads, any color
Nymo size B thread
Size 10 beading needle

Techniques and skills needed:

Fringe

It's not your grandmother's tea ball—or maybe it is! But now it's something else. Finding a use for something other than what it was intended for is always fun, especially when beads are involved. The kind of tea balls we're using here aren't the ones you see more frequently today. Those mesh herb and tea infusers are also full of beading possibilities (if you can get a fine-enough needle to go through the mesh); the ones I'm talking about are the egg- or acorn-shaped ones.

Pearls

Older tea balls can be really interesting. I found some in a thrift store for 25 cents. Look at garage sales, and ask friends what they have lurking in their kitchen drawers. The positioning of the holes dictates somewhat how your ornament looks. The more holes, the more "drippy" you can make your ornament.

With these few supplies, you can brew up one fancy tea ball!

You can use any seed beads on the inside of the tea ball, as they're strictly used as anchor beads and to protect the thread from being cut by the rough metal edges of the tea ball's holes. You won't see them, so use up your least favorite colors or the mixture that resulted from an unexpected "bead dump" you didn't feel like re-sorting. (My seed bead soup was the result of a slightly unstable beading surface and a very mischievous cat.)

1. Thread your needle and knot one of your miscellaneous seed beads at the end of your thread. Go through the center bottom hole of your tea ball from the inside out.

This is what the inside of your tea ball should look like after you knot on your first seed bead and put your thread through to the outside.

2. Add 1 (size 9) seed bead, a crystal, and another size 9 seed bead, and alternate 3 more times so you have 5 seed beads and 4 crystals, beginning and ending with a seed bead.
3. Skip the end seed bead and go back through the crystals and seed beads, back into the bottom of the ball, and through the hole you just came out of. If you recall, this is the same thing you've done in the past to make fringe. Also go through the inside seed bead.

This is what your first crystal and seed bead fringe should look like.

4. Continue making seed bead and crystal fringe until you've used up all the holes, adding a seed bead on the inside each time.

The pattern on my tea ball goes out in concentric circles. I used 4 crystals for the fringe for the first circle at the center bottom and the first circle around it and then shortened the fringe to 3 crystals going up the sides.

If you want to add loops between crystals fringes, you'll have to do a little "engineering." You need 2 seed beads inside to prevent the thread from touching the sharp edges of the holes.

1. Make your first loop after doing the first fringe in the row by going back through the inside seed bead as you did before, and then adding a *second* seed bead and going around the outside of it and back through the *first* inside seed bead.

Use 2 seed beads on the inside if you're going to make loops in between holes.

2. Come out through the hole and the first seed bead of your fringe, and add however many beads you want for your loops (I added 10). Then go into the next hole and add a size 11 seed bead and a second seed bead, and go back through the first, as before. Repeat this all the way around.

Crimps!

The holes in the tea balls are sharp, so be sure to use a seed bead on the inside *each time* to keep the sharp edge of the hole from cutting the thread. The goal is to never have your thread touching the sharp metal edges.

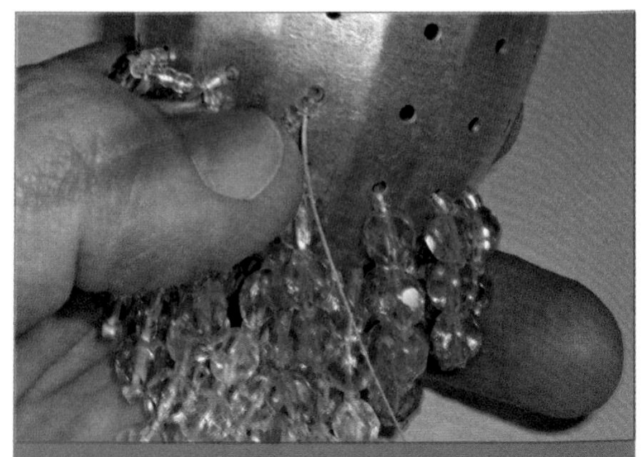

Adding loops adds interest, instead of or in addition to your fringe. I did both.

Crimps!

Keep everything fairly loose when you're doing the rows at the bottom of your tea ball so you can pull up the seed bead from inside and bring your needle through it. Then tighten up your fringe. Be sure your thread is always long enough to do this. Add thread as needed. It gets easier the higher up the sides you get. Before stepping up to the next row, go through the inside seed bead you started with in the row you're currently on (inside to outside), to anchor it, and go back through the fringe and back through that same inside seed bead. Then step up to the next row.

The top of my tea ball has a lot of holes. Some of the newer ones don't have as many. I used 3 crystals along the outside rows and shortened it to 2. I also added loops. You can decide what looks best based on your own taste and the shape of your tea ball, the configuration of the holes, and how many there are.

You can glue trim onto the outside of the screw threads of the tea ball and even bead that. (I added blue gimp trim to mine.) To finish, use the existing chain and hook of the tea ball to attach your ornament or bead a hanger of your own.

Variations

One tea ball ornament is not enough! These can become an addiction. I found tea balls in all different sizes, both vintage and new, and with different hole patterns and shapes. Another reason to check out your local thrift stores!

Burgundy and Crystal Sequined Ornament

Sequins add another dimension to beading. Maybe they could even be defined as a bead! The tea ball in this version was sprayed with paint and then beaded. A beaded hanger was added.

This version gets some of its richness from the burgundy paint on the tea ball. The crystal beads really stand out against the background.

Beaded Gala

Who says ornaments have to be "quiet"? This one shouts with color. Small colorful beads and seed beads riot around this ornament, finished with purple and silver trim and a beaded hanger.

Lots of color adds fun to this beaded tea ball, which has been left *au naturale.*

Resources

Tea balls: Silk Rainbow (www.beadornaments.com), Fantes Kitchen Wares Shop (www.fantes.com)

Crystal beads: Beads Galore (crystal AB; www.beadsgalore.com), Knot Just Beads (sapphire luster; www.knotjustbeads.com), 9 (3-cut) beads (crystal AB; Studio Baboo, www.studiobaboo.com)

Tea ball ornament kits available from: Silk Rainbow (www.beadornaments.com)

Champagne Charming

Skill level: Challenging

What you need:

- 4 wine glass charm holders in gold or silver
- 14 each (4mm) bicone crystals in 4 different colors
- 2 strands (size 11) seed beads, white
- 28-gauge beading wire to match charm holders
- Wire cutters
- Nylon jaw pliers

Techniques and skills needed:

Basic wirework

Champagne says "festive!" and rings in the new year, but why not kick it up a notch and add some sparkle among the bubbles? These champagne glass charms can be used on any winter's day to take the chill away. I made a set of 4 of these delicate snowflakes, but you can make as many as you like!

I used a few crystals in different colors and white seed beads to create these pretty snowflakes on prefabricated charm holders.

The reason this project is rated "challenging" is not because the wireworking technique is difficult, but because the thinness of the wire and the tiny scale of the snowflakes makes this one for experienced wireworkers who are used to handling a variety of wire gauges—or a patient beginner who is willing to take time and follow directions carefully.

1. Cut 4 pieces of wire, each 2 feet long. Run one piece of wire through your nylon jaw pliers several times to strengthen and straighten it. Repeat for each piece of wire.
2. Put 12 (size 11) seed beads on the wire, and bring them to the middle of the wire. Put one end of wire through all 12 seed beads and take it again through the next 2 (it goes through those 2 beads twice). Pull up to form a circle, but don't pull too tightly. You will need to go between the beads with wire later.

Your circle of beads should look like this, with 2 seed beads in between the 2 wires.

Crimps!

The 28-gauge wire used in this project can break fairly easily if you bend it too much. Be sure to keep it straightened whenever possible and avoid kinks. Use your nylon jaw pliers to straighten as needed. Remember to be *gentle* and *careful* as you work this project.

3. Using 1 wire of your circle and moving *away* from the other wire, * put on the wire 3 (size 11) beads, 1 bicone bead, 3 size 11 beads, another bicone, and 1 (size 11) seed bead. Bring the wire over the outside of the end size 11 bead and through the first bicone. Add 3 (size 11) beads, and go through the next bicone.
4. Keep things fairly loose up to this point and straight. Then pull the wire through all the beads slowly, using your fingernail to keep the beads down toward the circle base. Add 3 more (size 11) beads, count 2 beads on the circle from the wire you began with to make the snowflake "spoke," go through the circle from the back, and slip the wire in between the second and third beads. * Pull up snug and begin the next point of the snowflake, starting from the first *.

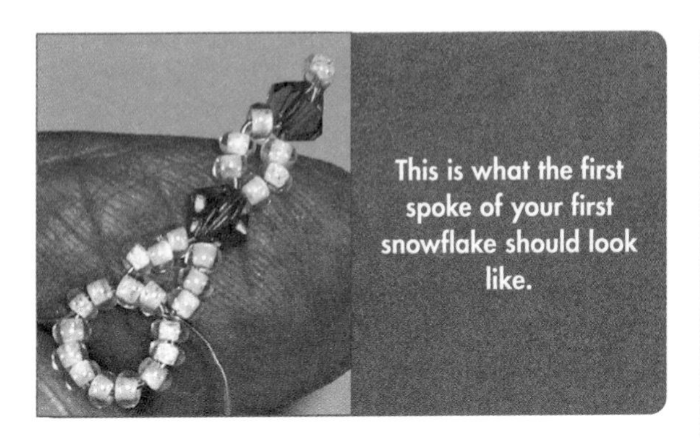
This is what the first spoke of your first snowflake should look like.

5. Repeat from * to * until you meet the other wire. You will have 5 spokes of your snowflake completed so far. Wrap the wire you've been working with an additional time around the space in the circle between the last 2 remaining beads, and cut off as close as you can.

This is what your snowflake should look like after you've completed 5 spokes with 1 wire.

6. Complete the last spoke with the remaining wire, following the instructions from * to *.

Pearls

For a star instead of a snowflake, make your circle from 15 beads and skip 3 beads between the two sides of your spoke instead of 2. You'll end up with a 5-pointed star.

7. When you complete the final spoke, wrap the wire a second time around the circle space and cut closely with your wire cutters, as you did before.
8. Cut a piece of wire about 6 inches long and fold it softly in half. Fit the wire between any two spokes, and twist the 2 wires together tightly until you have about ½ inch of twisted wire. Come back to the beginning and wrap the twisted around again, making a loop. Cut closely.

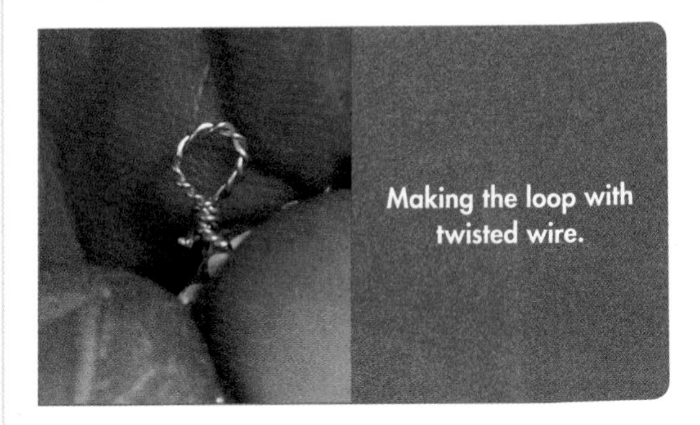
Making the loop with twisted wire.

9. Put on the charm holder 23 (size 11) seed beads, a bicone, your charm, another bicone, and an equal number of beads on the other side of the charm. You may need to adjust this number a bit, depending on the size of your charm holder. Bend the straight end of the holder to hold the beads on and so it fits into the hole on the flat end of the charm holder. (You might need chain nose pliers for this.) *Finis!*

Embellishments

Put the twisted wire loop at the end of a spoke, for a snowflake that dangles more over the edge of the glass. Use colored wire and clear glass seed beads. Use size 8 beads or 4mm round crystals in place of bicones. Try different snowflake patterns. Use 9 (3-cut) seed beads for more sparkle and a slightly bigger snowflake. Wear one snowflake as a pendant or two as earrings. So many possibilities!

Variations

Wine and champagne glass charm holders have really become standard at parties and make great gifts. Any beaded shape or charm can be adapted to this project. Remember the beaded beads used for the chandelier earrings in Chapter 1? Make them in different colors for yet another variation.

The two variations here are quick and easy. In the holiday rush, you won't have any trouble making time to whip out a set.

Geometry Rules!

These simple shapes are enhanced by bright silver beads. You can identify your glass by remembering not only which color your charm is, but also which shape!

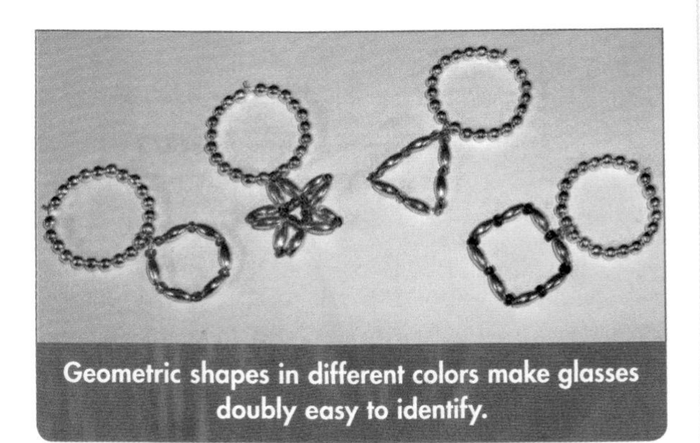

Geometric shapes in different colors make glasses doubly easy to identify.

Christmas in Silver

In a hurry? Just purchase a few of the many charms for every occasion and theme, and put these together in a jiffy. I did a Christmas theme, but you can choose a favorite sport or hobby, or anything that piques your fancy.

Purchased charms make for speedy wine glass charms for any theme or occasion.

These stemmed glass charms make great gifts for any host or hostess. If you don't have charm holders, put that ring-size memory wire to use and make your own. Or make a miniature charm bracelet with a length of chain, a clasp, and a wireworked dangle. How many other ways of making them can *you* think of?

Resources

28-gauge wire: Beadalon (www.beadalon.com)

Charm holders: Arizona Gems and Minerals (www.azgemsandbeads.com)

Easter Eggs Royale

Skill level: Beginner

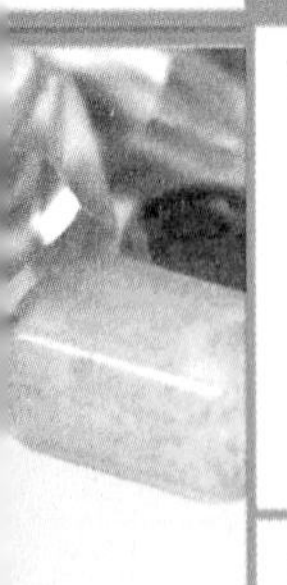

What you need:

- Styrofoam eggs
- Flat-backed aquamarine faceted stone
- 1 hank (size 9) 3-cut seed beads in several crystal AB
- Aquamarine bugle beads
- 2mm faux pearls
- 4mm faux pearls
- Tacky glue
- Nymo size B thread
- Size 10 beading needle

Techniques and skills needed:

- Bead stringing

I've always admired jeweled eggs, whether they be Fabergé or handmade with beads. Someday I want an Easter egg tree full of them; this project got me started.

Seed beads, pearls, a flat faceted stone, a needle and thread, and some glue transform a plain Styrofoam egg into a thing of beauty.

My foil-backed stone came in a lot of vintage beads from an eBay supplier (see the "Resources" section), but you can buy a nice variety at any crafts store.

Pearls

Glue only a little at a time onto your egg, and let it dry in between, especially after completing one side and before beading the other. And you might want to have a narrow box to set your egg in between drying times. It will want to turn over, as it'll be heavier on one side as you add beads.

1. Glue the flat-backed stone on one side of the egg in the center using tacky glue. Let it dry. You will be building your design around this center stone. If necessary, to get the stone to sit flat, you can rough up the Styrofoam egg to make it a little flatter or score it with your fingernail.

Find a place in the center of one side of the egg and glue on your flat-backed stone.

2. Thread your needle, but don't make a knot. Glue the ends onto the egg and let them dry. String on enough seed beads to go around the stone three times. You can use the "from the hank" method you learned in Chapter 4 or pick up the beads one at a time with your needle. I took my beads from the hank, to speed things up.
3. Working on a small area at a time, put glue around the stone and begin gluing down the strung seed beads. You can use a toothpick to help spread the glue. Don't put it on too thick, and remove any excess before adding your beads.

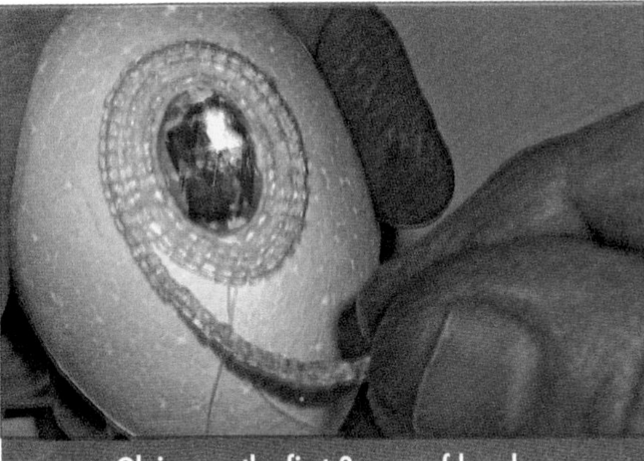

Gluing on the first 3 rows of beads.

4. String on enough small faux pearls to go around one time, and glue them down.

Add just enough pearls to encircle what you've already glued down.

5. Alternate between seed beads and the smaller pearls for 3 rows, and then use seed beads until you reach about halfway around your egg. Add 1 row of bugle beads.

This side view shows all the rows of seed beads, pearls, and bugle beads.

6. Add a final row of larger faux pearls, and let the egg dry for several hours.
7. Finish the back of the egg any way you want. I simply applied seed beads all the way from the outside to the center. Or you could cut your thread and repeat the same design you just did on the other side.

I chose to finish the back of the egg in seed beads. You can certainly do something different if you like!

A shortcut for stringing pearls is to use pearl trim. The pearls are already connected!

Embellishments

You can bead eggs in any number of designs or patterns. The stone you use will suggest ideas. Draw some possible designs on paper first, if you want to. You can glue the stone on and then lightly draw your design on the egg to guide you. Experiment with different sizes of seed beads. You can also use trim in between beaded rows.

Variations

You can use other kinds of eggs besides Styrofoam. Wooden eggs are heavier and look pretty with some of the wood showing. You can (carefully) blow the yolk and white out of real eggs, wash them out, and let them dry. (You'll have to make a hole on both ends, but they can be covered up with beads or trim.) You may be able to find papier-mâché eggs as well. And experiment with different sizes. You can add a hanger at the top and hang on an Easter tree or a Christmas tree. Or make a bunch and put them in a pretty bowl.

Here are three different examples of what a little imagination can do in a short time. Although these aren't entirely covered in beads like the featured project, they are pretty—and can be done in a jiffy!

The egg on the left is wood and was painted and then covered with beaded netting. The middle egg, also wood, was painted gold and decorated with strings of seed beads, flat stones, and larger beads. The egg on the right is Styrofoam covered with torn pieces of tissue paper glued down and then embellished with seed beads in two different sizes.

No egg need go unadorned if there's a beader in the house!

Resources

Styrofoam and wooden eggs: Jo-Ann Fabric and Crafts (www.joann.com)

Flat-backed vintage stones: eBay seller dyedye of DyeDye's Treasures from the Past (www.ebay.com)

Crystal AB size 9 (3-cut) seed beads: Studio Baboo (www.studiobaboo.com)

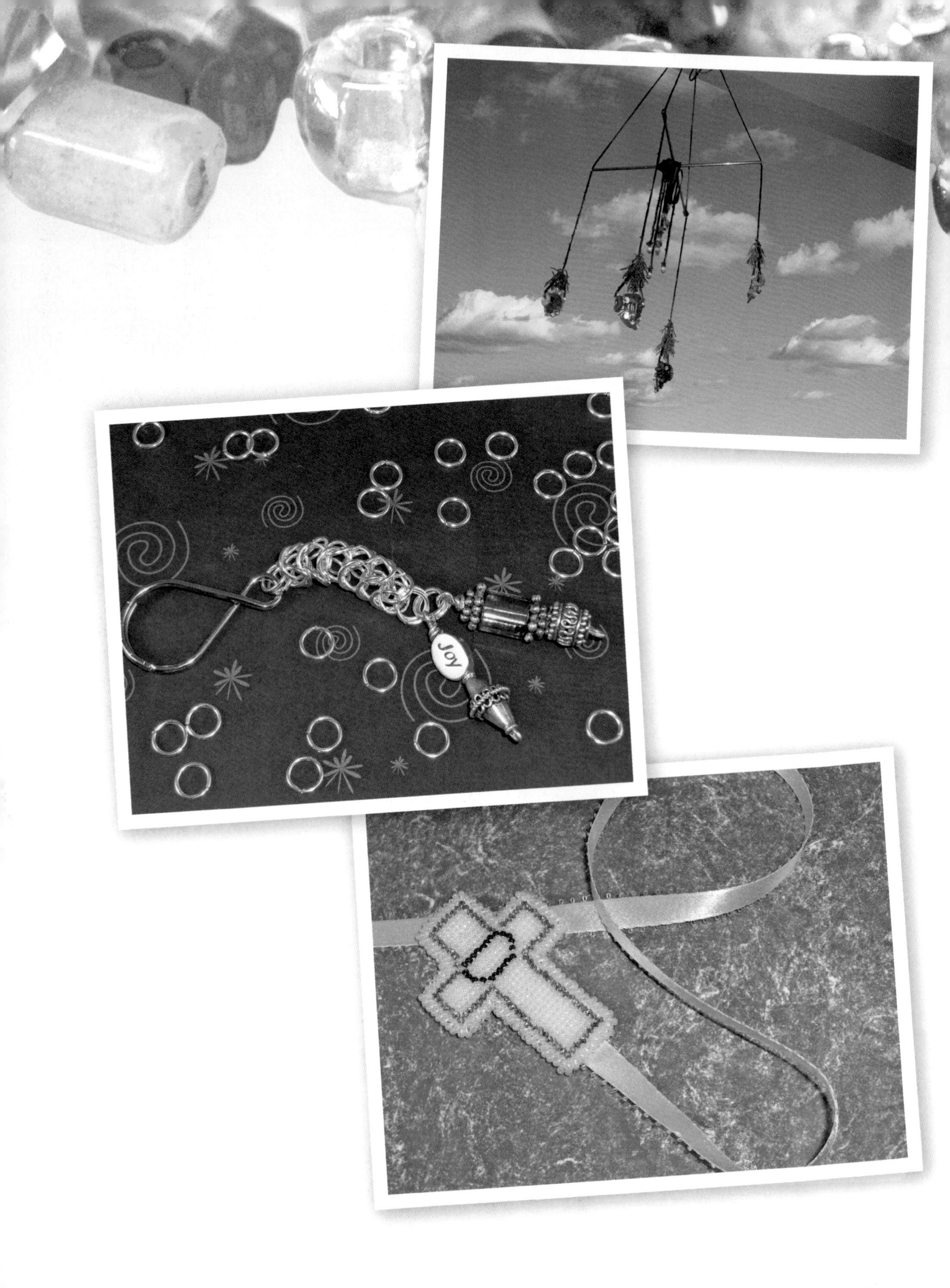
Joy

Celebrating Milestones

In This Chapter

- A beautiful lampwork glass fish mobile for baby
- Great graduation and birthday gifts for the guys in your life
- Mark her first communion with a beaded cross

Babies, graduations, birthdays, and other important passages are all opportunities to let your beadwork shine. The projects in this chapter are flexible. Use the basic structure and design and change the theme to suit the occasion. And most of all, have fun!

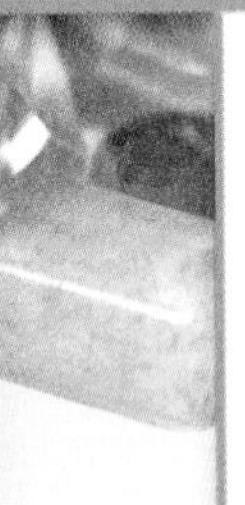

Baby Eye Candy

Skill level: Intermediate

What you need:

- 4 lampwork glass fish
- Assorted complementary lampwork glass beads and briolettes
- 1 hank each size 11 beads, charlottes, green, turquoise, and red
- Size 6 seed beads in complementary colors, as needed
- 12½ feet Hanah hand-dyed silk cord
- Approximately 2 feet Hanah hand-dyed silk ribbon
- 2 (12-inch) pieces copper tubing, ½cm diameter
- 12 inches (24-gauge) copper wire
- Size 10 beading needle
- Silamide thread
- E-6000 glue
- Scotch tape

Techniques and skills needed:

- Embellishment
- Branch fringe stitch
- Basic wirework

Designer and lampwork glass bead artist Rowena Tank made this intriguing baby mobile just for this book. The construction isn't difficult, and she'll be happy to make you a set of magnificent glass fish in whatever colors you choose. (Find out how to reach her in the "Resources" section at the end of this project.) Her fish are surrounded by branch fringe—don't worry. I explain how to do it in a minute!

The materials used in this project are both common and extraordinary. I've given you sources for the special ones; the rest you can find at your local bead shop or hardware store.

1. Hold the 2 (12-inch) pieces of copper tubing on top of one another, creating a cross of equal sides. Wind the 24-gauge wire tightly around the center of the cross in a figure eight to secure the tubing together. This is the main body of your mobile. Rowena recommends using a spot of E-6000 glue to help hold the assembly together until you add the cording, which makes it even more stable.

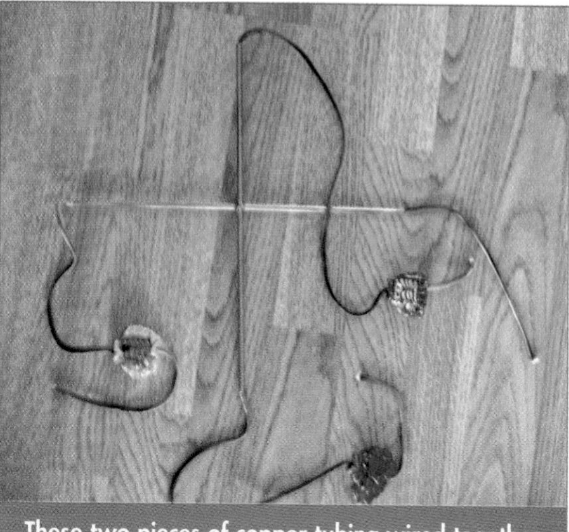
These two pieces of copper tubing wired together to make an equal-sided cross are the main assembly for the mobile.

2. Cut 2 pieces of silk cording 50 inches long, and tape the 4 ends of the cording. Cut a 13-inch length of 24-gauge wire, and thread it through one piece of the tubing. Wrap one end of the wire around the taped end of the cording and pull it through the tubing. Chain nose pliers might help you wind the wire more easily. Repeat this process for the second cord and piece of tubing.
3. Using the same technique you used in step 2, pull the cord through the fish. With each fish, sew the end of the cording above the fish, using the Silamide thread and the beading needle.
4. Now you can begin the embellishment. Starting with a size 6 seed bead, begin the first branch fringe. We did various fringes in previous projects, but this is a fun variation we haven't tried yet. Begin by threading on the desired number of size 11 seed beads, skip the last bead, and go back through the second bead from the needle. Decide where you want the first branch to begin. The more branches you make, the denser your fringe will be.

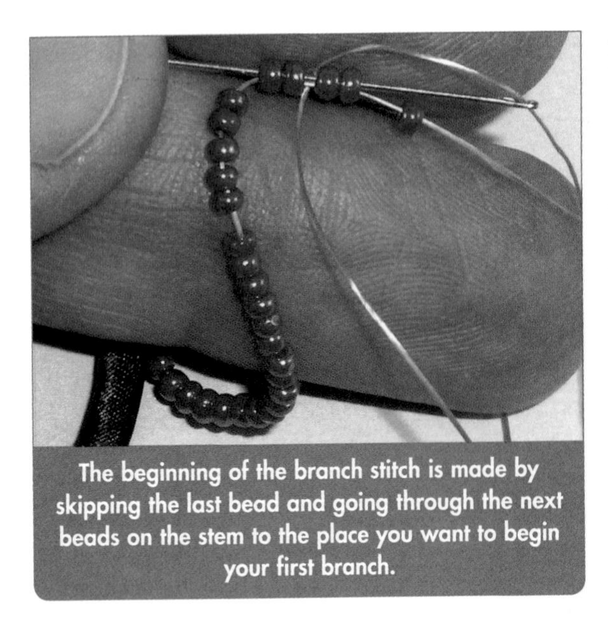

The beginning of the branch stitch is made by skipping the last bead and going through the next beads on the stem to the place you want to begin your first branch.

5. Add size 11 seed beads to the desired length for your branch, and skip the last bead, going back through the second bead from the needle to the main "stem" of your branch, going back down to the location of the next desired branch. Rowena used 28 beads for the main stem of her branch fringe and 10 beads for each of the branches. She made 2 branches on each stem.

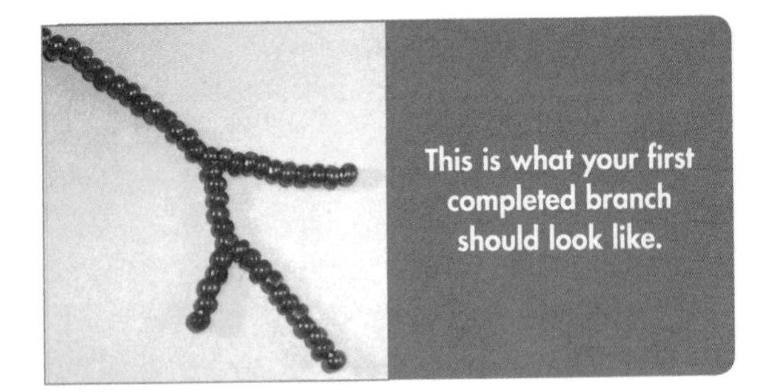

This is what your first completed branch should look like.

6. Add as much branch fringe as desired. You can sprinkle contrasting beads here and there, use a different color of bead at the end of the branches, or use any one of a number of other variations.

Pearls

Using a size 6 seed bead to begin your branch stitch creates a more dramatic branch and hides the bead thread.

Add enough branch fringe to look lush and cover the place where your cord is sewn together above the fish. Use size 6 seed beads to begin your branches if you want them to stand out more.

7. When you've done the desired amount of fringe over your fish, bring your needle and thread up through the cording and come out, adding 3 beads before you go back through, doing what Rowena calls a picot stitch.

Beaded embellishments give the silk cording a little more sparkle.

8. Now to add the top cording from which the mobile will hang: cut 2 (25-inch) pieces of cording. (You can make this shorter, if you like.) Pull the end of the silk cording that's holding the fish out of the tubing about ½ inch, and, using the Silamide thread, sew the end of one of the 25-inch pieces to the cord holding the fish. Pulling from the other side of the tubing, bring

the two sewn pieces back into the tubing. Repeat on the other end of the tubing with the other end of the 25-inch piece of cording. Repeat with the second piece of tubing and cording.

9. Hang the mobile to see if it's balanced. You can move the cords a bit until you feel satisfied it's balanced and knot the top or sew the cords together. If one cord is longer than you would like, Rowena suggests looping the cords holding the fish over the tubing until you get the desired length.
10. Add a drop of E-6000 glue at the center wired cross pieces of the tubing and wrap some silk ribbon and cording around it, tying bows and leaving tails. Embellish the cording with lampwork beads and seed beads.

Add more lampwork beads, ribbon, and seed beads to give the mobile even more interest for baby.

Hang the finished mobile in a place out of baby's reach, but where he or she can see it!

Embellishments

You can never add too much embellishment, according to Rowena. Add more beads and hang from the upper knot, if you want. Embellish the ribbons and anything else that will hold a bead!

Variations

Bobbi Wicks used inexpensive and simple materials to create this soft and colorful baby mobile. As you may have concluded by now, Bobbi specializes in making delightful things out of found objects and materials that are easy to find and not costly. Here, she transforms part of an embroidery hoop, some flexible wire, crimps, and several butterfly appliqués in different sizes into a lightweight butterfly show for baby. Any number of appliqués could be used for a different theme.

Your local crafts store probably carries the materials for this happy baby mobile.

Resources

Size 11 charlotte seed beads: Arizona Gems and Minerals (www.azgemsandbeads.com)

Hanah hand-dyed silk ribbon and cording; lampwork fish: Rowena Tank (www.rowenaart.net)

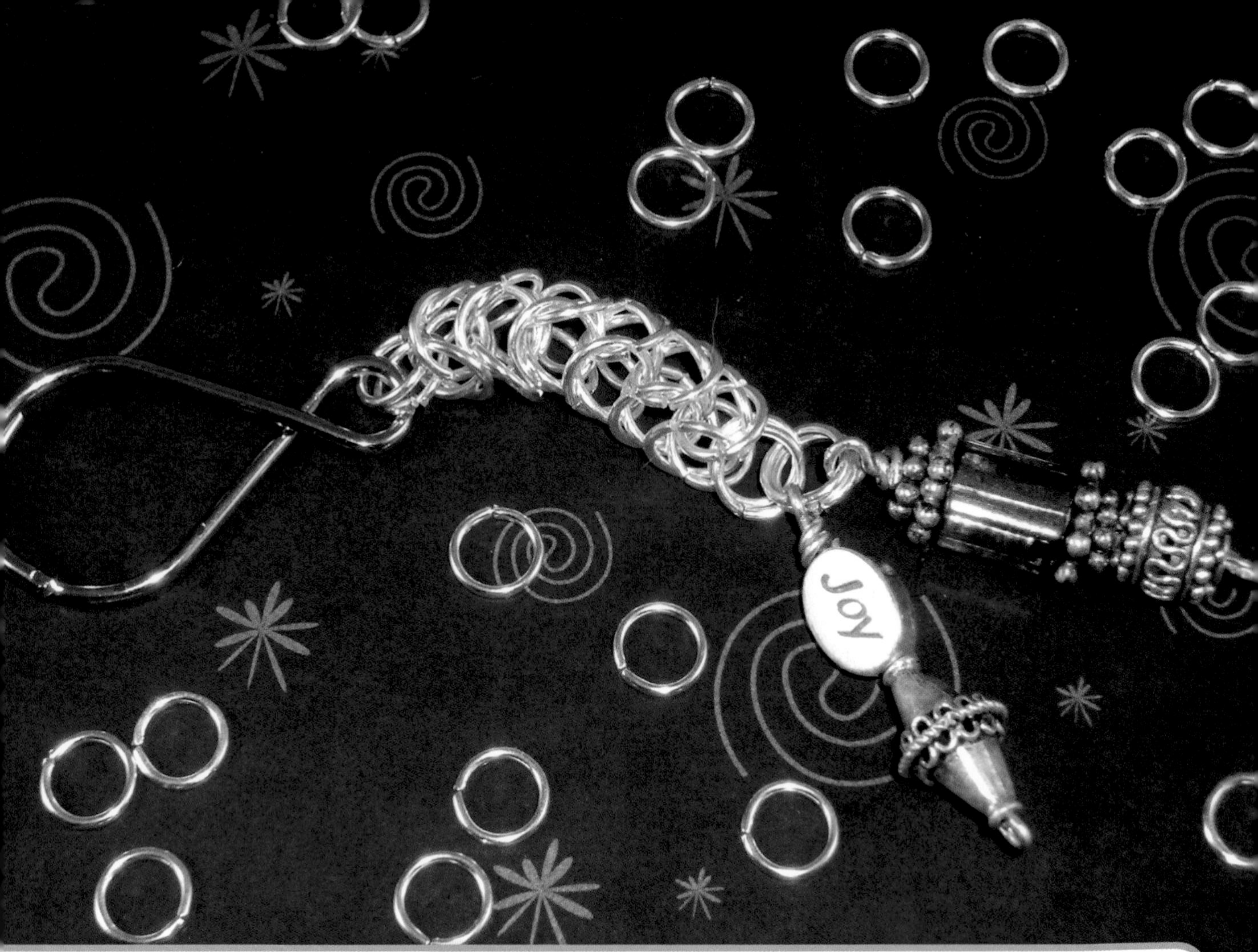

Knight's Delight

Skill level: Intermediate

What you need:

- 18-gauge silver-plated jump rings, 8mm
- Wire scrap, any gauge
- Focal bead, additional beads, charms
- Key chain finding
- 2 pairs chain nose pliers
- Ring closing pliers (optional)

Techniques and skills needed:

- Basic beadwork

When making a gift for a man, nothing satisfies better than these elegant but manly chains. They take their cue from ancient chain mail, a type of armor worn by knights to protect them in battle. (*The Lord of the Rings* movies might be responsible for the current trend in chain mail jewelry, but that's just my guess.) These chains are for a modern knight, whoever he may be, and can be personalized with beads and charms for graduation, birthday, or any other special occasion.

For this project, we're going to make a box chain. It's kind of like a little puzzle, but when you get the hang of it, the mystery is revealed and it's simple to do.

The materials needed for a box chain are simple and inexpensive. You do need 2 pairs of chain nose pliers to make this project easier.

1. Open 30 or so jump rings (always twist to the side; never pull). Keep 4 jump rings closed.
2. Put the 4 closed jump rings on 2 opened ones so you create a chain of 3 pairs of 2 rings.

Pearls

You can make your own jump rings (see Chapter 3). Just be sure to harden them by whacking them with a hammer under a block. It helps to have two pairs of chain nose pliers so you can twist them open easily. Using pliers and your fingers tends to cause pulling and is tough on your fingers. You may also like to have a special pliers made for closing. This just makes it easier if you do happen to pull some out of shape.

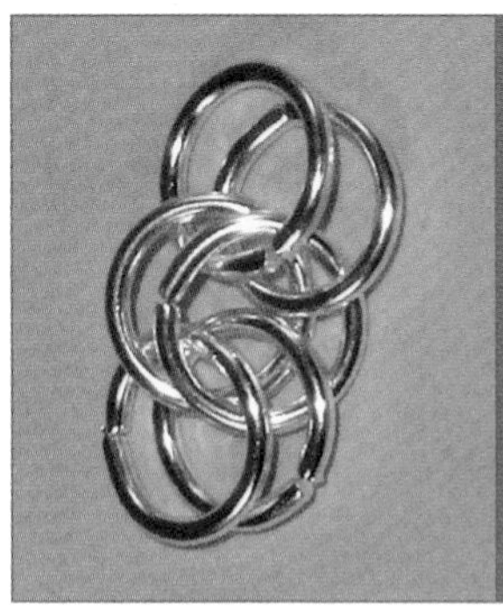

This is the basic 3-link chain you need to have to begin your box chain.

3. Lightly twist your scrap wire on one end of your 3-link chain. This is the first link in your chain, and the wire helps you grip it as you work.
4. With the tail you created with your scrap wire and the bottom set of rings held in the palm of your nondominant hand, flip the top 2 rings to either side of the middle 2 rings. You should now have 4 rings at the bottom (the 2 held by the scrap wire and 1 loose ring on either side).

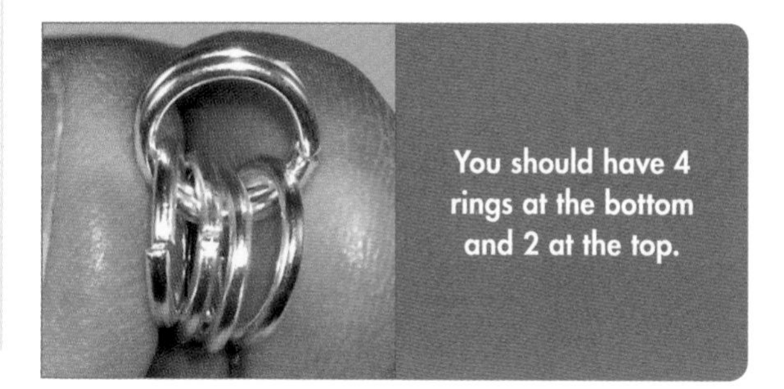

You should have 4 rings at the bottom and 2 at the top.

5. Grasp the 4 rings between your fingers and flip the top set of rings down to either side. The 4 rings will be standing up, but the ones on either side will stand up a little bit higher. These are called "stand-up rings," and it's through those that you slide the next 2 rings.

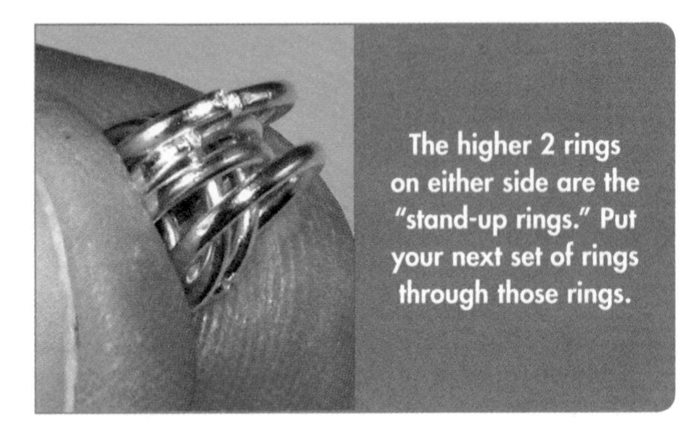
The higher 2 rings on either side are the "stand-up rings." Put your next set of rings through those rings.

6. Add 2 rings through the 2 stand-up rings and close. Now add 2 more rings through those you just added.

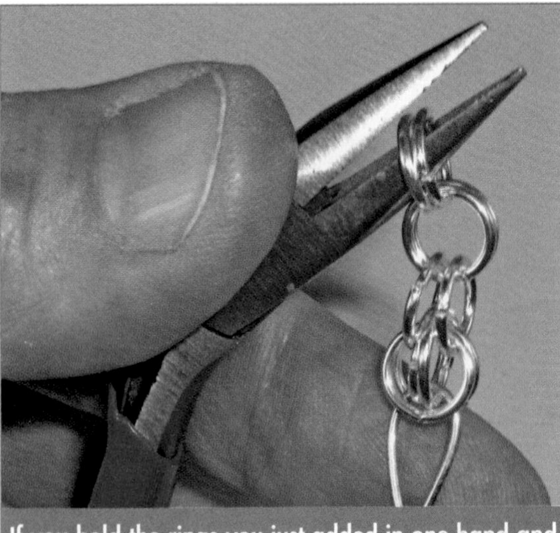
If you hold the rings you just added in one hand and the wire tail in the other and pull, you can begin to see the box pattern you're creating.

This is what your chain's first box link should look like.

7. * Flip down the top set of rings to either side. Grasp the 4 rings at the bottom you now have, and flip down the rings that are now at the top to either side. Add 2 rings to the stand-up rings and add 2 more to those. *

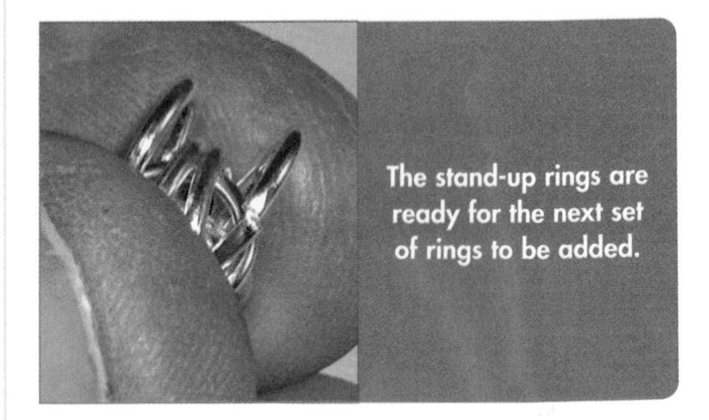
The stand-up rings are ready for the next set of rings to be added.

8. Repeat from * to * until you have the desired length. I decided on 6 complete boxes to our chain. You will end up with a chain of 2 sets of 2 empty rings at the top when you're done. Add a key chain finding before closing the final top 2 rings. Add a dangle "fob" or 2 to the bottom ring using closed-circuit wirework after removing the scrap wire.

Embellishments

You could add a photo charm instead of a dangle or a school charm. Or use his birthstone for your dangle. This chain would make a nice watch fob if he carries a pocket watch; just make it longer. It can also be lengthened to bracelet or choker length, or to hold keys from a pants loop to the pocket. You can also use it to make a charm bracelet. For a more delicate chain, just change the wire gauge for the rings and the diameter of the rings. Experiment with different wire gauges and sizes of rings. Also try using pieces of chain as links in between regular wireworked links with beads.

Chain mail has become a steady trend, not just the province of the Gothic crowd, fans of *The Lord of the Rings* movies, re-creators of medieval warfare, or belly dancers (just look at the costumes sometime!). It's here to stay, and its fun to make!

Variations

So many variations are possible with this project. I've worked four different key chains to give you some more ideas. The key chain on the top left of this photo is a different pattern, called the orbital chain, and is embellished with beads. The next one to the right uses a copper enameled focal bead hand-crafted by bead artist Christine Bricely. The chain is a box chain. The third one is made using 2 turquoise chips and a carnelian bead suspended from a box chain. The bottom key chain uses 20-gauge jump rings for a more delicate look.

By changing the beads, chain pattern, length of the chain, and gauge of the jump rings, a key chain can have a completely different look.

Resources

Silver-plated jump rings; sterling silver charm: Arizona Gems and Minerals (www.azgemsandbeads.com)

To learn more about chain mail and for supplies: www.dcwireworks.com, www.theringlord.com, www.mailleartisans.org

Divine Devotion

Skill level: Beginner

What you need:

- Size 14 paper or plastic canvas for cross-stitch embroidery
- Embroidery floss: gold, white, or blue
- Size 11 seed beads: gold, white, and blue
- Bead embroidery needle
- Ribbon
- Felt for backing
- Fabric tacky glue

Techniques and skills needed:

- Stringing with flexible wire
- Crimping

A small handmade object such as a bookmark can be used to commemorate an important rite of passage in a young person's life. Holy Communion, a bar or bat mitzvah, baptism, a sweet 16 party—these are the milestones for young adults.

The featured project is a Bible bookmark that can be given on any special occasion. Variations include a Star of David and a Celtic cross, and you can develop or find patterns for any symbols appropriate to your faith or spiritual leanings.

Beads in three colors, a needle and embroidery floss, plus some felt, ribbon, and plastic canvas are the raw materials for this project.

Crimps!

If you're using paper canvas for this project, you need to be a bit more delicate with it. The advantage of paper, however, is its light weight. I used plastic canvas in my version.

1. Decide on a design, copy it onto the canvas, and cut out the shape, making sure to cut carefully so as not to compromise any of the holes you'll be embroidering into. My cross, before adding the edging, was approximately 2¼ inches long by 1½ inches wide.

2. Using 2 strands of embroidery floss, thread your needle and bring it up from the back at a corner of the shape you'll be working. You'll work this project in beaded cross-stitch. Normally, when using only floss, the thread is worked in an X or cross shape. In beaded cross-stitch, only half of the stitch is worked. (I cover beaded cross-stitch in *The Complete Idiot's Guide to Beading Illustrated* if you need more in-depth information.)

   The trick to beaded cross-stitch is to remember that the stitches are really only half a cross-stitch and they must always go in the same direction. Also, remember to bring the thread to the top before you add the bead!

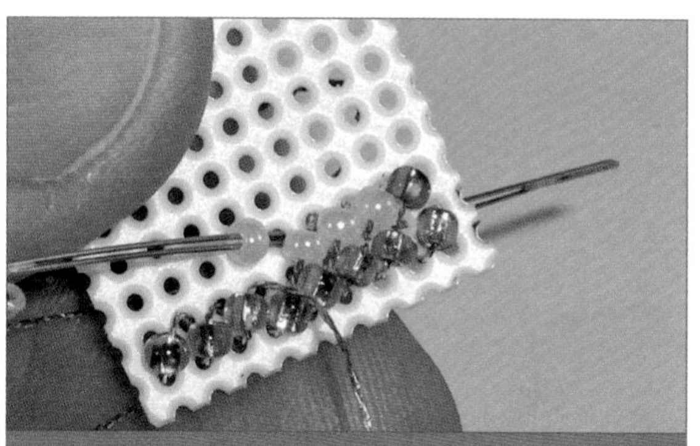

You'll work only half of the cross-stitch when beading, and you need to keep all the stitches going in the same direction.

Embellishments

You can include regular cross-stitch (using floss only) among the beaded cross-stitches for a different texture. This gives your piece raised areas where the beads are and depressions where only the thread is used. You can add a smaller motif at the bottom of the bookmark, too, if you like.

3. My design is a simple one. The cross shape is edged in gold and filled in white beads, and has a blue circle in the center. Edge the cross by doing a whip stitch around the entire shape, using 3 or 4 beads for each stitch. I doubled up the stitches at the corners.

A simple whip stitch creates a fancy edging.

4. Cut a piece of felt in a color complementary to your finished piece. You might want to trace the original shape before you begin to bead. Glue your ribbon to the back of the cross. I cut my ribbon approximately 13 inches long. Glue the felt to back of the cross and let dry.

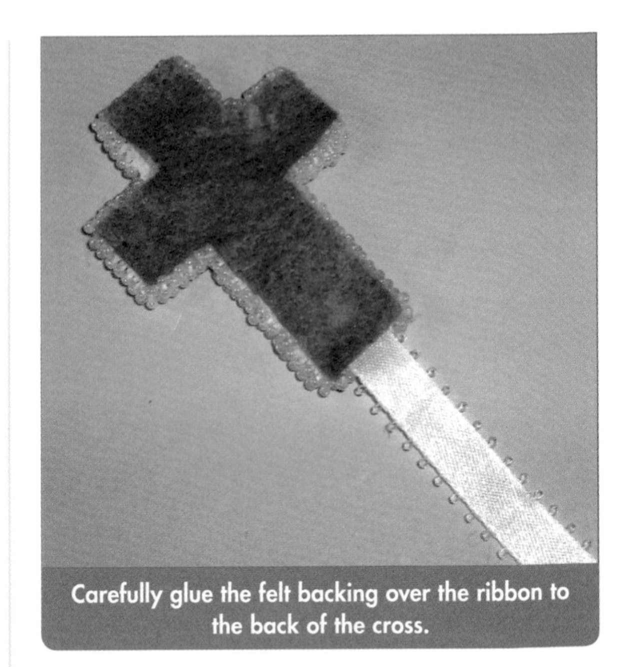

Carefully glue the felt backing over the ribbon to the back of the cross.

You may want to put some antifraying solution on the bottom of your ribbon, or turn it under and add a beaded edge to keep it from unraveling, depending on the ribbon you use and its tendency to fray.

Variations

These variations, a Star of David and a Celtic cross, are worked in a smaller size. What else can you think of creating?

Resources

Plastic canvas, embroidery floss, ribbon: Jo-Ann Fabric and Crafts (www.joann.com)

A Star of David and a Celtic cross are possible variations, as is any symbol of faith and spirituality appropriate to the occasion.

CHAPTER 11

Here Comes the Bride

In This Chapter

- A stunning one-of-a-kind bridal headpiece
- Complementary hair jewelry for the entire wedding party
- A simple but unique twisted wire bridal necklace and earrings set

A wedding is a milestone that warrants a chapter all its own. There are so many lovely and important details involved—something old, something new, something borrowed, and something blue—why not make some of them completely yours, beaded by your own hands? This chapter shows you how beadwork can add glamour, elegance, and beauty to your special day or that of someone you love.

Crowned in Beauty

Skill level: Intermediate

What you need:

- Size 10 champagne seed beads
- 26-gauge silver wire
- 30-gauge silver wire
- Tinted pearls
- Rose *montees*, crystal AB
- White floral tape
- Wire headpiece comb
- Bead spinner (optional, but recommended)
- Wire cutters
- Nylon jaw pliers (optional, but recommended)

Techniques and skills needed:

- French beading

What tops off a bride in a to-die-for bridal gown better than a fabulous headpiece only you can create? Nothing! In this section, I show you how to make it happen.

Many types of veils and headpieces are available for today's bride. In fact, many modern brides often eschew the veil altogether but still want something special to "crown" the event. You'll probably want to research what will look right with the gown you've chosen and what will suit your size, face, and style. Also consider your hairstyle for the big day and what type of veil you're planning to wear, if that's your choice.

Once you come up with some ideas, you can think about what beading technique will best manifest what you envision. Spend some time looking at bridal magazines, visiting bridal salons and shows, and searching the web to spark your imagination. For my vision of a beautiful wedding, I chose a gown embellished with champagne-colored lace and beading. And French beaded flower techniques seemed the perfect way to create my elegant headpiece.

In Chapter 4, you learned how to make simple looped flowers. I discussed materials and tools in that chapter as well. For this headpiece, you need to learn another French beaded flower technique, called the "simple basic" or the "center post method." Whatever you choose to call it, once you master making French beaded leaves and petals using this technique and learn to make a few other little embellishments, you'll have a whole new world of beaded components to add to your repertoire.

Beadwise

Montees are premounted rhinestones that come in a special setting with holes, allowing you to sew the stones onto material or string them with beading thread or wire.

You're probably already familiar with most, if not all, of the materials used for this elegant headpiece.

I used champagne seed beads in size 10, but size 11 would work just as well, and you could use white or ivory instead, depending on the color and style of the gown you're accessorizing. (I was working with a white gown with champagne lace.)

Pearls

Be aware that there are many, many different shades of white. Bring your fabrics (lace included) with you when you choose the beads for your headpiece and other accessories. Also, if you're a beginner in this technique, you might want to use slightly heavier 24-gauge wire for your leaves and petals.

I guide you through the simple basic or center post method of French beading for flowers as we make our first leaf. I learned this technique from various books but refined my skills in annual classes taught by Donna DeAngelis Dickt at Studio Baboo in Charlottesville, Virginia, so I tend to use her terminology and abbreviations. I highly recommended Donna's book, listed at the end of this project in the "Resources" section, for more instructions and tips.

Crimps!

Give careful consideration to weight. Beaded flowers en masse can get heavy! You can always combine silk or silk ribbon flowers with beaded components to lighten the weight.

For this leaf, you want a round bottom (RB, for short) and a pointed top (PT). You need 10 leaves in all.

1. Using your bead spinner (or other method outlined in Chapter 4), put approximately 18 inches of beads onto the spool of 26-gauge wire. *Do not cut the wire!* Keep it attached to the spool. Make a couple of loops resembling a knot at the end of the wire, to keep the beads from sliding off.
2. Slide up 4 beads (called the "basic beads"), leaving 3 inches of wire at the top of the wire (called the "basic wire"). Slide down the rest of your beads, and under the 4 beads, make a loop about the width of your palm. Twist the wires of the loop together about 1½ inches below the 4 beads on the center wire. This twisted loop is called "the stem," and the entire assembly is called the "basic framework."
3. Hold the basic framework so the knot is at the top, the stem loop is at the bottom, and the spool wire is on the left. Let the basic beads drop down to rest on the stem wire. If you're left-handed, you may find it easier to reverse this. Just remember to always set up the framework the same way.

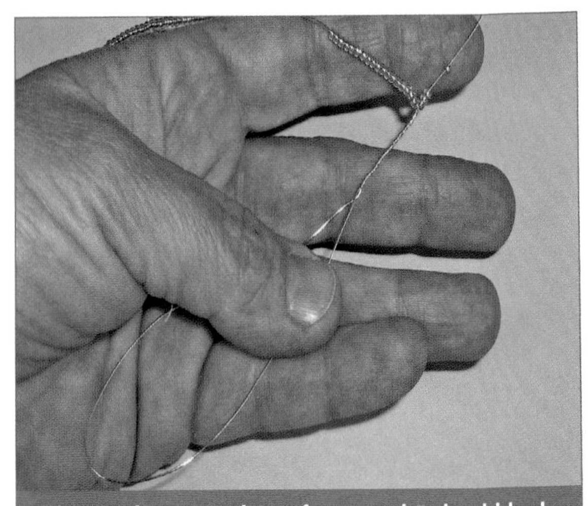

This is what your "basic framework" should look like as you prepare to make your first leaf.

4. Bring the beads on the spool wire up on the left side of the basic wire and, keeping it close to the 4 basic beads, create a row of beads from top to bottom and then wrap the spool wire around the basic wire from front to back, keeping the spool wire at a 45-degree angle. This is what creates the pointed top of your leaf.

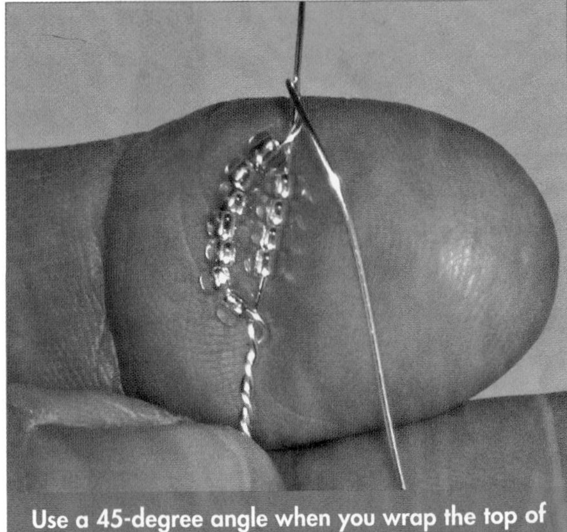

Use a 45-degree angle when you wrap the top of your leaf to create the point.

5. Bring the spool wire back down along the right side of the center basic wire, and wrap the spool wire around the bottom twisted stem wire at a 90-degree angle. This is what creates the round bottom of your leaf.

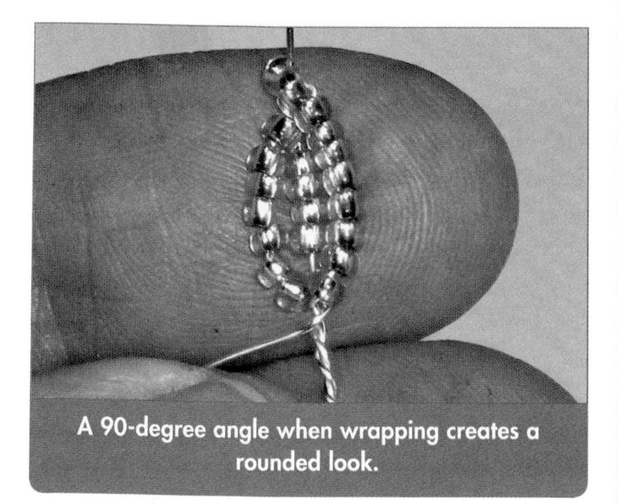

A 90-degree angle when wrapping creates a rounded look.

6. Continue in this way until you have 13 rows altogether and end at the bottom.
7. Twist the spool wire around the bottom stem wire a few times and then trim.

To end your leaf, twist the spool wire around the stem wire and trim.

8. Cut the bottoms of the loop wires and twist.

Trim the stem wires.

9. Leave about ¼ inch at the top of your leaf and trim the basic wire.

Trim the basic wire.

10. Fold the trimmed basic wire down to the back of the leaf.

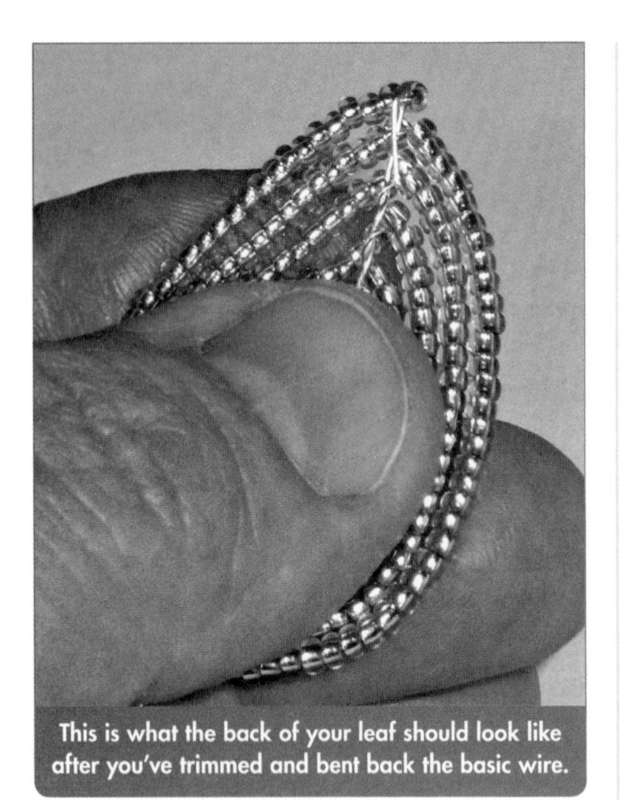

This is what the back of your leaf should look like after you've trimmed and bent back the basic wire.

11. Repeat steps 1 through 10 until you have a total of 10 leaves.

Now to lace each leaf, which you use 30-gauge wire for. This is not absolutely necessary with these leaves and petals, but it adds extra shape.

12. Cut a 6-inch piece of 30-gauge wire. Hold the leaf with the right side facing you. Thread the wire on one side of the basic bead row and the other end of the wire on the other side so you have approximately half of the wire on either side. Pull the 2 ends of the lacing wire to the back side of the leaf so it falls in between the 4 beads on the basic wire (2 beads above and 2 beads below).

Position the lacing wire.

13. Turn the leaf over so the "wrong" side faces you, and cross the 2 lacing wires, pulling them snug but not too hard.

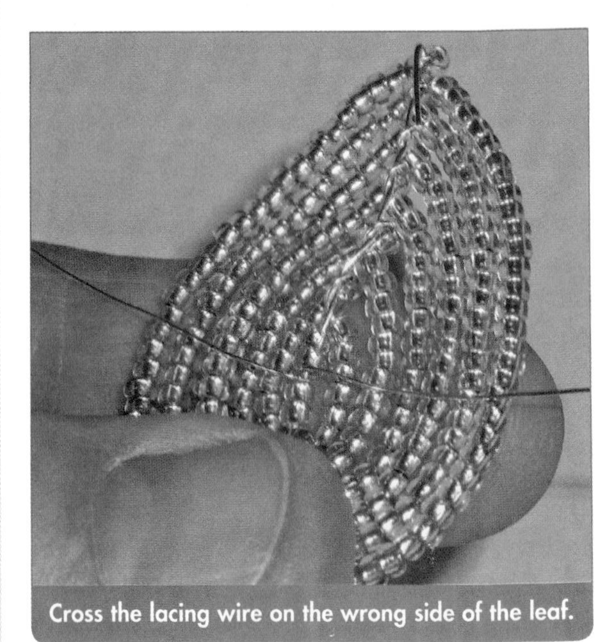

Cross the lacing wire on the wrong side of the leaf.

14. Working out from the center, one side at a time, loop the lacing wire around each row of beads (like a backstitch in sewing) at a slight angle until you reach the last row of the leaf.

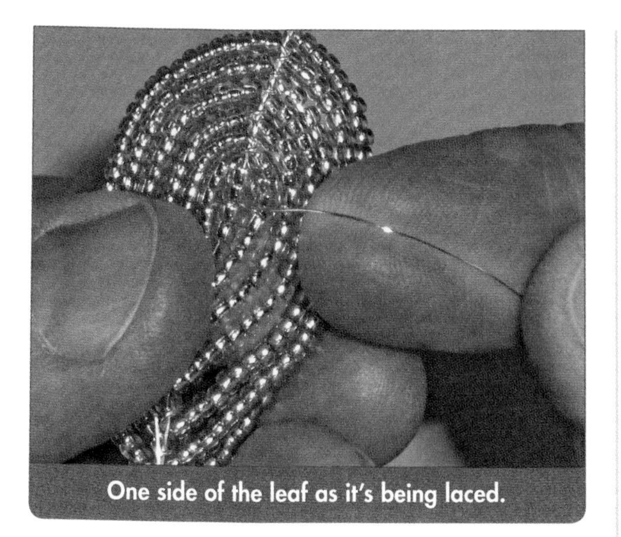
One side of the leaf as it's being laced.

15. Wrap the lacing wire around this last row twice, and trim it very close.

Pearls

Be sure you work from the *wrong* side of the leaf. This will make the lacing wire seem to disappear when you look at the right side.

16. Repeat the lacing process with the second half of the lacing wire, working out to the last row on the other side of the leaf.
17. Lace all 10 leaves.

The next component of the headpiece to make is the center flower. The process is the same as the leaves, only you use a round bottom and round top for most of them, so you wrap both the top and bottom at a 90-degree angle.

18. Make 5: RB, RT, 4 beads basic wire, 9 rows.
19. Make 3: RB, RT, 4 beads basic wire, 7 rows.
20. Make 1: RB, PT, 4 beads basic wire, 5 rows.
21. Using the same method you used for leaves, make the flower petals as directed earlier. Note that the center "petal" has a pointed top.
22. Trim and finish as you did before, lacing if desired.

Here are all the components for the center flower of the headpiece before lacing.

23. Twist the center petal with the front side facing out.

Make the center of the flower by twisting the single 5-row petal.

24. Begin to assemble the flower by joining the center and the 3 (7-row) petals with floral tape. Be sure the stems and bottoms of the petals align before joining.

Join the first section of the flower using floral tape.

Pearls

If you have trouble finding white floral tape, you may well have to turn to online sources. One I found is www.weddingflowersandmore.com/supplies-tape.html. You might also contact your local florist and ask if they have any suggestions.

25. Add the 5 (9-row) petals one at a time so the flower looks balanced, joining each with floral tape.

This is what my assembled flower looks like from the back.

26. Shape the petals and move them so they look natural and balanced.

Here's my flower, fully assembled.

27. Make the decorative pearl and montee "stamens" (also called "pips" in the flower arranging craft) using 2 pearls and 1 montee for each leaf. You'll need 10 montee stamens and 20 pearls.

Here are a couple of pips or stamens made from pearls and flat rose montees.

Embellishments

You can use any number of things to create centers or stamens for flowers. Try small bicone, round, or oval crystals, for instance, or loops made of seed beads. You can study real flowers or create fantasy flowers from your imagination.

Assembling the headpiece is a critical part of the process, and if you treat your individual components, assemble them, and attach them to the headpiece comb very carefully, you'll have something professional-looking and worthy of being handed down as a family heirloom. Don't hurry through this step!

28. Take 2 pearl stamens and 1 rose montee stamen, make a bundle, and twist. Add to 1 leaf and wrap with white floral tape. Repeat until you have all 10 leaves and pip bundles wrapped.

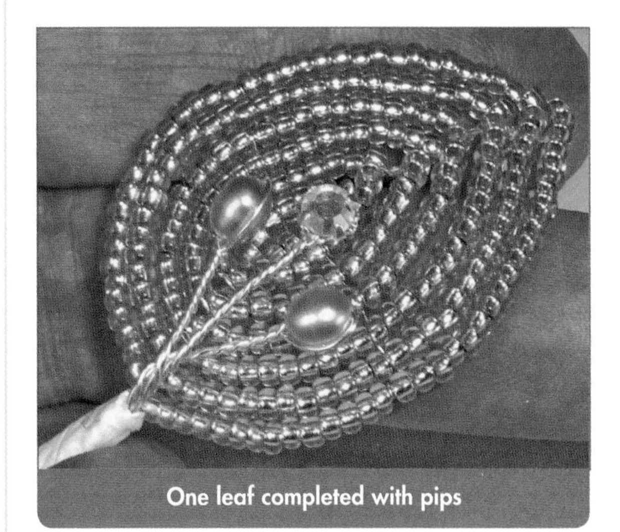

One leaf completed with pips

29. Hold 1 leaf bundle in your nondominant hand. With 2 leaves side by side, tape them to the single leaf, about ½ inch down the stem. Add 2 more leaves in the same way. Add the flower centered over the wrapped leaf "spray" in the same way.

Here's my finished spray of leaves and center flower.

30. Repeat step 29, excluding the flower, trimming the wires before wrapping where you can.
31. Using 30-gauge wire, secure the flower and leaves assembly to the headpiece comb by wrapping it around them both, in between the teeth of the comb. It helps to secure the wire first to the comb by wrapping it around one tooth of the comb several times. Fit the other leaf assembly up under the flower and leaf assembly already attached to the comb, and using the 30-gauge wire, repeat the process. Wrap the wire several times around one tooth of the comb again, to secure it, before cutting with your wire cutters.

Attach your veil (if you'll be wearing one) using whatever method you choose. My veil already had elastic loops sewn onto it, so I simply had to slide the loops over the teeth of the comb. You can also use Velcro or stitch the veil to the comb.

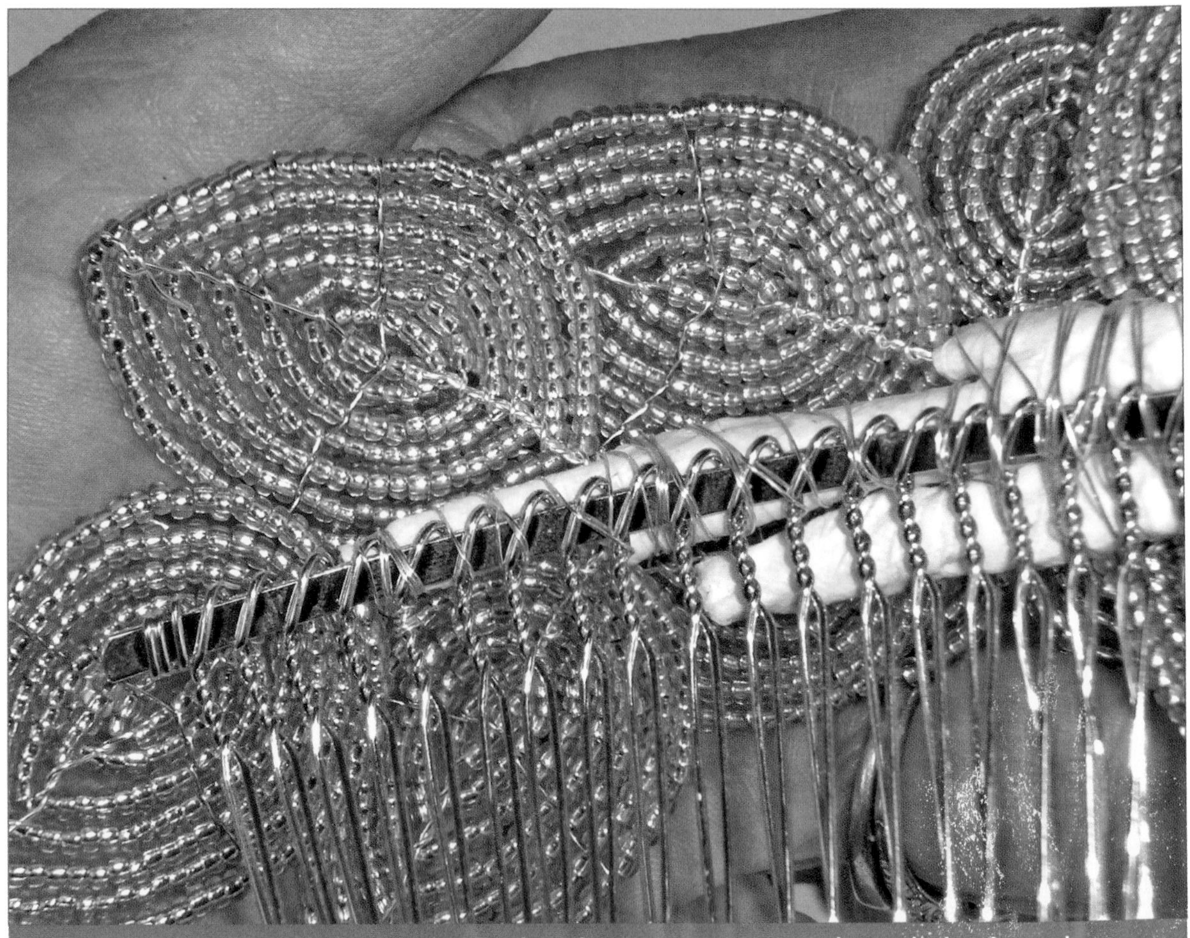

This view of the back of the comb shows how the two sprays are securely attached to the comb.

Resources

Books, videos, and DVDs: *French Beaded Designs* by Donna DeAngelis Dickt; *"I Do" Veils: So Can You!* by Claudia Lynch; *Veiled in Beauty: Creating Headpieces and Veils for the Bride* by the editors of Creative Publishing international, Inc.; *Rosemary Topol's French Beaded Flower Sessions* on DVD and video

Wire comb, veil: Jo-Ann Fabric and Craft (www.joann.com)

Seed beads and bead spinner: Studio Baboo (www.studiobaboo.com)

Wire: Artistic Wire (www.artisticwire.com)

Rose montees: tutu.com (www.tutu.com)

Side Interests

Skill level: Intermediate

What you need:

- Size 10 champagne seed beads
- Size 10 seed beads in complementary colors for attendants
- 26-gauge silver wire
- 30-gauge silver wire
- Tinted pearls in complementary color
- White floral tape
- Small wire comb(s)
- Bead spinner (optional, but recommended)
- Wire cutters
- Nylon jaw pliers (optional, but recommended)

Techniques and skills needed:

- French beading

Carrying on with the design I created for the headpiece through to the attendants, now let's make a hair comb (you can make a set, if you like) and a boutonniere. By introducing a different color for the flower but keeping the same color for the leaves, the attendants' hair accessories coordinate nicely.

Materials for the attendant's accessories are nearly the same, except for the use of a smaller comb and different colors of beads for the flower.

1. Using steps 18 through 29 of the previous project, make 2 leaves (RB, PT) of champagne beads, but use only 9 rows of beads for each leaf.
2. Make a simple flower by creating 5 petals (RB, RT) of 7 rows each, using a color to complement your attendants' dresses.
3. Make 3 pearl pips for the center, as you did in the previous project.
4. Twist the pearl pips together tightly. Attach the petals around all the pips one at a time using white floral tape.
5. Attach the leaves in the same manner.
6. Attach the wrapped stem to the comb, centering it. (See step 31 of the previous project.) Bend your flower and leaves so they cover the end of the comb.

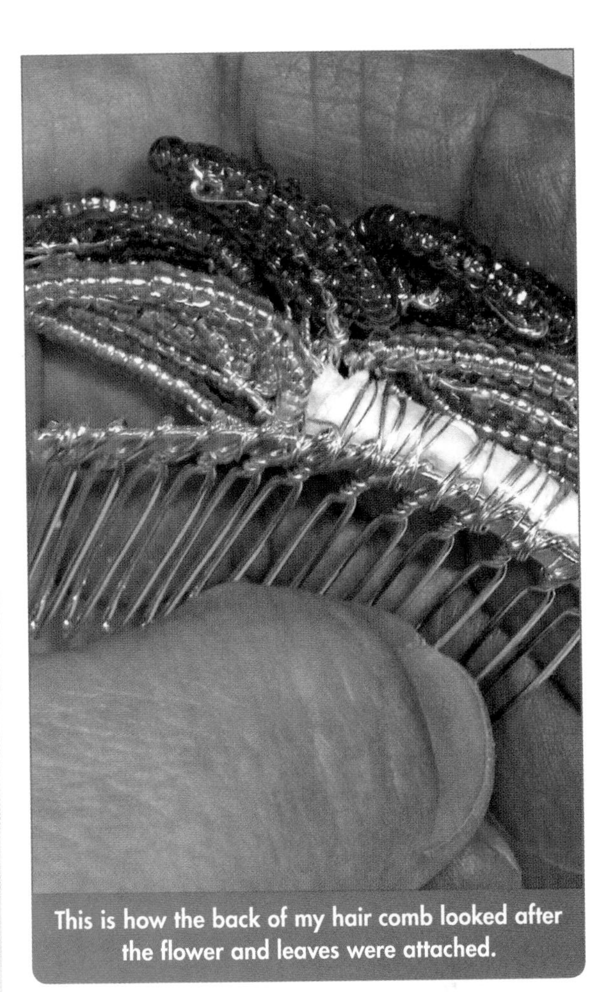

This is how the back of my hair comb looked after the flower and leaves were attached.

For the men's boutonniere, the materials are the same as for the wire comb, minus the comb and plus some silver embroidery floss, tacky glue, and complementary ribbon. I used the twisted bead center from the bridal headpiece flower (you could also use pearls) and added sepals.

You can easily create a boutonniere from the same beads and supplies as the attendants' hair combs.

1. Make 2 leaves using champagne beads with RB, PT, 4 beads on the basic wire, consisting of 9 rows each.
2. Make 4 sepals (basically, a small leaf) using champagne beads with RB, PT, 4 beads on the basic wire, consisting of 5 rows each.
3. Make 5 petals using pink (or color of your choice) beads with RB, RT, 4 beads on the basic wire, consisting of 7 rows each.
4. Make the center of the flower using pink beads with RB, PT, 4 beads on the basic wire, consisting of 5 rows.
5. Assemble the petals around the center, wrapping as you go. Add each of the sepals, wrapping one at a time, and each of the leaves.
6. Wrap the entire stem with silk embroidery floss and add a ribbon, if desired. Provide a pin for attaching the boutonniere to the lapel.

Tack on metallic embroidery floss in a color to match the champagne beads with glue, and wind around.

Necklace and Earrings

Skill level: Beginner

What you need:

Size 10 champagne seed beads
28-gauge silver wire
Tinted pearls in a complementary color
Rose montees in crystal AB
Silver French earring wires
Silver chain, desired length
Wire cutters
Nylon jaw pliers

Techniques and skills needed:

Basic wirework

This necklace and earrings set employs an even simpler wire-twisting technique than the first three projects in this chapter. Here, you construct several sprays of wire, pearls, montees, and champagne seed beads, and you twist together and loop the wire "stems" of the sprays to create a bail for a pendant necklace. The earrings are simpler still. I used champagne beads in this ensemble for the bride, but the attendants' colors could easily be introduced.

The materials for this lovely ensemble are the same ones you've been using, with some earring wires and a chain added, and a different-gauge wire.

Crimps!

If you have difficulty working with 28-gauge wire, you can substitute 26 gauge, but it will make the bail bulkier. Using good-quality wire means less breakage. You can handle the wire and twist quite a bit before it breaks. You may want to practice a bit on some small pieces to get the feel of the strength of the wire.

1. Make 2 of component 1: cut 1 foot of 28-gauge wire. Fold it in half and put on 10 seed beads. Make a loop. Add 10 more seed beads to 1 wire and push up about 1⁄4 inch above first loop you made. Make another loop. Repeat with same wire 1⁄4 inch away. Make 2 loops on the other side of the first loop you made, each with 10 beads, each 1⁄4 inch apart. Twist wires together about 1 inch.

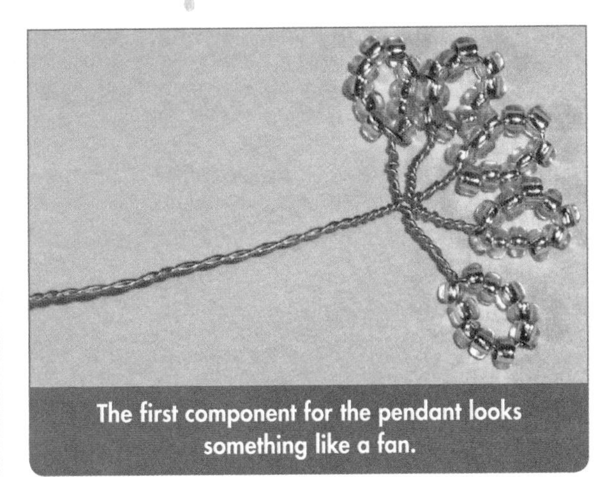

The first component for the pendant looks something like a fan.

2. Make 2 of component 2: cut 1 foot of 28-gauge wire. Fold in half and put on 10 seed beads. Make a loop and twist wires together about 1⁄2 inch. Add 10 beads to 1 wire, push up approximately 1⁄4 inch, and make a loop. Twist wires approximately 1⁄8 inch. Add 10 seed beads and make a loop approximately 1⁄8 inch above the main wire. Repeat these 2 loops using the same measurements with the other wire. Twist the 2 wires together about 1 inch.

The second component for the pendant looks like a branch.

3. Make 4 pearl pips and 4 montee pips, as you did before.
4. Make a little bouquet with all these components, putting the pips at various intervals. Twist all the wires together using a nylon jaw pliers, if you need to (I did!).

Assemble all the components together in a "bouquet" with the stems twisted together.

5. Make a loop with the twisted bundle of wires and then wrap the stem around the bottom of the loop to make a bail. Be sure to leave a large enough loop that you can thread through a chain and clasp end. (Or add the chain first and then make the bail.) Smooth down any wires that may be sticking up or clip closely. You can also use your nylon jaw pliers to gently smooth things down where necessary.

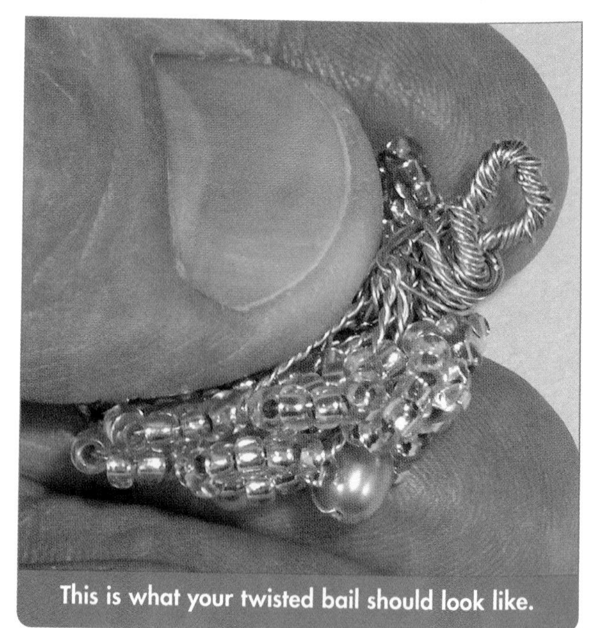

This is what your twisted bail should look like.

6. Spread and twist your tiny "bouquet" to make a pleasing form. You can keep the form close and dense or spread it out, as I did, for a more "fanned" effect. Add the chain.

By spreading out the branches of your beaded bouquet, you get a different effect for your pendant than if you bend them closer together.

Now for the matching earrings:

1. Fold a 6-inch wire in half and add a pearl. Twist about ¼ inch. Add 10 champagne beads to 1 wire and make a loop close to the main wire. Do the same on the other side with the second wire. Twist both wires together approximately ¼ inch and add a montee to 1 wire. Put the other wire behind and twist tightly approximately 1 inch.

This simple earring complements your pendant and adds a delicate sparkle.

2. Make a loop to hang from an ear wire, and wrap as you did with the pendant.

The loop for your earring should look like this.

3. Open an earring wire, and add the wire drop you just made.

Repeat to make the second earring.

Variations

Wire twisting is a highly versatile technique, and you don't need to know advanced French beaded flower techniques to create beautiful wedding jewelry. If you're just learning the simple basic technique, you can still add a few small leaves and a loop flower like the one you made in Chapter 4, and you'll have an ensemble that's equally enchanting.

Pink and Green Hair Confections

Bobbi Wicks created these hair accessories by starting with a long piece of 26-gauge wire folded in half and twisted around a pearl or loop of seed beads. She then made branches along the way. Then she wired these sprays of pearls and seed beads in pink, green, and champagne to a hair comb. The small hair jewelry spirals she made in a similar manner. Even bobby pins can be decorated with beads.

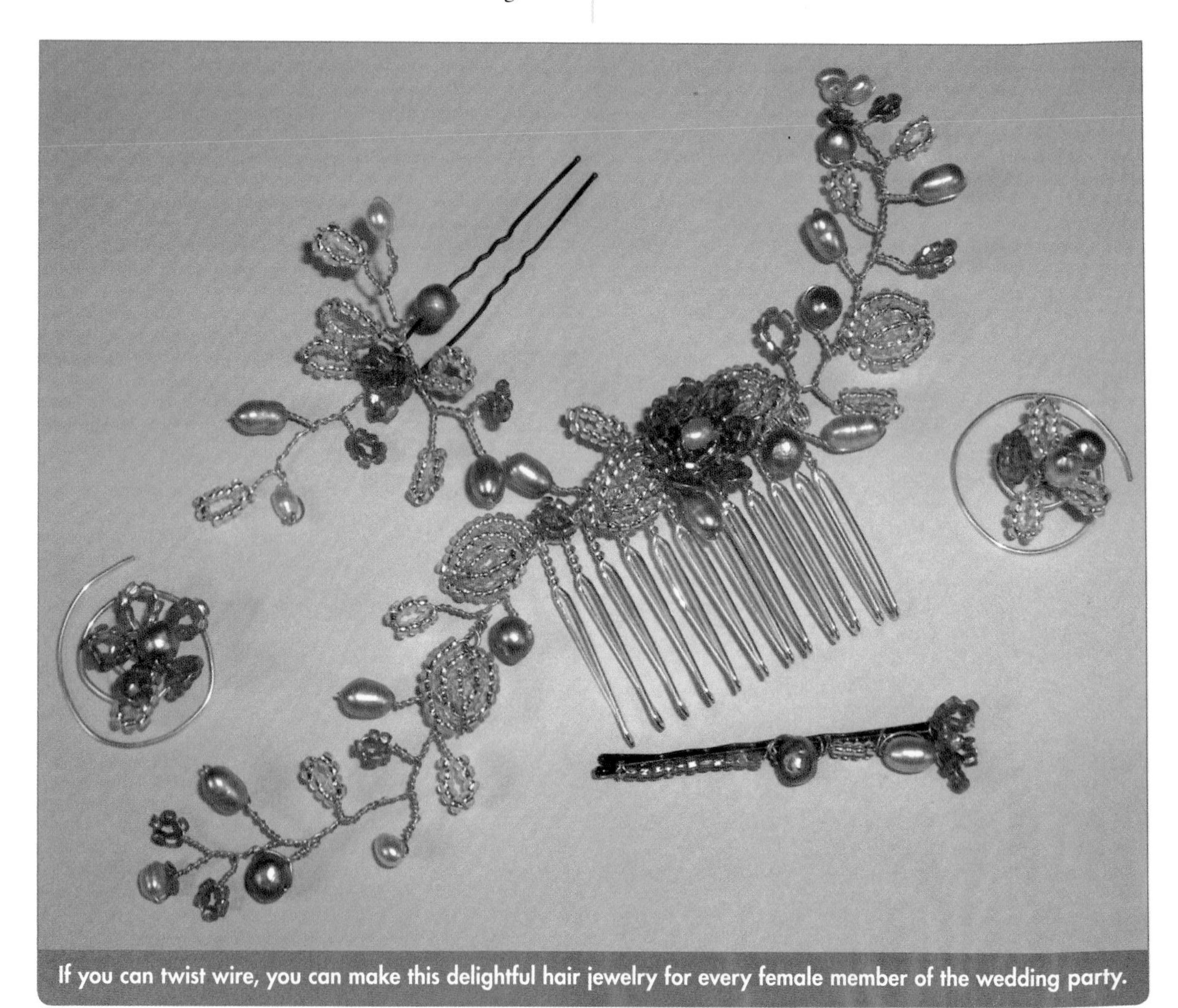

If you can twist wire, you can make this delightful hair jewelry for every female member of the wedding party.

Necklace and Earring Delicacies

Bobbi used the same technique for the Pink and Green Hair Confections to create this necklace and earring set. Wouldn't this be pretty on a flower girl or for a spring dance? (By the way, all of the accessories in the chapter are adaptable to evening or prom wear. Think black and white or silver!)

So wire a gorgeous wedding for yourself or someone you love. Whatever your skill level, there's a wire and bead project for you.

This delicate jewelry is easy to make and appropriate even for the younger members of the wedding party.

Afterword

It's my sincere wish that this book has ignited a fire in you to pursue your beading projects well into the future. The world of beading is so wide and full of challenge that you can spend your lifetime learning and creating.

Now for a few final things to say ....

Organizing Your Beads

As your beading hobby grows, so will your supplies. But how do you store everything so you can find it again when inspiration strikes? Everyone has his or her favorite storage containers and organizational tools, and many of us who have been beading a long time have tried some and moved on to others. Ultimately, you need to find a system (or, more likely, several systems) that works for you.

First, I advise taking inventory of what you have. Are you a seed beader? Then your storage needs will probably be quite different from those of someone who does mostly stringing or wirework. Do you do a variety of techniques? Then you'll probably need to come up with a variety of storage and organization solutions. How big is your stash? Even if it's small now, you will probably want a system that can grow with you. Believe me, beads are like small living creatures—they seem to multiply! Do you want to organize by color? Material? Type of bead? Finish? Or maybe you want to organize several ways within a category.

Perhaps the best way to help you start thinking about your own organization needs is to describe my beading studio and some of the methods I use to organize my large beading stash. Because I do a great variety of beading techniques, I have had to organize almost every type and size of beads and findings. Some of these may work for you!

I had the luck of inheriting a large map-filing cabinet from my husband. It is perfect for storing beads in a way that makes them easy to see and retrieve. The five large but shallow drawers are perfect for most larger beads and findings. I purchased inserts with dividers and sorted them first by type (two drawers for findings, two drawers for larger beads, and one drawer for crystals). Within each drawer, I sorted by color. When I'm working on a piece, I can look for the color I need and see just about everything I have available in that color. The drawers are labeled so I don't have to remember what's where.

I have a separate box just for pearls, which I sorted by color. Right now they're in individual baggies, but I may ultimately change that.

I then have a rolling cart with deep drawers that I've labeled for all my supplies, including threads and other stringing materials, glues and tapes, polishing clothes for silver, and the like.

Seed beaders have different storage needs. I do French beaded flowers, so I have large quantities of seed beads and wire. I also do off-loom and loom weaving, for which I use smaller quantities of many different colors or seed beads. For large quantities of seed beads, I use plastic shoe boxes and sort by color and seed bead sizes. I keep half-kilo hanks in plastic closeable bags and broken hanks in smaller bags. I use the same boxes for wire, sorted by gauge.

For smaller quantities of seed beads, I like the Tic Tac candy–style boxes. You can even purchase a unit that fits into another larger box. These containers come in different sizes; I like the little ones for travel. You can take out only the ones you want and leave the rest in the larger box.

Some people like stacking circular containers for bead storage. I have found these sometimes come apart, I find them cumbersome, and I have a tendency to tip them over. Be sure the lids screw on rather than just fit together if you try these containers. I have retired these altogether and rarely use them.

Plastic resealable storage bags work well if you're not going to be handling the bags a lot. Eventually, they'll wear out and not stay closed or simply get "cloudy" and hard to see through. I still use them for half-kilo hanks of beads, but I prefer a system I can see clearly and don't have shuffle and reshuffle through for most of my beads and findings.

Another favorite storage container for beaders is a divided box with a hinged lid. These are sold specifically for crafts, but I have found them in hardware stores for less money. Be sure the ones you buy have dividers that either are permanent or really fit snugly. These containers work better for larger beads and findings, as seed beads tend to migrate over the tops or underneath the dividers.

Another container I like is a box made by Craft Mates, which has locking compartments. I use these for small beads and crystals when I'm traveling. You can use them for seed beads, but it helps to have a little scoop or spoon to get them out.

Some systems are made specifically for beading or other small components. They are similar in principle to my map cabinet, but are nice wooden cabinets with custom-made drawer inserts. These are expensive but might be worth investing in, especially if you're going to be storing your beads in plain sight in a room where family and guests spend a lot of time.

It also helps to organize your tools so you don't have to hunt for them when you have a moment to bead. I have a tool rack for the tools I use all the time. I also have a circular holder for other odds and ends.

I'm always looking for new and better ways to organize my supplies. After all, I wrote *The Complete Idiot's Guide to Organizing Your Life!* and, as you might guess, organizing is my thing. But it's also an individual thing, and you need to do what works best for you, your personality, your circumstances, and your needs. As you meet other beaders and peruse magazines and online groups, you'll learn many other clever solutions to bead-storage challenges.

Your Computer to the Rescue

Even if you're very organized, your bead stash can grow so much that it's difficult to remember where things are. Plus, as you become more accomplished as a beader and experiment with your own designs, you might want to start selling some of your work. One of the greatest challenges if you begin selling your beadwork is how to price your pieces.

Enter *Jewelry Designer Manager* from Bejeweled Software Company. This computer program is, in my opinion, the key to better organization and better business. It's easy to install and can be customized in a variety of ways. With *Jewelry Designer Manager*, you can organize your components and your suppliers, keep track of your customers, and even create a catalog with photos, all with the same program.

I am slowly inputting my inventory, which is probably the biggest task, but already I have found this program extremely useful for my jewelry design business. Just go to www.jewelrydesignermanager.com and take the online tour to see if it's right for you.

Have Beads, Will Travel

As you bead more and more, you'll want to be able to take your beading with you. Because beadwork is generally small, it's relatively easy to transport, *but* those little rascals do have a way of rolling away.

For traveling with bead projects, I've used everything from an Altoids tin (for making a set of earrings or a ring) on an airplane, to a huge rolling toolbox on wheels (to do beaded flower demonstrations). I regularly bead on an airplane. So far, I've dropped only a few small seed beads. I use the top of a wooden cigar box fitted with a Vellux sheet I cut out of an old blanket. It has a lip just high enough that the beads don't roll off, but my hands can rest comfortably on it. I carry a small locking container with crystals and seed beads, and I put out only a few beads at a time. If the ride gets bumpy, I pack everything up and wait for smoother sailing!

Some well-known designers take their seed bead work in a padded handgun case. Yep, a *gun* case! I've tried it, too, and it works. If you have a sectioned tray (some of us use porcelain watercolor trays), you can keep your seed beads separated by color and simply lay them between the foam layers of the gun case. Press it closed, and the beads will stay put.

Many totes and cases are made specifically for beaders. Keep your eyes open, but always remember to ask yourself, "Does this work for the kinds of beading I do?"

Have fun thinking of new and clever ways of transporting your bead projects. There's no reason why you can't bead just about anywhere!

Education and Inspiration

The beading world is constantly changing. New materials are constantly being introduced, new techniques are being developed, and new takes on old techniques are emerging. There are bead gatherings, shows, and conferences. Classes abound. By looking at the work of other designers, you might be inspired to create designs of your own. But how do you keep up?

Beading magazines and online beading sites abound and are perhaps the most economical ways to explore the beading world. (I've given you a list of my favorites in Appendix A.)

And look for inspiration everywhere. Travel can become part of your beadwork. I love to buy a few beads that are unique to places I visit and make a piece of jewelry that forever reminds me of my trip. Visit museums that show the craftsmanship and artwork of your destination. Exploring new cultures is always an inspiration.

Books on costume and handiwork from the past are another source of ideas. Don't just confine yourself to beading, but comb your library and bookstores, both new and used, for designs and influences.

I love period films, and I'm almost always excited by the clothing, interiors, and jewelry that designers present in them. Films like *The Age of Innocence*, *Bleak House*, or *House of Mirth*, or even fantasy films like *The Lord of the Rings* can provide inspirational material to get your creative juices flowing.

And of course, there's always nature. A trip to your own backyard can inspire you with shapes, forms, colors, and textures to add life to your beading.

Now, go forth and *bead!*

APPENDIX

A

Resources

All those little things! You'll need to know where to get them. This list of resources points you in the right direction for suppliers of components and equipment, sources of information and free patterns, as well as ways to connect with other beaders, both online and through local organizations.

Don't forget to add your own when you find good ones!

Suppliers

Arizona Gems and Minerals, Inc.

6370 East Highway 69
Prescott Valley, AZ 86314

1-800-356-6903

www.azgemsandbeads.com

Beads, findings, tools, and equipment.

Artgems, Inc.

4860 E. Baseline Road, Suite 101
Mesa, AZ 85206

1-800-408-0032

www.artgems.com

Watch faces and beads.

Anvente Enterprises

8093 N. Highway 99 West
McMinnville, OR 97128

1-877-ANVENTE (1-877-268-3683)

www.weddingflowersandmore.com

Floral tape, especially hard-to-find white.

The Bead Cellar

6305 Westfield Avenue
Pennsauken, NJ 08110
856-665-4744

www.beadcellar.com

Home of The Bead Cellar Pattern Designer.

Bead Spinner Lady

Judy Kintner Gilmartin
1005 W. 17 Avenue
Spokane, WA 99203

509-624-7938

www.beadspinnerlady.com

Wooden bead spinners in three sizes.

Beadalon

440 Highlands Boulevard
Coatesville, PA 19320

1-866-4-BEADALON (1-866-423-2325)

www.beadalon.com

Flexible wire, tools, and accessories.

Beads Galore International, Inc.

3320 S. Priest Drive, Suite 3
Tempe, AZ 85282

1-800-424-9577

www.beadsgalore.com

Beads, findings, and tools.

Blue Moon Beads

7855 Hayvenhurst Avenue
Van Nuys, CA 91406

1-800-377-6715

www.bluemoonbeads.com

This brand is available at several chain stores.

Buckaroo Bobbins

PO Box 1168
Chino Valley, AZ 86323

928-636-1885

www.buckaroobobbins.com

Patterns for period bags to bead embroider.

Butterick Patterns

www.butterick.com

Butterick patterns are available in most major craft and fabric stores.

Check out their patterns for bags to bead embroider.

Cabela's

1-800-237-4444

www.cabelas.com

This is where you can get FireLine if you can't find it at your local Wal-Mart or fishing store. Order a free catalog or use the store locator to find a retail outlet near you.

DeCordené WireWorks

Charles Gragg
PO Box 701
Springfield, MO 65801-701

417-832-1350

www.dcwireworks.com

Jump rings and chain mail supplies and instruction.

Dover Publications

Customer Care Department
31 East 2nd Street
Mineola, NY 11501-3852

www.doverpublications.com

Great source for vintage design and beading book reprints.

DyeDye's Treasures from the Past

eBay seller and store

www.ebay.com

Vintage beads, cabochons, and findings.

Eclectica Beads

Main Office/Mail Orders
18900 W. Bluemound Road
Brookfield, WI 53045

262-641-0910

www.eclecticabeads.com

Vintage beads.

Fante's Kitchen Wares Shop

1006 S. 9th Street
Philadelphia, PA 19147

1-800-44-FANTE (1-800-443-2683)

www.fantes.com

A good source for tea balls.

Fire Mountain Gems

1 Fire Mountain Way
Grants Pass, OR 97526-2373

1-800-292-FIRE (1-800-292-3473)

www.firemountaingems.com

Everything for the beader.

Frontier Natural Products Co-Op

PO Box 299
3021 78th Street
Norway, IA 52318

1-800-669-3275

www.frontiercoop.com

Herbs for your dream pillows and sachets.

Jo-Ann Fabric and Crafts

www.joann.com

Beads, findings, tools and organizing supplies.

Kmart

www.kmart.com

Lamp shades.

Knot Just Beads

515 N Glenview Avenue
Wauwatosa, WI 53213

414-771-8360

www.knotjustbeads.com

Beads.

Lacy's Stiff Stuff

Happy Jack's Trading Post, Inc.
4905 West Second Street
PO Box 2646
Roswell, NM 88202

505-623-1544

happyjacknm.tripod.com

Foundation material for bead embroidery.

Maille Artisans League

www.mailleartisans.org

A resource for chain mail and jump ring jewelry making.

Margo's Beadie Critter Collection

www.BeadieCritters.com

Lots of free patterns for beaded critters.

McCall's Patterns

www.mccallspatterns.com

Patterns for bags to make to bead embroider.

Michaels, The Arts and Crafts Store

www.michaels.com

Beads, findings, tools, and organizing supplies.

Out on a Whim

121 E. Cotati Avenue
Cotati, CA 94931

1-800-232-3111

www.whimbeads.com

Beads, especially size 8.

Paramount Wire Company

2-8 Central Avenue
East Orange, NJ 07018

973-672-0500

www.parawire.com

Wire for beaded flower making.

The Ring Lord

290C RR6
Saskatoon SK S7K 3J9
Canada

306-374-1335

www.theringlord.com

Jump ring jewelry and chain mail supplies and instruction.

Rings & Things

PO Box 450
Spokane, WA 99210-0450

1-800-366-2156

www.rings-things.com

Wholesale supplier of everything for the beader. You don't need a tax ID to order.

Ross Stores

1-800-945-7677

www.rossstores.com

A good source for scarves and bags to embellish with bead embroidery. Call or go online for store locator.

Rowena Tank, Glass Bead Artist

928-899-3574

www.rowenaart.net

Rowena made the glass fish used in the baby mobile in Chapter 10.

San Francisco Herb Co.

1-800-227-4530

www.sfherb.com

Herbs for dream pillows and sachets.

Scottsdale Bead Supply and Import Inc.

480-945-5988

www.scottsdalebeadsupply.com

Great clasps and beads.

Shipwreck Beads

8560 Commerce Place Drive NE
Lacey, WA 98516

1-800-950-4232

www.shipwreckbeads.com

Everything for the beader. A good source for size 9 (3-cut) seed beads.

Silk Rainbow

5195 Waterlynn Drive
Lake Wylie, SC 29710

1-800-848-8501

www.beadornaments.com

Beaded tea ball ornament kits and supplies.

Silver Charms, Inc.

2715 National Circle
Garland, TX 75041

1-877-926-4788

www.silvercharmsinc.com

Charms for charm bracelets and wine glass charm holders.

Simplicity Pattern Co., Inc.

www.simplicity.com

Patterns for bags to bead embroider. Also available in most craft and fabric stores.

Soft Flex

Soft Flex Company
PO Box 80
Sonoma, CA 95476

1-866-925-FLEX (1-866-925-3539)

www.softflexcompany.com

Flexible wire, tools, and other beading supplies.

Studio Baboo

321 East Main Street
Charlottesville, VA 22902

434-244-2905

www.studiobaboo.com

Beads and bead spinners.

Tandy Leather Factory, Inc.

3847 East Loop 820 South
Fort Worth, TX 76119

1-800-433-3201

www.leatherfactory.com

Leather for hat bands, buckles, and tips.

Tuesday Morning

www.tuesdaymorning.com

A good source for tassels and other things to bead embellish.

Tutu.Com

PO Box 472287
Charlotte, NC 28247-2287

1-877-888-8266

www.tutu.com

Rose montees and some other novelties to experiment with.

Via Murano

Pamela and Ira Israel
PO Box 10081
Newport Beach, CA 92658

1-877-VIAMURANO (1-877-842-6872)

www.viamurano.com

Home of the Tornado Clasp.

Vogue Patterns

www.voguepatterns.com

Patterns for bags to bead embroider. Also available in most craft and fabric stores.

Wal-Mart

www.walmart.com

Some beads, findings, and organizing supplies.

WigJig

PO Box 5124
Gaithersburg, MD 20882

1-800-579-WIRE (1-800-579-9473)

www.wigjig.com

Wire jigs, wirework supplies, and instruction.

Magazines

My favorite magazines for instruction and inspiration are *Bead&Button*, *Beadwork*, *Bead Unique*, and *Step-by-Step Wire Jewelry*. But there are many more magazines for you to choose from, including some on just about art jewelry or polymer clay. For a comprehensive list of beading and related magazines with links, go to beadwork.about.com/od/beadingperiodicals/Beading_and_Bead_Related_Magazines_and_Periodicals.htm.

Websites

We all have our favorite websites. Here's a list of mine:

Auntie's Beads

www.auntiesbeads.com

Susie Henderson's company is a full-service supplier, and her site is an online catalog. But she also has a "university" and lots of good instructional material.

About.com's Beadwork

beadwork.about.com

Paula S. Morgan is your About.com beading guide. Check in here often.

The Bead Bugle

www.BeadBugle.com

Super twice-monthly online magazine and beading community, plus great deals on beads and findings.

Bead-Patterns.com

www.bead-patterns.com

Rita Sova's bead pattern site has lots of free patterns and instruction sheets, plus patterns to buy from some of the best designers.

Bella Online

www.bellaonline.com/site/beadwork

Bella Online is actually an online women's magazine on a wide variety of topics. The main site has subsites for all kinds of crafts. The beading one is a gem.

Candy's Beading Links

www.candysbeadinglinks.com

Lots of great links here, and Candy does her best to keep them up-to-date.

Online Groups

Beadchat

groups.yahoo.com/group/Beadchat

There's an online group for every kind of beading. My favorite general online group is Beadchat.

Learn2Bead

groups.yahoo.com/group/learn2bead

Learn2Bead is a good group for beginners. Follow along with one technique at a time and lots of help from fellow beaders.

Bead Guilds and Societies

Beading societies and guilds are all over the country (and outside the United States as well)—too many to list here. But to find one near you, go to one of these online sites for lists of groups to join:

www.thebeadsite.com/GUI-LKBS.html

www.rings-things.com/BEAD-SOC.HTM

www.justbeads.com/user/societylist.cfm

www.beadlady.biz/beadsocieties.htm

Bead Events

Shows, conferences, and other beading events are great ways to buy supplies, learn new things, and have fun with other beaders. One of my personal favorites is the annual To Bead True Blue show in Tucson, Arizona. There's bound to be a bead show near you! *Lapidary Journal* has a full listing, including gem and mineral shows (www.lapidaryjournal.com/cal1.cfm).

Storage Solutions

Map Filing Cabinets

Home Decorators

www.homedecorators.com

Check here for nice wooden ones in 5-, 9-, and 11-drawer versions. You can also try your luck on eBay. These are usually "for pickup only," but if you happen to be in the right place at the right time, you just might nab one in your area at a great price.

Storage Boxes

Oriental Trading Company

www.orientaltrading.com

or

Whim Beads

www.whimbeads.com

These folks have the flip-top containers in a variety of sizes.

Bead Trays

Fire Mountain Gems

www.firemountaingems.com

Software

Jewelry Designer Manager

Bejeweled Software Company

www.jewelrydesignermanager.com

Further Reading (and Viewing)

I owe a debt to many beaders who have come before me. Listed in this appendix are the many books I referred to for inspiration and instruction when writing this book, as well as others I recommend to you for further reading. I've also listed some visual media you might find helpful.

Further Reading

Bhatt, Sonal. *Beaded Critters.* New York: Sterling Publishing, 2005. (ISBN 140270416X)

Davis, Jane. *Bead Embroidery: The Complete Guide.* Iola, WI: Krause Publications, 2005. (ISBN 0873498887)

Detrick, Kristin. *Making Jewelry with Scrapbook Embellishments.* Cincinnati, OH: North Light Books, 2006. (ISBN 1581806892)

Dickt, Donna DeAngelis. *French Beaded Designs.* New York: Sterling Publishing, 2005. (ISBN 1402716036)

Editors of Creative Publishing International. *Veiled in Beauty: Creating Headpieces and Veils for the Bride.* Chanhassen, MN: Creative Publishing International, 2002. (ISBN 1589230477)

Fitzgerald, Diane. *The Beaded Garden: Creating Flowers with Beads and Thread.* Loveland, CO: Interweave Press, 2005. (ISBN 1931499551)

Lockwood, Georgene. *The Complete Idiot's Guide to Beading Illustrated.* Indianapolis: Alpha Books, 2004. (ISBN 1592572561)

Lynch, Claudia. *"I Do" Veils—So Can You!: A Step-by-Step Guide to Making Bridal Headpieces, Hats, and Veils with Professional Results.* Rocky River, OH: Harpagon, 1996. (ISBN 0965081362)

McNeil, Suzanne. *Beadie Babies.* Fort Worth, TX: Design Originals, 1998. (ISBN 157421148X)

———. *Beadie Babies 2.* Fort Worth, TX: Design Originals, 1999. (ISBN 1574217518)

———. *Beadin' Critters: Fun Faces.* Fort Worth, TX: Design Originals, 1998. (ISBN 1574219294)

Further Watching

Rosemary Topol's French Beaded Flower Sessions and Patterns

Rosemary is an accomplished beaded flower designer, and she has both a session for beginners and one for advanced beaded flower crafters (available on videotape or DVD), as well as a CD of all 27 of her beaded flower patterns. To order, go to www.geocities.com/roetopol.